PITFALLS OF THE MODERN CAREER

by: R.J. Pulma

ACT I

Chapter 1

The Beginning

A medium built kid is running across the street towards his home. Upon reaching the door of the house he had been living in as far as he can remember, the boy made a last-minute check at the position of the sun. The sun was going down but is still fully visible, with some distance before it dips into the horizon. At his quick estimate, it was around 5:00 PM and just in time for the show he hurried home to watch.

He quickly opened the door and the sound of the television quickly reached him. His younger brother was already watching the television and the show they both wanted to watch was just about to start.

"Wow, I made it just in time," said Stan to his younger brother Gram.

"Why are you so early?" said Stan.

"Our teacher released us early. I went home immediately once Miss Carol said we could go. Drum already reached the base of Grin and a big fight will happen for sure in this episode," excitedly replied Gram.

"I don't want to miss this episode for anything in the world" said Gram with a big grin on his face that showed both excitement and pride for being able to watch the highly anticipated episode he can't stop thinking about.

Stan and Gram watched the episode with all their focus. After thirty minutes and the episode has already ended, their grin and excitement were even greater than before. They both couldn't wait until the next day to watch the next episode and talked and debated about what would happen next, and which part of the episode hyped them up more.

After a few minutes, their mom, who was already in the house before Gram arrived, told the boys to change clothes and help her prepare dinner. The boys changed into their house clothes and helped their mom chop some vegetables and set up the dinner table. As the food was already simmering and things were already set, the boys went out to play with the neighbor kids in the street. They chased each other and also discussed the latest episode of "Drum Quest".

The kids took an interest in a tall tree with no branch from the ground to its lowest branch, at about ten feet up. "Hey, do you think we can see the whole town up that tree?" Said Lloyd, a friend of Stan and Gram.

"I think we can even see the other town from there," said Sheen, another friend.

"Who wants to try climbing?" Asked Gram.

Sheen tried climbing first but just slipped and fell without barely getting out of the ground. Gram and Lloyd also had a go, but both failed to get to a significant height. The three kept trying to get up, but more than fifteen minutes lapsed, and no one was able to rise up.

Stan was just watching the others try and fail at climbing the tall tree. But he did take note as to where they stepped on the tree trunk, and how they grasped it as they tried to climb up. He tried to see if it was really possible to climb this big tree, or if it was just a waste of time. Then suddenly, Sheen made some improvement in climbing the tree and Stan noticed how Sheen grasped the trunk as he progressed. Sheen eventually lost the grip however, and fell to the ground without getting past eight feet up.

"Wow, you were almost there!" said Gram. "Yeah, I was there but my hand slipped," said Sheen. Let me try again. And they tried again but they were still not able to get up. Then Stan got curious and decided to try climbing up.

"Hey, let me have a try at it," said Stan. "I think you were just doing it wrong," again said Stan.

"Nah, I think it is just impossible to climb. With the branch that far away and with nothing to hold on to, I don't think it's possible to get up there," said Lloyd.

"Maybe, but let me just try," said Stan.

Stan tried climbing up with his body upright and his feet and hand positioned as if he were hugging the tree copying the way Sheen climbed the tree during his most successful try. He positioned himself well that he slowly but surely progressed up the trunk, little by little. At about nine feet up, the skin of the trunk he was holding onto peeled which caused him to fall. Undeterred, and with an idea as to how to better climb the tree, he tried again, more cautious and focused, this time around. After a few minutes, he was able to have a firm grip at the lowest branch of the tree and was finally able to climb up and sit on said branch.

"Wow that was hard!" said Stan with a laugh. "Wow, you were great! You looked just like a monkey climbing up that tree!" shouted Sheen, with a laugh and a slight frown.

"I'm part gorilla! Let me climb to the top of the tree and let you know if I can see the other town from here" said Stan so innocently with a laugh.

"Yeah, go higher!" Said Gram and Lloyd almost in unison. "Check if there are bigger buildings in the other town!" said Gram.

Stan climbed higher and higher until he reached the very top of the tree. The top was precarious as the branches were thinner than those at the lower part of the tree, and a moderate wind swayed the top ever so gently.

Stan did not however notice the danger, nor was he minding the wind. To him it was like entering a new world up in the trees that he has never seen before. As he climbed up, he saw branch upon branch from all sides of the tree, as if they were roads or ladders that allowed its users to access different regions within this tree world. It was like he was travelling in a world that moved up and down, instead of the side-to-side travel that he was accustomed to, all his life.

The view was also different. For the first time in his life, Stan was able to see the world from about forty feet above the ground. "The world looked different," he thought to himself. "Hey, I can see the roof of houses! I think the leaves can provide protection for me during rainy days and shade during sunny days. And the breeze and view are great! This could be a great place to live in", he said to himself.

Entering and exploring a new world excited him further. He transferred to the different sides of the tree and tried to peek at the view that each side of the tree offered. Despite a sudden breeze, Stan enjoyed the swaying of the branches, as though the branches were cradling him while he was up there. As he was there, he tried to enjoy all the new things the vantage point had to offer. Finally, he tried to look for the other town from his position.

"Hey Gram, I can't seem to see the other town from here", said Stan.

"That's impossible! This is the tallest tree I know, so you should already be able to see the other town from there," said Gram.

"All I see are fields, trees and houses and nothing more. Maybe this tree is not tall enough", replied Stan.

"Yeah, maybe you're right. Anyway, you should go down from there now. It's almost dinner time and mom will be mad if we are not back soon," said Gram.

"Okay, will be right down!" said Stan. And he slowly climbed back down until he was on the ground.

"You were amazing!" said Lloyd.

"Yeah, you are the only one I know who was able to get to the top of this tree!" said Gram.

"Not a big deal! I could have easily gotten to the top if I did not get a splinter on my first try climbing," said Sheen.

"Yeah, I think you could have gotten up the tree if not for your injury Sheen. I actually copied how you climbed this tree, that's why I was able to get up there," said Stan.

"See! He was just copying my technique, that's why he was able to climb to the top. I could have easily climbed this tree if I wanted to!" said Sheen.

"Yeah, I think you could easily have done so!" Said Gram.

"Wow, that's cool Sheen!" Said Lloyd.

"No doubt about it!" Said Stan.

"Well, I think we should be going," said Gram.

"See you again tomorrow! Hope Drum defeats Grin tomorrow, so that he can become the highest ranked hero in the kingdom," said Lloyd.

"Bye!" said Stan and Gram.

Chapter 2

Life Moves On

A couple of years later, Stan woke up to the sound of the alarm set at 5:30am. Stan woke up, did some push-ups and went on a short jog. After taking a bath, he did a short meditation and ate a light breakfast.

Stan got to the office and was greeted by the guards and staff of their law office.

"Good morning Stan! Pretty intense game last night" said Mike, the lobby security.

"Not as intense as the look on the coach's face since the rumor of him being cut, spread", said Stan.

"Yup, lucky for him they won that game!" said Mike, while violently laughing.

Upon reaching his office, he quickly saw his secretary who was there, earlier than usual.

"What are you doing this early in the office?" said Stan.

"Just needed to finish some work before the day starts so I can get home early for my daughter's birthday" said Shirly, Stan's secretary.

"Well, you could have just told me that it was your daughter's birthday and I would have told you to stay home. As easy as that!" said Stan jokingly.

"Well, that's why I came early because I knew you were going to say that" Shirly replied jokingly.

"Wise guy huh! Tell you what, just finish completing the work on the Raymond case and get the hell out of here! And greet Maggie for me will you!" Stan said.

"You're the boss!" replied Shirly.

After a few hours, Shin entered Stan's office. "Stan, where are we on the Grace case?" said Shin.

"Was able to read the relevant laws and decisions and we don't have a great case in our hands. We can maybe insist on the old decisions of the court to support our claim and hope the court and the opposing lawyers don't raise the recent court decision on the matter.

"It's not that the recent decision squarely applies, but still, a new decision still has more weight that an old one. Our best chance is if we can convince the court that the old decision is an exception to the new one, and that our case falls within the purview of the old decision", said Stan.

"Well how do we convince the court to use the old decision?" asked Shin.

"Well, we don't. We make the other party insist that the old decision is applicable, and then capitalize on that mistake", said Stan.

"The lawyers on the other side are known to be old and ruthless, but they are not known to be stupid. I also don't think we can casually just say hi and say 'can you please use the old decision' because I don't think they will bite, so how do you suppose we convince them to use the old decision?" sarcastically asked Shin.

"To be honest, this is a very risky move and very dependent on how the opposing lawyers will draft their pleading, but I am confident that I can put them in a spot wherein they have no choice but to use the old decision.

I am thinking of hammering them on the 'mistake of fact' angle so they won't have a choice but to use the old decision as their argument", sincerely replied Stan.

"As Mike would always say..." continued Stan, as they looked at each other with a smile as they recited "a good lawyer can use the law to force what he wants, but a great lawyer makes people agree on his arguments, using language and the law".

"You got that right!" loudly said Shin.

After they shared a laugh, Shin looked back at Stan and said "despite all that, you know this is a very risky move. This client may be new to the firm, but we already have several proposals worth millions that are pending signature. And based on my discussions with them, they are waiting on how this Grace case goes before they sign the pending proposals. So, it is an understatement to say that we badly need this win.

"That being said, we know what you're capable of. You are on deck to be the youngest partner in this firm because of your work ethic and talent, not to mention your credentials. But considering the impact this win or loss might make on this firm, complete the draft of your pleading, and let me have a look at it", instructed Shin.

"I wouldn't have it any other way" said Stan jokingly.

After a few more reviews and discussions, Stan and Shin finalized their pleading.

"Well, this could work. But are you sure settling would not be the better and safer option?" asked Shin.

"Negotiating a deal with the other party is safer, but considering the lawyers representing them, they would try to insist on some unreasonable deal that would be very painful for the client to swallow. And even if the client agrees to accept an unreasonable offer, I think the client would have second thoughts in signing the proposals we have, if we went with the settlement route. So, to be honest, this is the best shot we have of making sure we get the client, and make sure they agree to the large fees we proposed", calmly said Stan.

"I guess you're right. Go big or be mediocre, right?" said Shin.

"Couldn't have said it better" said Stan jokingly.

After a few weeks, Stan was at the office, working. At around 2PM, Shirly came inside Stan's office to give a mail. "Another package just came", said Shirly.

Stan was drafting a pleading when he saw the package with what looked like a thick file of papers inside the mail. "Thanks, Shirly" Stan said but his mind was already racing, as he was suspecting that the mail contained the opposing party's pleading, in reply to the one he and Shin drafted on the Grace case. As Stan was taking the scissor from the drawer, he was already anticipating what was written in the opposing party's pleading.

Did they take the bait? Did they use the old decision to defend their position against the mistake of fact argument they insisted? If they did not use the old decision, would trying to settle be already off the table? If we settle, how do we convince the client to agree without compromising the proposals that are pending their signature? All these thoughts poured in, as Stan was able to open the envelope, despite the pounding of his heart, in what he felt like a constricting chest. Stan took a deep breath and began reading the pleading.

"Mr. Shin, Shirly is asking if you are not tied up as of the moment" said Jean, Shin's secretary.

"Yeah, I can spare a moment. What's this about?" asked Shin.

"Shirly said that the pleading on the Grace case came and if you have time, it's in Stan's office", said Jean.

"Oh yeah it was supposed to come this week! Thanks Jean", said Shin.

Shin quickly got up and walked straight to Stan's office. "I hope they were sensible enough to use the old decision. If there is no mention of the old decision in the opposing party's pleading, maybe we can just quote the old decision in our reply and invoke it during hearing" Shin kept thinking to himself as he continued walking to Stan's office.

Upon opening Stan's door, he saw Stan frowning and in deep thought. This made Shin worry as Stan is normally a cool and collected guy, even during high pressure meetings.

"So, did the guys from across the pond use the old decision?" Shin asked, while trying to sound cool and composed.

"Hey, didn't notice you came in. Try knocking sometimes!" Stan said jokingly.

"Stop with the suspense and spill the beans already", a slightly irate Shin replied.

With a sly grin from his lips dashing to his right ear, Stan said "Yep! Those guys not only used the old decision, they anchored their whole defense on it."

"What?! Are you sure?" said Shin in excitement.

"Well, you can read it for yourself" said Stan as he reached out to give the pleading to Shin.

Shin took hold of the pleading and began reading the thing intently without talking for a few minutes, while Stan sat there watching Shin read.

"You're right! We sure got them good" said Shin, with a grin extending from ear to ear. Then suddenly, Shin frowned and asked, "wait a minute, then why were you frowning when I got to your office?"

"Oh that, I was just thinking of how best to write our reply so that we can close this case quickly and get our other proposals signed. Also, had a few thoughts on what I would buy this end of year, once I get the payout on the big contracts this case will be bringing" said Stan with a big smile on his face.

"Shut up and get this done already!" said Shin jokingly.

"It still amazes me how focused and composed you are, even in a big win like this. But at the same time, still in awe at how relentless and a perfectionist you can be. I mean you already have this in the bag even without the trial starting, and yet you are already looking ahead and trying to make sure you have every contingency planned out. I mean that's disturbing!" said Shin jokingly.

"Anyway, try to get some rest. You deserve it after all the work you did for this case", continued Shin, in a more serious manner.

"Sure! Will just finish some work and head out to get some fancy restaurant you keep talking about", said Stan.

Chapter 3

Progression

It was a minute before 5:30am and Stan woke up before his alarm went off. For some reason, he just gained consciousness and alertness on his own without the need for the alarm clock going off. He remembers how this sometimes happen to him when he had a field trip or sports competition and he was excited to participate in the next day's activity. Remembering his days as a child brought an involuntary grin in Stan's face, which he tried to tone down but tried to savor just the same.

Stan again remembers the big win he got the week before when the opposing lawyers used the old doctrine to support their position, which he is now heavily capitalizing in drafting their firm's reply.

"Not sure if the lawyers at the other side of the pond just don't realize how much I can take advantage of this position, or if they just didn't put enough time into this client? But who cares, right? Their loss is my gain," he said to himself.

"I just need to check again the other relevant decisions, to make sure that we did not miss anything," again said Stan to himself, as he positioned himself to do some push-ups.

Stan skipped his jog, had a light breakfast and took a shower, while simultaneously conceptualizing how he would complete their firm's reply. He could have had his staff draft the reply for him to review, but considering how important this case was, and how much he wanted to get his ideas reflected in the reply, he went ahead and drafted the reply on his own. This made sense to him since there would still be some fresh eyes to review them in Shin.

Driving to the office, Stan kept strategizing how best to present their position in the Grace case to the Roe family.

"Good morning Shirly!" greeted Stan. "Is the conference room available for the 10am meeting later?" asked Stan.

"Yep! Already have the room in place with every seat having a copy of the reply and our proposal letters," said Shirly.

"Great! See you later," said Stan.

Shortly after Stan went inside his office and as he was tidying up his hair, an elderly man in the mid-fifties opened the door and entered.

"Stan, are you ready for the 10am meeting?" said Mike, the managing partner in their law office.

"Good morning Mike! Yes, I already have the presentation reviewed and already have the contracts placed in the seats of the Roe family," said Stan, who was a bit surprised at the sudden entry of his boss, but maintaining a calm face so as to ease any anxiety that Mike may be feeling about the 10am meeting.

"Great to hear because we really want to get those acceptance fees in our books as soon as possible. Those are really big fees, and getting them will definitely secure your partnership this year," said Mike.

"I am confident that we will get them to sign those contracts once we present to them the favorable situation that we got them in the Grace case," said Stan.

"It's not that you don't have a good chance of getting admitted to partnership this year, Grace case or not, but just getting this Grace case and the Roe accounts will really convince the other partners that you are more than ready to be partner," said Mike before pausing to choose his words.

"Securing this account just leaves a lot less to chance, and can give you better peace of mind, I guess, in being admitted into the partnership. Not that I doubt you or anything like that, but you get the idea," Mike continued.

"I perfectly understand and don't want it any other way. I do badly want this win and I honestly hope that after this presentation, we get the signed proposals by end of the week," said Stan, and afterwards stares at Mike intently.

"You do know that I have already checked with my broker for the best estate in the neighborhood, right?!" said Stan half serious and half-jokingly.

"Of course! That's all I needed to hear! See you later" laughingly said Mike, as he went out of Stan's office in a good mood.

After a short moment, Shin entered Stan's office. "Saw the old man leave your office with a grin. What did he want?" asked Shin.

"He was just checking if I got things in order for the meeting later. I just told him that we had a good chance of impressing during our presentation later, and that if the meeting later works out, then we may already get the proposals signed by the end of the week," said Stan with a grin.

"I guess he is also excited to spend the cash we would be collecting once we have the proposals signed," jokingly continued Stan.

"I can't argue with that. Anyway, do your best, soon to be partner," said Shin with a wink.

Once Shin left, Stan once again browsed through the draft reply as well as the pertinent decisions researched by his staff. After a few minutes of serious review, Stan noted down some ideas that he may later consider adding to the final reply. It was an hour before the meeting, and Stan was in his office conceptualizing how the meeting would go and how best to approach different situations or questions as they would come.

"Although the Roe family's inclination for a definite victory is common knowledge, they still want to avoid any unwarranted publicity whatsoever. Not sure if I should just present our position as a sure win endeavor and capitalize on them being in awe to get them to sign our proposals, or just play it a little more composed?" Stan thought.

Stan weighed on his options and ran through several scenarios in his mind, on what to expect and how to carry himself, should different situations come up. But after almost thirty minutes of going back and forth with how he should approach the situation, he decided to gauge first the Roe families' reaction to his presentation, before deciding how he will present the Grace case to the Roe family. On the occasion however that it is unclear how the Roe family may prefer the Grace case to be handled, he decided to go with the 'definite victory' way of handling the case, as it at least projects great confidence and competence on their firm's part in handling the Grace case. "Hope this works," said Stan with a sigh.

"Has the Roe family arrived?" Stan asked Shirly.

"The lobby security just called saying that the Roe group just got dropped off," said Shirly.

"Ok, please call Shin and Mike and tell them of the arrival so we can welcome them at the elevator," said Stan.

"Got it!" said Shirly while dialing on her office phone.

Stan checked his hair and tie one last time before going to Shin and Mike's office. All three of them went to the elevator opening and waited for the Roe family to arrive.

A few minutes later, the elevator opened and revealed an elderly gentleman around the age of seventy-five to eighty in appearance but still had some miles in his step and intense sharpness of mind. Along with him in the elevator are his daughter and two sons, who were also as well dressed as their father.

"Good morning Mr. Paul! Hope you did not have any problem getting here," greeted Stan.

"Stan, it has been a while since I last saw you. You are looking good!" pleasantly greeted Mr. Paul.

"Thanks Mr. Paul! I have to thank my bosses over here for taking good care of me all these years," said Stan jokingly, as he introduced Shin and Mike.

"That's good to hear. Say hi to your grandfather for me will you. And tell him not to buy the lot he talked to me about last week, as that was extremely overpriced," replied Mr. Paul.

"Not again! I'll tell him you said hello and also give him a piece of my mind about buying another overpriced land," said Stan jokingly.

"Good! Your grandfather needs to get an earful because of how stubborn he can be. By the way, hope you still remember Julie, Jan and James?" said Mr. Paul as he introduces his three children.

"Of course, I do!" said Stan as greeted the three.

After a few more pleasantries, Mike led the group to the conference room where Stan began discussing the status of the Grace case, as well as the possible issues that may arise during the trial. After a few question and answer in between his presentation, Stan still could not figure out how best to leverage the positive development in the Grace case, to make sure that the Roe family agreed on all their pending proposals. Stan however noticed that Mr. Paul asked twice about how the win in the case might affect the other party.

"For a rather intense businessman such as Mr. Paul, asking for the consequences of a pending lawsuit seemed unusual. Is he worried about some negative publicity this might bring to his business? Or is Mr. Paul working on an angle that may double his benefits in the long run?" said Stan to himself while Mike was now discussing about the details of the proposals, that were pending the Roe Group's acceptance.

"They are really hard to read, and despite my close relationship with their family, I may have to be cautious with them on this" said Stan to himself.

"Thanks for the discussion Mike, and thanks as well for taking on the Grace case for us, on such a short notice Stan. As much as we like to work with you on the other cases, our group really would like to have a better appreciation of how your team would handle the Grace case first, before we sign off on the other engagements," said Mr. Paul sternly.

"Although we know and trust you Stan well enough to give you a chance to handle the Grace case for us despite our limited appreciation of your firm's capabilities, I hope you understand that I also have to make decisions that would promote confidence in me by the other shareholders in our company," Mr. Paul continued.

"We perfectly understand Mr. Paul, and we don't want it any other way," said Stan calmly, but his mind already frantic as to how to push through with the other contracts while at the same time trying not to sound defensive about their capabilities as a firm.

"This sounds like Mr. Paul trying to politely back out on the other engagements. Should I continue to sell just half of the proposals or just package them to a more affordable bundle? Or should I give a discount for all the offered services?" said Stan to himself while still trying to figure out where Mr. Paul is going with his statements.

With about a second or two of momentary silence, which to Stan, Mike and Shin seemed an eternity, Stan motioned to speak so as to try to break the deadlock and possibly try to reduce any awkwardness that resulted due to the silence. Before Stan could however muster a sound, Mr. Paul proceeded with his statement.

"Nonetheless, based on how well you handled the Grace case thus far, and of which we are really thankful, we are convinced that your firm is capable enough to handle the many jobs that we have asked you for your proposals. But before we can proceed with moving forward with taking your firm as our counsel, we hope you can enlighten us on how you intend to close this Grace case?" said Mr. Paul, who was composed but had a dead serious expression.

With his mind racing a million miles an hour, trying to get a feel of the situation and trying to find the best response to not only close their proposals, but also make a good impression on his grandfather's close friend, he remembered both Mr. Paul and James looking at the news about the Grace case in their phones. It is still unclear to him if this was an indication that Mr. Paul and the Roe family was sensitive about the publicity that the Grace case would bring on their group, but based on Stan's understanding of the profile of the Roe family and how they would like to protect their business at the end of the day, it seemed to him that they we more cautious about the negative publicity this case would bring, should the trial proceed. Despite being overly cautious as well, this was a situation that left Stan with no choice but to gamble on an option and try to make the best of the situation.

"To be honest Mr. Paul, we really have a very good legal defense to counter all their arguments in court. To me, we have them right where we want them and we can easily capitalize in our favorable footing to make a statement to everyone not to mess around with the Roe family moving forward with this case," said Stan with conviction. But after a very brief pause and a short sigh of sorts, Stan continued "but at the same time, I believe that the better way of closing this case is by trying to make a deal with the other party and use the favorable position we have to make sure we get the most favorable deal possible for our side. In this way, we can try to keep this case as far away as possible from the public's notice to avoid any unwarranted publicity, and just kill this case as quietly and as quickly as though this never existed. And if we play our cards right, settling can also guarantee that there would be less animosity between the parties in the future."

With a short pause and after looking at Mr. Paul's eyes once more, Stan continued, "but of course we would only proceed as discussed as per your group's go ahead."

Mr. Paul paused a bit and frowned, with eyes fiddling about and in deep thought as to how to respond. And after looking back eye to eye with Stan, as if trying to peek inside his brain, Mr. Paul responded. "I like that plan," said Mr. Paul. And after looking at Julie, Jan and James to check if they had other opinions, Mr. Paul continued, "and I believe our group and the board agrees with me that this should be the better way to proceed with this matter. I understand the need to send a message across, that our group is not a pushover, but our shareholders are very wary at how unpredictable public opinion can be. It sometimes doesn't even matter if you did the right thing or not. It seems that everyone has a knee jerk reaction to anything that is brought to the venue of public opinion. And I know you can defend and justify your side later on, but the immediate damage any wrong publicity brings, may be greater than any positive publicity you receive later on, once you clear your name.

"It's really not worth it to risk going to that arena, unless you are one of the underdogs in the situation, right?" said Mr. Paul with a sarcastic grin.

"Besides, even if you eventually prove to everyone else that you were right, no one would even try to rectify the collective wrong action of the public. Worse, the public would probably just remember the initial wrong conclusion and just ignore how you were able to vindicate yourself in the end. Let's face it, no one wants to admit that they are wrong, right?!" said Mr. Paul with a laugh.

"Couldn't agree more!" said Mike also with a laugh. "Unfortunately, that is the world we are dealing with right now!" quipped Shin with an awkward smile.

"Anyway, with your answer, I can confidently express our group's trust and confidence that you will handle our cases not only in the most capable way, but also in the manner that will sit well with our interests," said Mr. Paul a short while after the laughter settled down.

"As I have already been given the authority by the board to decide whether or not we can proceed with our contracts with your firm, I'd be happy to proceed with the signing of the contracts today," said Mr. Paul with a tempered smile. "Kindly just assist me on which copies do I need to sign to get our partnership with your firm rolling," Mr. Paul continued.

After a brief moment of surprise from both Shin and Mike, and a moment of relief and awe from Stan, they proceeded to discuss with the Roe family delegation on how to proceed with the contract signing. All the proposals were signed and the Roe delegation eventually left the meeting.

After ushering the Roe family to the elevator, Stan, Shin and Mike had a short meeting in Mike's office to discuss the next steps on the new accounts. After settling on the steps to be taken, Mike jokingly quipped, "well, all that's left is for Stan to be admitted to the partnership."

"Let's finally cut all the suspense and get this over with Mike. Are all the paperwork ready?" said Shin, with a big smirk.

"Yes, everything is all set and I guess the partners were just waiting for the Roe accounts to be signed before proceeding with Stan's admission. To be honest, all the partners are excited to have Stan join our ranks and wanted this to happen soon, and so we really planned to have the admission done within the week. I know how impressed the partners are with Stan's track record but I think even they did not expect the Roe family to sign the proposals in our meeting today!" said Mike jokingly.

"But no matter. We already did the paperwork on this and I already asked Melany to give notice to the partners that we will be admitting Stan to partnership this evening," Mike continued.

"Are you serious?!" said Stan, with some seriousness but still not fully believing what Mike just said.

"Do I sound like I'm joking?" sarcastically said Mike.

"I guess not," replied Stan.

"Do you know about this Shin?" asked Stan as he looked over to Shin.

"Yes, the legwork has already been done on this and the other partners were really just waiting for the signature on the proposals before we went ahead with your admission. But even if we somehow had a hitch in this proposal negotiations, the admission would have come regardless. But hey, not only do you become partner, you also get to immediately share on the profits of the Roe accounts you just closed. Good deal, am I right!" said Shin with an immediate soft elbow to Stan's right rib.

"Not really sure what to say," said Stan while still in disbelief.

"You don't need to say anything. This is happening because you deserve this. No one in this firm has worked as hard as you all these years. And to add to that, no one in this firm is as talented as you are, to be honest. So, it is our great pleasure to welcome you to our ranks" said Mike with all sincerity.

"I can't thank you enough Mike and Shin for the support and the opportunity. I hope I can live up to the lofty expectation you have for me," said Stan.

"You deserve it and more, so don't sweat it. Just don't forget to treat us afterwards!" jokingly said Shin.

"Of course!" emphatically replied Stan.

Still refusing to believe the good news, Stan went back to his office to try and rationalize the events in his mind. Despite the news coming straight from the managing partner's mouth, in Stan's mind, he will only accept his admission when the partner's meeting is already done, and only after he has already signed the new articles of partnership, with his name on it. For him, a lot could still happen from now until the partner's meeting and who knows what unexpected setbacks might happen along the way. At the same time, he was also in awe as to how smoothly things panned out.

He recalled how he was guided by his parents during his elementary up to his college days to go to the best schools and programs, because they were confident that he would do good. He looked back as to how much trust they gave him during those days and how much he wanted to live up to those standards every single time. He fondly remembered how much fun he had during his school days because of how much he outperformed and dominated his classmates not only in academics, but even in sports and politics. In his mind, those were enjoyable memories because he was able to compete with his classmates on a daily basis. The stakes did not bother him one bit because he did not think about those activities as must win situations with dire consequences later on in life, but just considered them as just another form of play with friends, with bragging rights as the only reward.

He also recalled how he was eventually talked into law school by his parents, because they were convinced that he would be able to overcome it, and how he agreed to it because it seemed like the better plan at the time.

After becoming a lawyer and getting into the firm, he knew he had to work not only on his technical skills but also on his marketing skills, for him to get admitted to partnership. He knew that he can tap into their family network to gain enough accounts to make him partner, but also understood that he would have to save the bigger ones for when he was already at the doorsteps of the partnership, just to have an ace when the time comes.

Now that everything went as he planned, he couldn't believe how smoothly it went. In the back of his mind, he was thinking of how all this could still go wrong and what he can do to avoid any anticipated shortcomings. He was still in awe as to how well it all went, that he thought to himself that maybe some bad luck or tragedy would strike him once he already achieved the life he planned. That maybe, just maybe, with all the right things that went his way, he was due for some bad things to happen in his life.

And while the day moved forward, his thoughts continued on.

Chapter 4

Glimpse Of Life Beyond

A few more hours passed and evening came about. Despite several email invitations for a partner's meeting to promote one to their ranks and of which Stan was the only one in the invite who was not a partner, Stan still entertained some skepticism on his promotion. Unless and until the papers are signed, I won't assume anything, he thought to himself.

And then it was 6:30pm and all the partners were at the conference hall, while all the seniors and staff were making murmurs outside the conference hall. As Stan made his way to the conference room, seniors and staff alike all gave their congratulations. Not to be impolite, Stan gave generic remarks to thank them for their well wishes quipped with some humor.

Entering the room of partners, Shin directed Stan to a chair at the edge of the table near Mike. Stan noticed the partners looking at him with excitement and glee, as though a favorite child of theirs is about to be named valedictorian. Despite all this, Stan remained calm and composed as is his style, as though trying up to the last moment to present a good demeanor to the partners.

His mind was again racing at that moment to try and finalize a short message he had been preparing in his mind, just in case he was asked to deliver one.

"Good evening once again partners, and thank you for making it on such short notice," started Mike.

"As we have discussed several meetings ago, it has been resolved that one of our managers has already proven himself that he can not only take on the role of a partner in this firm, but even excel at it, should the role be put upon him. As I have emailed and discussed with several of you earlier, the Roe account, which has been marketed and won by Stan a few hours ago, has confirmed what we already knew for so long. And I believe this win solidified the case for Stan to be promoted to partner in our firm, and serve within our ranks. As part of our tradition and under our bylaws, I am nominating Stan to be a partner in our firm. As stated in our bylaws, all partners should signify their agreement to have Stan as partner, otherwise, the nomination will not push through," said Mike with a pause at the end, as he looked the partners in the eyes with his slow gaze, from one side of the room to the other.

"With the recent win of the Roe case and with an exceptional track record, I am formally nominating Stan to be a partner in our firm. All those in favor, please raise your hands," said Mike.

Despite being on the good side of all the partners, and having worked himself to the bone to get to this point, part of Stan still was not sure if he would become a partner. "All it takes is one vote to ruin a perfectly executed plan," Stan thought to himself. "I may have shown that I am ready to be a partner, but who knows what any of the partners is thinking right now," he again thought, as he tried to avoid looking at the other partners at that moment.

As the vote was being cast, there was a short pause. Stan, after trying to initially avoid looking at the hands that decided his fate, eventually decided to check the voting and maybe move on with the rest of his life, regardless of the result. And with a very soft sigh, he raised his gaze.

His eyes did not believe what they witnessed. Not only were all the partners raising their hands, they were standing as well to show their strong agreement with Stan's admission to be a member of their ranks. They were smiling as they looked at Stan with joy.

"Well, it seems like all partners are in agreement. Stan, under the authority provided me by our bylaws, and as confirmed by a yes vote of all the partners in our meeting today, I am formally accepting you as partner to our firm. Congratulations and well deserved!" said Mike with a great grin as he motioned towards Stan.

As the partners and the staff outside the conference room applauded, Mike said "now Stan, kindly say a few words for us."

Still a bit surprised at the overwhelming appreciation he got from the partners, Stan stood up and faced the partners.

"First and foremost, thank you Mike for accepting me to your firm and giving a kid like me a shot to show what I can do. Also, I would like to thank all the partners, managers and staff that I have been fortunate enough to work with. I learned a great deal working with you, not only in the field of law, but also in the field of life. And I am truly thankful for the great many lessons and learning I gained working with all of you.

"I believe that it's not the ends, but more importantly the means, that matter more in any endeavor. I am fortunate to have great people to guide me to be the best lawyer I can be, as I journeyed on towards this partnership. And I cannot thank you enough from the bottom of my heart for believing and staying with me from the beginning up to this point. I hope and pray that I live up to your expectations, and be able to make you and your predecessors proud. Thank you, and more power," said Stan as the partners clapped and cheered to his admission to partnership.

As Stan was speaking and even after he delivered his speech, flashes of the hours he put on and the plans he conceptualized came back. He was happy to finally know that his patience and dedication paid off, and that he can now confidently claim this accomplishment as his own. With a short sight before he began shaking everybody's hands, he felt a great relief knowing that his risk to push on with his plan to be a partner, finally came into fruition. And that finally, he no longer needed to work a single hour, just to achieve his goal.

The whole office had a festive mood, as people joyfully celebrated an accomplishment that only a few were persistent enough to achieve. Food was ordered in and drinks were also provided, and everybody celebrated well into the evening.

Once the food and beverage fizzled out, little by little the staff and partners bid their goodbyes and went home. When only a few people were left, Stan shook Mike and Shin's hands and bid his farewell.

"I should probably be going. I want to avoid being late on my first day as a partner tomorrow," jokingly said Stan.

"Of course, you don't!" said Mike with a big laugh. "Well, see you again tomorrow, partner", slowly said Mike, but now more seriously and with conviction.

As Stan proceeded home, he called his parents to tell them the news about his promotion. His parents were overwhelmed with joy knowing how hard Stan worked to become a partner. They congratulated Stan with great joy, but also told him to always keep his feet on the ground and never look down on anyone no matter how high his status further becomes.

"Yes mom, I will," said Stan. "Thank you for everything, and I owe this all to both of you. You take care always," said Stan as he said his goodbyes.

Entering his house, Stan recalled how glorious the day was. He felt a great sense of achievement, knowing that he finally reached partnership. In his mind, he marveled at how great of an accomplishment he achieved by becoming not just a partner, but the youngest partner in their firm. He also felt a sense of accomplishment, knowing that he was the fastest to become partner in a big firm, among all of his contemporaries in law school.

But more than anything, he relished in the thought of finally making his parents proud. "I know that my parents have always been proud of me, regardless of my performance. But finally, I am able to accomplish something tangible and monumental enough for my parents to brag to their friends. They deserve as much," said Stan to himself, with a smirk.

"But I wonder what happens now?" said Stan as he gazed outside his window, pondering how his life would go on.

Chapter 5

Celebration

With his alarm clock ringing, Stan woke up and tried to look back again to what he accomplished just last night. Turning off his phone alarm, he stared at his window contemplating the events that went down. "Can't believe I am already a partner now. Still can't believe things went out just as planned," said Stan to himself as he slowly went up and did his workout routine.

After tidying himself up and getting ready for work, Stan went off to his new role and his new life.

When Stan got to the office, he went to his old office room and was greeted by Shirly at the door. "You don't need to keep coming to the office this early anymore, Stan. You're already a partner!" said Shirly jokingly.

"Can't let you have all the perks of being early," countered Stan jokingly.

"Oh, come on! Honestly, you should have given us more time to change things while you take your sweet time relaxing at this point. We were actually in the middle of changing your office room, and of course mine, at this very moment. Of course, we anticipated you'd be early, so I scheduled the movers and handymen to come early, but we were not expecting you to be this early!" said Shirly.

"Oh, was that scheduled to be done today? I thought it would have taken it at least a few days before we moved to a new room. Which room are we moving into?" said Stan.

"Yup, your life as a partner starts today. The partners already selected a room for you. Come let me show you," said Shirly, as she motions Stan to follow her.

They went up another floor, through a majestic and old fashion looking stairs, up to the floor wherein all the partners conduct their day-to-day business. The walls were covered with artwork both old and contemporary, as well as some contemporary sculptures. The interior design was both sophisticated and old fashioned.

Walking along the hallways of this floor, reminded Stan of the few instances when he would be able to walk these halls. As this floor has a separate elevator than the one Stan and the other employees were using, they were only able to come up to this floor during special meetings and some occasional discussion with partners. On a normal day, the partners will just call them through landline, if they wanted to clarify some of their work, or just go down to their floor to discuss matters with them. As they know that the partners normally have very busy days, it was a treat for any of the staff or manager to get a visit from any of the partners. And through Stan's experience, getting called up to the partner's floor could mean you either did a good thing, or you did a bad thing. Now in awe, Stan could not believe that a day after he got promoted, he would already be doing his day-to-day business on this floor, and in one of these rooms.

As they got deeper inside the partner's floor, Stan saw the partner's names inscribed at the door of the room that each partner was assigned to, with their respective secretaries at the door greeting Stan a good morning, as he walked by. Finally, he got to a door wherein his name was already inscribed. His eyes widened, and for a very short moment, he was lost for words.

"With all the days of work and the meticulous planning to get to this point, finally, I have tangible proof that says it wasn't all for nothing. Before me is proof that I was able to succeed!" said Stan to himself, as Shirly opened the door.

"Well, what do you think of your new room, Boss? Well, as you came in very early, we have not yet completed transferring all the files and things at our previous room into this one. But your new table, chair and furniture, and of course the table, chair and furniture of yours truly, are already here. We will complete the transfer, and probably a little interior designing by lunchtime today. So, you should have stayed home and had a few more drinks, so I could have given you a grander office reveal than the one you are getting now!" said Shirly, teasingly.

While Shirly was discussing, Stan went inside his new room and looked around in amazement. He looked through the big window of his new room, which gave him a great view of the city. This was the same view he often enjoyed whenever he had a meeting in one of the conference rooms of the partner's floor, or whenever he was called up by a partner to discuss one of his works. Stan was caught aback, as he stared deeply into the landscape offered by the window of his new office, and expected this new view to give him a lot of relaxation and perspective, as he takes on his new role in the firm.

"This is perfect," said Stan in an almost hushed tone.

"Glad you like it Boss!" said Shirly with a big grin.

As things were still being moved from his old room to the new one, Stan stayed at his old office room to get some work done. As the days went on, some of the partners called Stan asking how he liked his new office and teased him about why he still came super early on his next day as a partner. After lunch break, Stan got a message from Shirly saying that all is now set in their new room, and that she and Stan are now required to use the elevator reserved for the partner's floor.

While masking his glee, Stan finished his lunch and went back to their office, but this time going into the farther side of their building lobby, to use the elevator reserved for partners. Upon entering the elevator, he was greeted by Billy, a well-groomed man of probably thirty-five years old.

"Good afternoon Stan! Hope you had a great lunch!" said Billy.

"Yup, had a great lunch. Thanks Billy!" said Stan, after catching the name in Billy's name tag. Before Stan was able to tell Billy the floor he wanted to go to, Billy already pressed the button to the partner's floor. And Stan understood that this will likely be his new normal, now that he was a partner.

Reaching the partner's floor, the elevator door opened to a grand hallway, eliciting a sense of class and grandeur that was the very intention of the design. Walking through the hall, Stan still could not fully absorb the fact that he is now walking through these halls as a partner, at that moment. But he believed his good fortune more and more, as he walked through the partner's floor, as each time he walked by a partner's door, the partner's secretary and the partners that were also by the hallway, congratulated and teased Stan on his promotion. Finally, Stan reached his door, with Shirly welcoming him with a big smile.

"Glad you're here! We can now better give our new room a welcoming ceremony," said Shirly, while discretely raising a champagne bottle from under her table.

"Then let's not keep our new office room waiting!" said Stan with a big smile.

Stan and Shirly immediately went inside their new office, locked the door, and silently opened the champagne. Raising his glass to make a toast, Stan said "cheers to a great year that passed, and cheers to brighter years to come! May we pleasantly endure the work that is before us, and fully enjoy the triumphs that are to be reached!". With a slight nudging of their glasses, and hearts over pouring with joy, they made their toast.

"Now don't go changing your attitude on me overnight now," said Shirly with a joking frown.

"As long as you don't become overly dramatic on me, I think I'll be alright," said Stan jokingly.

"Wise guy, huh!" said Shirly, again in jest as they both shared a laugh.

After finishing their drinks, Shirly went back to her table in front of Stan's office, while Stan began to explore the nuances of his new room. Shortly after, Shin and Mike came to his office.

"How does the new room feel?!" said Shin excitedly. "Do you like your new view?!" said Mike before Shin could finish his statement.

"Yes, I like the view a lot, but I just got here half an hour ago, so I really haven't gotten used to this new room yet," said Stan.

"You should like this view. I wanted to get this room when I got promoted to partner, but Jake was still a partner that time. You were lucky you got promoted just in time that this slot got vacant, you son of a gun!" said Shin jokingly.

"Stop complaining already. Your room is amazing. The view here is exceptional, but still, I doubt you would have wanted to delay your promotion just to get this spot, now would you?" said Stan.

"Guess you're right," said Shin.

"Well, glad to know that you're enjoying your new room. Hope you don't let up and keep getting more wins for our firm," said Mike.

"Of course, I will. That's what I was trained to do after all," replied Stan.

After Shin and Mike left, Stan began to get a feel of his new room, and get a feel of the work that was on his plate at that moment. As Stan was conceptualizing how to approach his workload and his new track, he took a moment to pause and appreciate the great situation that he was given. "What a blessing to be in this situation. Now time to make the best of it," said Stan to himself before he started working.

Stan continued on with his day, planning and working how to complete the tasks before him. Late into the night, and Stan was still in his new room working.

"Mike is still working, and so are some of the other senior partners. Although I am pretty much done with most of my tasks, I can't just leave before the senior partners. Besides, I also have to show the younger staff that are still working below, that I am just as hard working as they are, if not more. I can't give an impression that just because I became a partner, I can already slack off," said Stan to himself.

"Besides, I really need to strategize how to reach more clients so I can exceed the given target for this year," said Stan as he jotted down "Notes – Marketing Plan" in his laptop.

He continued working on his plans, far later into the night. Eventually, all the staff and partners already left, leaving only Stan in the office. Having listed down a significant number of ideas, Stan called it a night and prepared to leave. As he was about to shut off his computer, he was prompted to a new message he got from Mike. Wanting to show that he was still working at that time, Stan checked the email to see if it needed a reply. The email had the subject "Welcome to the Partnership" in it, and all the partners were tagged.

When Stan opened the email, it wrote:

"Hi Stan,

"Congratulations on your new promotion and we welcome you with open arms into our small brotherhood of stewards of our firm. We hope that you would continue with your relentless pursuit for perfection in all your new endeavors as partner.

"Your profit share as partner in the Roe Family engagements has already satisfied your capitalization requirement for partnership, and the excess from the capitalization requirement has already been credited to your existing bank account.

"The whole partnership group would like to extend our gratitude for this big win, and to show our appreciation, and to also welcome you to your new role, I will be sending you a separate email enumerating the bonus, we as a firm, are happy to extend to you.

"Sincere congratulations,

"Mike"

Stan quickly emailed back to all the partners, giving his thanks and assuring them of his continued hard work. He then opened another email also coming from Mike, but this time with no other partner copied, and with an attachment labeled "Bonus". When Mike opened the email, it only had the following words written "Enjoy!" written on it with Mike's email signature.

When Stan clicked on the attachment, it showed a table with the benefits that Stan is now allowed because of his promotion.

"Wow, these are great," said Stan to himself as he browsed through the table.

"I get to drive a Porsche as a bonus on top of all these perks?! Wow, they did not hold back," said Stan, in shock at the benefits he will now get to enjoy.

"And Mike said that some money was credited to my account as my first earnings as a partner. Wait, let's also check that out," said Stan, as he opened his mobile banking application to check his balance.

His jaw almost dropped, when he saw the large amount of money that was just transferred to his account that day.

"With this, I can now put my down payment on that house and lot I have been eyeing these past few months," said Stan with excitement.

"The mortgage will tie me up for a long time, but that neighborhood is worth it," said Stan with conviction. "Can't believe I can already enjoy these things, this young, and this early in my career. Maybe it's best to hold off on the gloating, so I don't upset anyone. Well except for Monica. I think I'll enjoy gloating my accomplishments to her," said Stan to himself while making a deviant smirk.

After a short while, Stan eventually packed up and headed home with a very happy heart, but with his mind still racing, trying to figure out how best to spend the money and benefits, he now gets to enjoy.

A few months later, in a bar near the downtown area, a well-groomed and power-dressed woman entered the door of a high-end bar. She had a pretty face and a fit figure, but still looked elegant and professional at the same time. She carried herself in a dignified and poised manner, but not over the top as to call any attention to herself. Yet despite her composed and unassuming demeanor, she gets people's attention when she enters the room, because of just the right combination of sophistication and presence. She continues to walk further inside the bar, towards a table occupied by four men and two other women.

"How are the best lawyers of this town holding up?!" the woman greeted. "Hey, Monica! How are you!" greeted Jason, one of the men at the table. "Couldn't be better!" greeted Lloyd, another one of the men at the table. "We should be asking how you are holding up, with how hectic the practice in your city is!" greeted Ben, another one of the men at the table.

"Hi Monica!" greeted the two ladies at the table. "It's been a while. You look great Jen! Are you still going to yoga? Wow, you look fit," said Monica, as she looked in amazement at Jen. "And how have you been Mary? Is that Junior partner at your firm still giving you a hard time at work?" said Monica, as he looked with compassion at Mary.

"Well, I am no longer getting any problem from that junior partner, after I kind of lashed out at him a few months ago," said Mary, with a coy expression. "Good for you!" said Monica. "Now where is our superstar?" asked Monica, as she looked around the table.

"I wouldn't call myself that just yet," said Stan, as he greeted and joined the group. "Hey 'Mr. Big Shot', how is life in paradise?" said Lloyd playfully. "I definitely wouldn't call the life of a partner like that. There are great perks, don't get me wrong, but the day-to-day grind is more hell than heaven, if you ask me," said Stan in a sarcastic manner.

"How are you all doing?!" said Stan, as he greeted the people at the table. "Wow, you guys are early to say the least! Is work that bad, or do you really want to drink that bad?" said Stan, again in a sarcastic manner.

"Well, some of us have to work so that our firms can get things done you know!" said Jason as he looked at Stan condescendingly. "And what does that supposed to mean?" said Stan as he looked at Jason with a blank expression. "And I don't want to hear that from the guy caught sleeping in his office by his boss in the middle of the day!" said Stan jokingly. And the group, along with Jason, burst to laughter after hearing Stan's remark.

In the brief pause that followed the group's laughter, Jason countered with a blank face "you're still the same prick you used to be during law school". "I learned from the best, sensei," countered Stan, while making a traditional bow to Jason, as if to spoof a student paying respect to his master. And the group burst to laughter again.

"Wow, boys will be boys!" said Monica to the other women. "Yup, they never change," said Mary. "And we probably never will," said Stan in reply, as he looked at Monica. "I guess some cases are just hopeless," countered Monica, with a laugh. And the group continued with their lively catching up.

"It's been a while since I last saw these guys. Never knew that things worked out for a lot of them, despite their fairly bad performance during law school. And Jason actually handled and won a landmark case as a lead counsel in their firm. Maybe he did learn a thing or two during law school, despite him constantly being at the bottom of the rankings," said Monica, as she listens to the group discussing their current professional standing.

"But Stan is still impressing us by becoming the youngest partner in their law firm to become partner. I mean he was always relentless and talented way back in law school, not only in academics, but even in politics and the occasional sports events, that people called him a beast or nicknamed him 'Superman'. But becoming a partner in a large firm this young, that was unheard of until he went and did it. I wonder how he does it," though Monica to himself, as he reflects on his days during law school and compares his time then, with that of Stan's. "I know I didn't lose in effort to this man, but still stings a bit to constantly end up in second place. Would have given me at least a relief if he looked terrible and fat, but damn, he looks more handsome and fit than ever. He better not let up just yet, or I will jump ahead of him in no time," further though Monica, as their group kept eating and drinking on.

"I wonder if Stan and I as a couple would have worked? We had moments during law school, but we probably had a different set of priorities back then," thought Monica.

"Anyway, glad that all of you made it tonight, despite the short notice and heavy traffic," said Lloyd, as he abruptly shifted the light-hearted conversation of the group. "Why the sudden serious tone? I just came here because you promised free beer," said Jason, as he tries to lighten the mood of the conversation. "Yeah, nice try Jason. You're paying for your dinner and beer," said Lloyd, as the group again burst into laughter.

“As I was saying,” said Lloyd, as he tried to get back his composure. “I would like to make a toast to our dear friend who has time and time again seemed to defy and exceed all expectations, and accomplish things never heard of before. As you know, growing up with this chump was never easy, as he almost always was the best at the things we did together. It didn’t matter if it was in our games, school, and even with the ladies, this chump for one reason or another, always seemed to be ahead of us all,” continued Lloyd.

“As if you had a chance!” shouted Ben jokingly, to a restrained chorus of laughter from the group.

But undeterred, Lloyd continued, “and despite the heavy defeats, of which there were many, this guy represented us well, and always made us proud. And even after we already graduated from law school and become lawyers ourselves, this guy continues to represent us and our school, and has once again made us proud. I guess just to give recognition to a great milestone for Stan here, I just wanted to share a toast and celebrate a great achievement you did, buddy. For Stan, the new partner, cheers!” As the group made a committed toast, and loudly shouted “cheers!”

“Thanks man, you almost made me cry there,” said Stan teasingly. “Oh, shut the hell up and drink already,” countered Lloyd.

“Anyway, if you ever need a new assistant, or your firm can no longer handle all your cases, feel free to reach out to me, or subcontract any work my way. I’ll make it your while, if you know what I mean,” said Lloyd, with a sly wink.

“Thanks for the offer man, but I need to keep getting more clients if I want to quickly pay off the big mortgage for the house I just got,” said Stan. “Oh, you already got a down on that house inside the exclusive area?! Nice! I hear there are a couple of celebrities and politicians living in that area,” said Ben.

“I guess you won’t be getting any business from Stan anytime soon, so better give it up Lloyd,” said Mary. “Besides, I call dibs on any client of Stan's that becomes available. Isn’t that right Stan?” said Mary, while jokingly raising a first at Stan as if to intimidate him. “Not a chance, we go way back than you so just shut it,” said Lloyd, with some irritation.

“Appreciate the offer, both of you. I’d have to decline for now, because I actually need more clients as of the moment. But just in case any case comes up which our firm can’t or is not allowed to handle, I’ll give you guys a call,” said Stan, to mellow the topic and move past it.

“Let’s stop talking about work already. It’s not so often the whole gang can get together like this. And we are here to celebrate a great accomplishment by one of our very own. So, let’s drink this bar dry while Stan does all the paying. Right ‘Superman’”, said Monica with a wink.

“Nice try Monica! You pay for what you ate and drank,” said Stan, as the group again laughed. “But I guess I’ll take care of this round for now. The next ones back on our own tabs,” said Stan coyly.

“Best announcement I heard all night!” shouted Monica. “Cheers!” shouted the group in chorus. And they continued on to enjoy each other’s company well into the night.

As they merrily bonded, Stan felt satisfied and at peace at that very moment. He knows that reaching partnership was the biggest accomplishment he’s reached thus far. But he could not help but wonder why, despite the great sacrifice and success he attained chasing the partnership, somehow someway, that very moment meant more to him than the time he got announced as partner. And they merrily bonded on.

Chapter 6

A Chance Encounter

A few months had passed since the ruckus reunion with the gang, and Stan was again at the office trying to figure out how to approach a new case he is handling. His staff was at his office discussing the key points in their pleading for Stan to resolve, but Stan knew from experience that the pleading still needed further research on it.

"Have you already checked all the recent rulings on software royalties?" asked Stan.

"Yes, I believe all applicable rulings have already been taken into account when we drafted this pleading," answered Jake with vigor.

"Well, I was expecting to see last month's ruling on software royalties involving newspapers in your draft, as that would have been very favorable to our arguments. Not only do I not see that ruling, I am also only seeing the old ruling that was already superseded by the last month ruling", discussed Stan to a surprised Jake.

"I may have missed that ruling in our research. Let me check on that again and change our draft accordingly. Apologies for that", said Jake with a lowered head.

"Be careful next time. We never want to lose a case just because we were out researched by the other side. Worse, we don't want to lose a case by not knowing the recent decisions in our field. So, I hope you will be more careful next time", said Stan in a calm and caring manner.

"Yes, I perfectly understand. I won't let this happen again", said Jake once again in an almost hushed voice.

"Also try to iron out some of the clerical errors in your draft. Even with a quick scan, I was still able to see a lot of clerical errors in your draft. And also, try to dial back the tone of your draft. I don't like the lawyers on the opposing side, but the general tone of your draft was very aggressive, if not angry at times. We are adversarial, but still civilized in our profession. Let's just gloat through phone once we get the win, ok?" advised Stan in a serious, but also playful manner.

"This manager has been with the firm for a few years now, and although he does not seem to be the most talented in his batch, but he is the hardest working and most coachable of the bunch. So, I guess, I'll give him a pass this time around and try to lighten his mood a little bit", said Stan to himself, as he gives further instructions to Jake.

"That's it for now. Let me see your draft by tomorrow morning, ok?" said Stan. "Got it!" said Jake.

After Jake left the office, Stan made a big sigh as he slouched back to his chair. "What a hectic day. I've only been a partner for a few months, but I have never been this drained before. It's like I have to constantly convince myself that I need to go to the office everyday just to get by. It's still just 5:30pm, but I need to have a change of scenery for the moment, just to pace myself for the three other drafts I have to review", thought Stan, as he stands up and checks the view through his window.

A few seconds after standing up, his phone began to ring. After a short hesitation, Stan answers the phone. "Yup, what can I help you with Shirly?" said Stan.

"The Goodwill Corp. board called earlier asking if you can discuss with them the latest on the merger this week. I told them that your only available schedule was Thursday but I need to check first with you on the available time that day for a meeting. On your calendar, you only have 9am-12pm and 1pm-2:30pm available for the day. Which slot would I give for the Goodwill Corp.?" asked Shirly.

"12pm-2:30pm on Thursday will be our meeting with the Cherry Stove Group, so give the Goodwill Corp. board 9am-12pm if they'll take it. If they are not available, I think the earliest schedule I can give them is Friday next week, unless they are ok if only Manny will discuss with them on the merger?" said Stan.

"They insisted on having you there to discuss the merger with them and they already said that they are available from 9am-12pm, so I will go ahead and schedule this in. And just like that, your week has been fully booked again boss, this early in the week. It's like your week never had a free hour in it since you got promoted boss", said Shirly jokingly.

"I guess it comes with the territory. At least it pays well!" countered Stan.

"Anyway, kindly hold off any calls or reviews that come up from now until you're off the clock. I'll just go outside to get some fresh air and probably some dinner. But no need to wait up. You can go when you're already done with your -" said Stan before being cut by Shirly. "I know what to do boss. Just go on ahead before anyone shows up", said Shirly.

"Thanks, Shirly. See you tomorrow", said Stan before dropping the call.

Stan quickly got his wallet and some other personal effects and went outside. As he was still very drained from his long day, he could not think well enough to decide where he wanted to go. Too exhausted to decide, he just continued walking from his office, until he reached a small park just a few blocks from his office.

This small park used to be his go to destination when he was an associate and manager, and he needed a place to refresh or collect himself after a grueling day in the office. The past months since becoming a partner however, have been so busy, that he didn't even have the time to walk to this part of the city.

"Wow, it's been quite a while since I last went here. It's only been a few months, but this park changed quite a bit", said Stan to himself. "I wonder if my favorite donut stall is still here?" he thought, as he continued walking to a section of the park with food stalls.

After a few minutes of walking, Stan finally saw a familiar sign. Upon reaching his desired destination, he immediately saw the doughnut shop he had been looking for. In a far corner of the food section of the park, lies a small but welcoming doughnut stall which serves freshly fried doughnuts. The owner was an unassuming but passionate chef, who was beloved by his patrons. Although he did not know the names of most of the customers, he approached them as if they were family, and always checked with his customers to see how their day was.

"I guess more than the food, I think I came here because of how the owner connects with his customers. He even gave me a free doughnut when I got totally buried in work when four of the twelve new associates from our batch had to go across the country for three weeks to resolve an immediate labor case", said Stan with a subtle smile.

Going in front of the owner to order his usual doughnut and coffee order, the owner noticed Stan and gave him a warm smile. "How you been doing! Haven't seen you in a while, but got to tell you, you're looking good", greeted the owner fondly.

"Never better!" replied Stan while also giving a subtle but warm smile.

"You look better than ever. Must be hustling a lot these past few months, huh? Just don't forget to get some sleep every once in a while, ok?" said the owner with a subtle hint of concern.

"Yeah, work's been overloading as of late, but I do get to slip in a few snoozes every now and then", said Stan in a joking manner so as to disarm any concern from the owner, and at the same time being careful not to reveal any personal or work matters into the conversation.

"Good to know!" said the owner followed with a laugh. "So, what will you be having?" asked the owner. "I'll have the classic and regular coffee combo", replied Stan. "Ok, got it", said the owner.

The owner immediately proceeded to prepare Stan's order. Stan however noticed that the owner discretely got a classic doughnut and a chocolate coated doughnut and placed one on top of the other, as if to pass off the two doughnuts as just one. "I really appreciate the owner trying to brighten my day up again, but I can't keep getting these freebies at his expense", said Stan to himself as he signaled the owner about the additional doughnut.

Already with an idea as to what the owner is planning, and in an attempt to discourage the owner, Stan said jokingly "you have got to stop spoiling me already".

"What are you talking about?" said the owner in a coy manner. "At least let me pay for the additional doughnut", said Stan as he handed out a bill that covered both his order and the additional doughnut.

"Don't sweat it! I was going to throw the leftover doughnuts anyway if I can't sell them today. Might as well give them to one of my regulars, if only to make their day," said the owner with a bright smile, as he gives Stan's change insistently, without charging for the chocolate doughnut.

"I can never win an argument with you, can I", said Stan, with a big smile. "This owner is really special", thought Stan to himself.

As he was walking away from the doughnut stall to look for an available bench to eat, he kept recalling the genuine gesture of the doughnut shop owner. And each time he recalled the gesture, he couldn't help but smirk.

"I guess the owner noticed that I looked better dressed than I was, before I was partner. But I guess, I still looked like a kid in a whole lot of mess, despite how well I looked", thought Stan, as he kept looking for an available seat. "Maybe to him, we are all just customers, waiting to satisfy, not only our hunger, but maybe even more. Must be nice to look at others beyond race, color or bias. And I guess to a point, we may all just be stomachs, just waiting for our hearts, minds, and of course actual stomachs, to be satisfied", said Stan to himself.

Before Stan could fully complete his thoughts, his phone vibrated as an email was received. Stan quickly checked his email and reviewed the communication. "Do they really expect us to make a decent pleading in just half a day?!" said Stan, visibly frustrated as he dialed a number in his phone.

"Hi Nathan, did you get the email from Marly? The one with the documents we asked three weeks ago", asked Stan through the phone. "Yeah, we gave them several reminders on this and the last one was two days ago. I even called Mason to remind them of the deadline and the need for these documents. Yeah, Mason said that they were really flooded with work, of late. Anyway, since the deadline to submit our pleading is the day after tomorrow, and Mason wants to review first our pleading, can you check on the documents they sent and make the necessary changes to the draft pleading accordingly. Also, kindly give me a summary of the documents they sent so we can easily reference them as we review tomorrow. I understand it's already 6:30pm, but can you push through again tonight for this one so we can give Mason the draft by tomorrow afternoon? Ok, appreciate it. Will wait for your draft tonight or tomorrow early morning. Thanks", said Stan as he ended his call.

Checking again at his designer watch, partly hoping that if he stared hard enough, time would stop, while partly trying to map out the tasks that needed to be done and how much time he had to be able to do them. "I guess this donut and coffee will do as dinner for tonight", said Stan to himself as he looked for an empty bench.

Stan scouted the park to look for the perfect spot to consume his dinner. He only saw two benches at the spot and the nearest one was already occupied by a middle-aged man, who looked like the typical salaryman who took a coffee break before commuting home. Past the salaryman's bench however was an empty bench.

"Perfect! An empty bench, just what the doctor ordered!" said Stan to himself as he darted towards the empty bench. "It's best to eat on the bench alone so I can check on my emails and also avoid appearing snobbish to a seatmate", again said Stan as he was just a step away from the salaryman's bench.

As his gaze was so focused on the empty bench, Stan was not able to see a jogger running towards him from his right. As the jogger herself also got distracted by a sudden wave from a jogger running the opposite direction, she only noticed Stan when they were a meter apart. With quick reflex however by the jogger, and Stan also noticing the jogger a meter away, the jogger was able to side step away from Stan before making contact.

"Sorry about that", said the jogger as she continued to jog on, convinced that she did not make contact with Stan.

"Oh, come on! Watch where you're going!" said Stan in an irritated voice, as he was able to dodge the collision. "Sorry again!" said the jogger, now several meters from Stan, as she continued to jog on.

Despite his reaction to dodge the collision, his reflexes however caused some of his coffee to spill to his sleeves. Upon noticing the mild spill on his sleeves, Stan stopped to wipe the coffee with the dry portion of the table napkin from his coffee.

"Maybe this can help", said the salaryman, while extending his hand from his seat to give some of his table napkin from some food he also got from the park.

"Thanks", said Stan hesitantly, as he continued to wipe his sleeve. "Hope I did not get any of my coffee on you", politely said Stan to the salaryman, in an attempt to reciprocate the kindness.

"Nope, the coffee only got you this time", said the salaryman jokingly. "Sorry about that. She just ran into me and I barely got away from that without a scratch", said Stan with a smile.

"Well, it seems like you won't be getting the empty bench because of that near collision", said the salaryman as he pointed to the bench that Stan was targeting. As Stan looked at the direction of the salaryman's point, he saw a couple now sitting on the bench he was eyeing.

As Stan sighed while his shoulders and head fell in defeat, the salaryman said "well, if it's any consolation, you can sit with me."

"Are you sure it's fine with you?" asked Stan with a slight delight in his tone. "Yeah, there is plenty of room in this bench for us both", said the salaryman, as he cleaned some of his stuff from the bench.

"Thanks a lot for offering your seat", said Stan, as he now sits on the bench with the salaryman. "I guess this should be enough, so I can get through with dinner, and begin working on the Wiseman case", said Stan to himself, as he lays out his meal.

Stan began munching on the doughnut while chasing it every now and then with his coffee, while making an awkward smile to the salaryman, every once in a while. As Stan began to settle into his meal, he was puzzled as to how the salaryman knew that he was aiming for the open bench.

"By the way, sir", said Stan gently. "Yep, what is it?" asked the salaryman. "How did you know that I was aiming for the empty bench just a moment ago?" asked Stan.

The salaryman made a short pause, then said "well, isn't it obvious?", as he looked Stan in the eyes. "I'm your stalker", said the salaryman, in a soft and serious voice.

As he said that, Stan paused and intently observed the eyes and facial expression of the salaryman, who was still staring seriously at Stan. And after a brief moment, "it was that obvious that I was gunning for that seat, wasn't it?!" said Stan.

"Yup, pretty much! When I saw you darting from towards this direction, I knew you wanted to get that bench for yourself. I know I would have done the same, if I were in your shoes", said the salaryman, as they both cracked to laughter.

"Anyway, I hope you get to enjoy your doughnut before you go back to work", said the salaryman. "That's a very tasty doughnut you have there. One of my favorites as well", continued the salaryman.

"Now how did you know that I was going back to work again?" asked Stan with a puzzled look. "Well, you just simply look the type", said the salaryman, as he and Stan again shared a laugh. As their laughter settled, they continued with their meals.

"If I may ask though. Why do you work so hard? What keeps you moving, day in and day out?" seriously asked the salaryman.

After getting caught off guard with the sudden seriousness of the question, Stan collected his composure and thought about how best to respond. "Why do I work hard?" Stan asked himself as he pondered for a reason, any reason, why he does what he does.

"I'm actually not sure. I guess that's just how I was trained growing up. If I were to pursue an endeavor, I should pursue it to the best of my ability", said Stan with energy, despite some reservations to his answer. "I think, at the end of the day, the discipline and learning you gain by going about your activities in the right way, is what matters", continued Stan.

The salaryman listened and thought about what Stan said, and after a brief pause, he said, "well, I agree with you that the journey is very important in any endeavor. But I also think that the destination is equally important."

"Imagine training and eventually participating in a long jump event, and realize when you are no longer able to stand, that you were actually meant for track and field? I think what would have been a regrettable life", said the salaryman, as he also tried to ponder on the thought.

As both Stan and the salaryman thought about the question, despite the joggers around them at that moment, it seemed as though there was complete serenity in the environment, as both of them wondered in their heads.

After a brief moment, in what seemed to be a lifetime for both of them, the salaryman noticed the silence. "Or maybe not. Maybe he still would have lived a full life despite being in the wrong event", jokingly said the salaryman, in an effort to lighten the mood once more.

Stan simply nodded and smiled politely back at the salaryman. "Anyway, as I am already through with my dinner and so I don't miss my bus, I'll leave you to your dinner", said the salaryman, as he tidies his things. And before Stan could reply, the salaryman was already standing up.

"Thanks for the company! See you around!" said the salaryman, as he waved goodbye. "Thanks for the napkin, and you take care", replied Stan as he also waved goodbye.

Stan watched the salaryman walk away from him until he was no longer in sight. And although the salaryman was already gone, his words lingered on.

Chapter 7

A Never-Ending Cycle

As Stan was walking back to the office, he was still reflecting on the salaryman's questions. Reaching his office and turning on the lights, he sat down at his table and opened his computer. "Why do I work so hard every time? I guess because my client's trust deserves no less than my absolute best", said Stan to himself as he checked his emails and tried to do some work.

"And I guess for the most part, I really want to earn a lot of money so I can take it easy later on in my life. I think it's only wise to capitalize on my youth and energy now to earn a few bucks, so that I'd have something to draw from, later on in life. It also won't hurt to build a network and establish a good reputation this early in the game", said Stan to himself with a smirk, as he tried to resolve his thoughts. Feeling satisfied with his conclusion, he continued to work further into the night.

The next day at almost noon, the partners just finished with their monthly meeting. During the meeting, Stan sat next to Shin since they were the two youngest partners of the firm and have had the most work together, thus far. As they were going out of the conference room, Stan whispered to Shin "how are the Franze and Enigma cases doing?"

"The cases are very active of late and so we had to pull a few all-nighters just to get by", answered Shin in a hushed voice.

"With all the old cases being active, and several new clients pouring in, how do you keep up?" said Stan without trying to sound too snoopy. After Stan asked that question, Shin stopped walking, turned his head towards Stan, and stared Stan in the eyes for a moment.

"Is it the new partner mentorship time already?" asked Shin in a joking manner.

"I'm not sure what you're talking about?" asked Stan while a bit baffled. "Was there supposed to be a mentorship time for all new partners? Because I'd like to get some of that right now, I guess", continued Stan.

Shin did not respond to Stan's question, but instead walked towards Mike and had a short discussion with him. Shin and Mike then walked back to where Stan was standing, as Mike made a smile.

"I guess it's already time for us to talk about you and your career", said Mike to a still confused Stan. "Let's have lunch at my office", said Mike, as he walked past Stan before he could even respond. Mike then went to his secretary and instructed her to bring three portions of their pre-ordered meals into his office.

"Let's not keep our managing partner waiting", said Shin, as he motions Stan to follow them. And they walked until they got inside Mike's office.

Mike's office had a separate sofa and table to receive guests or conduct meetings with. As Mike's secretary laid down the pre-ordered lunch at the separate table, Mike motioned for them to sit down, as he joined them.

"I know we already discussed the benefits, job, and targets for you as a new partner during your initial orientation to the partnership role. We even had some discussions on the possible issues you may encounter as a partner and even some tips from me and Shin, on how to make good being a new partner. But to be honest, you can only appreciate the role, once you are actually doing the job. And so, we normally do counselling sessions every now and then with the new partners, to check on them and give them more tips on being a partner, as well as to try and answer any questions they may want to ask by that time", said Mike with a smile.

"It actually didn't occur to me to initiate this discussion, as you seemed to be a natural at the role, so I thought maybe you no longer needed any of our advice. Not to say that it's a bad thing if we have to counsel you, all I'm saying is that you actually managed quite well for an extraordinarily long time, before you had to ask for any guidance. But still, everyone needs to ask for help eventually, and so we are here, and we would be happy to give you any tips", said Mike.

"I'm a bit surprised that we ended up in your office to talk about my career. But I am very grateful for this opportunity to get some guidance from both of you on how to do better in my role", initially said Stan. "I guess I was asking Shin earlier about some of his personal tips on how he manages the workload he has right now. And I guess I was also trying to underhandedly get some tips on how Shin handles the stress that comes with the bonuses", Stan clarified with a laugh.

"Of course. It's only natural to ask about these things. All the partners here have been through what you are going through right now. No matter how well we start off, the workload and pressure eventually get to you", said Mike with a laugh.

"I can't agree more. I remember just my third month as a partner, I already had more on my plate than I can ever ask for", said Shin with a smile. "But if you just continue with it, you sort of get a second wind and eventually get through it. And after a busy stretch, the bonus at the end, more than makes up for it", Shin continued with a wink.

"Knowing Stan, I don't think he needs any convincing about the payout in the end. But just in case you have any doubts, I'm telling you now, with the number of jobs you are getting in, your bonus at the end of the year may easily be the highest bonus for a new partner we will have since the start of the firm. So, I guess, if you were asking how any of us are able to keep up with all the work, then the easiest answer would be our trust that after our hard work, we will reciprocally be rewarded in the end. Knowing that the harder we work, the better we get paid, is more than enough motivation to keep at it day-in and day-out", said Mike with a serious conviction.

"Now, just because we have a good drive, doesn't mean we won't have down times, or moments when our whole being just wants to stop working altogether. Times when we are so overcome by stress and pressure that we just want to give it all up", said Mike, as he stared intently at Stan. "And I think it comes to all of us, although to varying degrees and at different periods in their career", continued Mike.

"In those moments, that's when being in a partnership really counts. In those moments, that's when we support you and tell you that it will be fine later on. That's the time that we impart some of our wisdom to you and encourage you. As we already understand that even the most passionate partner can lose their fire at any given time, it's the time wherein we come together and try to ignite a fire once more in your heart, through the burning passion we have for our chosen calling. Because law is a calling, a vocation, wherein we make sure that the rights of our clients are properly represented. And in so doing, we hope that order and the law always prevails in our society", said Mike with a subtle but fierce conviction.

"This is who we are, and who we intend to be in the years to come. And more than your talent and your dedication, we also chose to welcome you into our ranks, because you represent these values and we have confidence that you can pass it on to the next generation of partners, long after we are gone", said Mike with eyes starting to redden and water a bit, but still being able to control his emotions, and withhold any tears.

With a brief pause as Mike tried to compose himself, Mike continued "so we hope that you can trust us and trust the process, and know that we want nothing but your best interest in mind".

Silently listening and passionately absorbing the words and emotion of Mike's statements, Stan was deeply moved at the wisdom and passion of Mike's words. Stan intently listened to every word delivered and nodded at the words to express full belief and trust.

"Thanks, Mike, for all that you said, and I am truly humbled by the trust you have for me and what I represent. These times have really been draining for me due to the workload and the pressure of delivering on the targets, so I really needed those words to remind me of why I am doing all the things that I have been doing so far. I really needed those words to put things into perspective so that I can continue on", said Stan, as he paused for a moment as he reflected back for a moment on the words he just heard.

"I hope you guys won't get tired of ushering us new partners until we fully mature into the best partners we can be", said Stan with a smile.

"You don't have to worry about that. We will always be here every step of the way. And we'll also count on you to usher us into the new generation, when we are no longer strong enough to keep up", said Shin.

"We will do our best", said Stan. "That's all we need to hear", said Mike as the three of them nodded in agreement.

"So, I guess the only thing left to be done is for us to have lunch?" said Shin jokingly, as he attempts to lighten the mood. "That and have a few drinks later tonight, so we can drink some of Stan's stress away", said Mike in a coy way, before they all burst into laughter.

"Sure! I'm paying", said Stan while still laughing. "You should! You are due for a big payday. Might as well start celebrating as early as now", said Shin now with a big grin. And they began eating their lunch, as Stan asked for some practical tips on how to handle demanding clients and unreasonable deadlines, among other things.

As they were just about done with lunch, Stan remembered the statements of the salaryman. "Given Mike and Shin's wisdom and experience, I think it's best to get their thoughts as well, to get some perspective, and to finally get over it", said Stan to himself. He gathered his thoughts and tried to phrase his statement the best way possible. Considering however that the lunch break is almost over and Shin is already cleaning himself up to leave, Stan hurriedly said, "before we leave, can I ask you one last question?"

"Sure! Have at it", said Mike.

"Well, I guess I think it would be a treat for me as a new partner, to know why two of the most esteemed and hardworking lawyers in the country dedicate their time and energy to this demanding vocation?" said Stan while stuttering a bit.

As the two partners pondered on the question, and unsure if he was able to ask the question clearly, Stan tried to quickly clarify "I mean, why did you enter such a demanding profession, and work hard day in and day out? I mean, essentially, I just wanted to know the reason why you work this hard?"

"Well…" said Mike, followed by a pause, as he tries to come up with the answer to best address the question. "As you know, I am not one of the founders of this firm and took over the stewardship of the firm when the founders were a few years away from retirement, so I guess I can only tell you about their motivation based from my interactions with them", said Mike as though trying to gauge if Stan is ok if he spoke on behalf of the previous partners.

"Ah, of course I wouldn't expect you to know what was in the hearts and minds of the founders, and I guess to clarify, I wanted to hear more about your personal motivation as you work here", said Stan.

"Well…" said Mike, as he paused a bit as he tried to give the best answer he could to the question. "I guess I work hard every day because I am motivated to work for a firm that rewards people for their hard work. I mean, I started out as a staff and worked long and hard to get to this point. And now that my long hours and stress has finally paid off, I think it's only right that I get to enjoy the good life brought about by my perseverance. And I can tell you honestly, now that you are yourself a partner, the pay you get here will more than make up for your sacrifice during the early stages of your career", said Mike as he smiled and gave a wink.

"I can't agree enough", said Shin as he also gave Stan a wink and a big smile, while Stan's expression did not change. "But seriously, coming from a poor neighborhood, I had to study and persevere to get to this point in my life. And the reason I stayed and persevered was the faith that my hard work will pay off. Now as a partner of several years now, I can tell you that the hard work, absolutely pays off. I can testify to that. And now that you are a partner, you'll know soon enough what I am talking about", said Shin, as both him and Mike made very big smiles.

"Now that you are already a partner, it's time for you as well to have a taste of the fruits of your hard work. All that's left is for you to keep pushing, so that your bonus at the end of the year will be the biggest check that you have ever seen in your life. Am I right?" said Mike, as he nudged Shin.

"I couldn't agree more!" echoed Shin.

"I guess you're right", said Stan, as he tries to match Shin and Mike's enthusiasm, while trying to hide his reservation.

"Glad you agree. Now let's go out and earn our paychecks", said Mike as they all ended the lunch meeting and the two went to their respective offices.

Stan slowly enters his office, still trying to ponder on the lessons and thoughts brought about by his lunch with Mike and Shin. As he walks towards his table, he scans some documents for his review and his laptop, as he tries to recall what his tasks were for the day. He then shifts his gaze towards the side of his office made of glass and gives him a great view of the city, as his thoughts return to the conversation he had with Mike and Shin.

"I guess they are both right. This already came from two aged partners who have already seen most of what life can offer", said Stan, as he walked past his table and looked at the busy city streets through his view.

"I have consistently worked hard since childhood up to now, to be able to attain my credentials and reputation, and I have dedicated a good part of my life to be able to reach this point in my career. I was blessed with talent that falls second to none, and still put in the work to make sure people would know that I have not taken my gifts for granted. More importantly, I have cheated no one, and have done my studies and work the right way. I think it's only fair that I get to enjoy all the benefits which I have sought out to attain", said Stan as he breathed deeply while his view was still fixed on a busy pedestrian crossing.

After a brief pause, Stan made a big sigh and smiled. "I guess I over-thought this one again. I work hard because it is the right thing to do. It wouldn't be fair to my parents, to my clients, and to those who look up to me to give anything less than a hundred percent. So, I work my ass off every day, so that I can leave a better world than before I found it", he said to himself with a smile on his realization.

"As Mike said, the only thing to do is to earn that paycheck so that I can maybe inspire others to do it the right way", he said to himself with conviction.

With an energized morale and with conviction pumping through his veins, Stan mustered in a deep breath, and again began working.

Chapter 8

The Road More Travelled

Three months have passed since Stan had that lunch with Mike and Shin, and Stan just finished a meeting with one of the oldest clients of their firm. After Stan shook hands with all of the executives of the Marc Group, he ushered them towards the elevator, while pleasantly talking to their president about the tennis varsity programs of some of the prominent colleges in the country.

No sooner than the elevator completely closing, Stan checked his designer watch and saw that it was already 11:56am. Taking a second to map out how he should approach the remaining part of the day, he then walked to his office.

"Shirly, what time did the JaCu Group say they would arrive at the office?" asked Stan as he passed by Shirly on his way to his office.

"They said they would be here by 1:15pm later", said Shirly.

After a brief pause, with Stan's eyes deep in thought, he asked "what time does the partner's meeting end?"

"It's scheduled from 4:00-6:00pm later, but considering the loaded agenda for tonight, it may end later than that", said Shirly with a concerned look at Stan.

"Don't worry about it. Got to earn my paycheck at the very least", jokingly said Stan.

"And you also have the 3:15pm-4:00pm call with the prospective client", said Shirly, as Stan was about to step into his office.

"Yup, already checked the documents they sent for that boss", said Stan sarcastically.

"If you got that, then get to work already", replied Shirly as they shared a laugh.

"But seriously, thanks for sparing 15 minutes between the meeting and the call. With the way these days have gone, I need those 15-minute breaks in between", said Stan as he stepped into his office after Shirly gave a thumbs up.

"Wow, that meeting took longer than expected. I guess being one of our oldest clients, guarantees some freebie advice. I just never thought they'd have those questions, this early in the merger", said Stan to himself with a deep sigh.

"I thought I could finish my review of the draft pleading on the Tyler case before lunch, so I had enough time tonight to review the two other drafts on my plate", thought Stan, as he paused to think for a second.

"I'll just have to work again through lunch then", he said to himself with some disappointment, as he dialed his phone to ask Shirly to get him some light lunch.

As he puts the phone down, Stan begins separating the documents and the printed draft of the Tyler case pleadings. As he lifted the Tyler case documents, a financial statement for "Farmer's Charm" corporation was revealed. He paused for a moment, and lifted the "Farmer's Charm" financial statements after he stacked the documents on the Tyler case on the center of his table.

"Can my team even handle this new work? Do I even have the time to handle this work?" said Stan to himself with a frown.

“I don’t think working through weekends would be enough to get this job done”, said Stan as he analyzes the financial statement. “How much does this company make?” he thought, as he flipped the pages to the “Income Statement” portion of the financial statement.

“Wow, didn’t expect an agricultural business to gross this much in a year. They must be doing something right over there”, thought a surprised Stan.

“Despite that, I still don’t see how we can handle this much new work for their group. I’ll just have to propose a big fee for them so that it would at least be worth our while, should they decide to work with us”, thought Stan while still scanning the financial statement. “I guess my first agricultural client is my 3:15pm call. This may get interesting”, said Stan with a smile.

Shortly after, Stan worked on the Tyler case as he had lunch. He then proceeded to attend his 1:00pm meeting and again ushered the JaCu Group executives to their elevator.

As the door of the elevator closed, Stan checked his watch and thought “it’s still just 3:09pm. I’ll just take the toilet and have a short discussion with Brad before the call”. Upon entering his office, Brad was already there with the files on the “Farmer’s Charm” corporation.

“So, what have you seen on their company information and documents?” Stan asked Brad. “Well, it seems like this company grew astronomically overnight, so their corporate structure is not ideal, and their legal and tax compliance systems are all over the place. It also appears that they had several departments in their sole corporation, which has their own separate operations and profit.

“That being said, the company earns a lot and has very big and sustainable margins across their departments. On top of that, the company owns several intellectual properties, although seemingly controlled by their respective departments.

“I had an initial call with their head of accounting the other day, when I asked for the required documents, and the ask for this call, is for us to give them an overview of the regulatory compliance requirements for their type of business, and for us to point out the specific areas in their current structure, that needs correction and improvement”, discussed Brad.

“Who would be joining this call?” calmly asked Stan, albeit with eyes deep in thought. “Their head of accounting, Patty, would be joining the call, along with Marvin, the founder and owner himself, would be joining the call”, reported Brad.

“Were you able to fish out what their budget is for this project?” asked Stan again. “I wasn’t able to get their budget for this project, but what I can tell is that they really want to iron out their operation and make sure that they are not only complying with the existing laws, but make sure that their structure and operations are protected from any future risks.

“They probably would appreciate a few savings here and there, but the general direction seems to be for us to tell them what they are doing wrong, or how they can improve on their current structure, and offer our services to solve and improve their situation. Patty asked us to give them a list of the services we can offer and the respective fees for each service”, discussed Brad.

“Haven’t we already given them a list of services and the corresponding fees?” asked Stan. “Yes, we gave them our list and the corresponding fees last night. I think one of the possible discussions for today’s call would be our fee prices and possible details of our scope of work.

"Patty did allude that the owner may have some questions here and there and depending on his questions, new work may come up. So, just in case new work comes up, then she is asking us to put that in our list of services and quotes", discussed Brad.

"The list of services we provided are pretty standard, so I don't think there would be any need to add any more to that. As for the fees, we may have to insist on the fees we already quoted because it seems to me that getting this company's compliance in order will require a lot of time on our part. We may agree on a discount for the less complicated work in our list, but for the most part, let's just stick to the fees we gave them", replied Stan.

After a brief pause, as Stan was deep in thought, he directed Brad to make the call. As the phone rang through loud speaker, Brad and Stan waited on, as both thought about how best to approach the potential client.

"Hello?", said the woman who answered the call. "Good afternoon Patty. This is Brad again, and I am joined by Stan, one of the partners in our firm", greeted Brad.

"Good afternoon Patty! This is Stan, Brad's partner in charge of this engagement. Nice to meet you!" greeted Stan.

"Good afternoon Brad and Stan! Thanks for having us. By the way, I am joined today by our owner, Marvin", greeted Patty.

"Hi Good afternoon Stan and Brad! Thanks again for having us", greeted Marvin. "Hi Marvin, pleasure to be here and glad to finally talk to you", replied Stan.

"So, how can we help you?" asked Stan.

"Well first of all, we are a start-up company that heavily invests in R&D to develop cutting edge agricultural technology that improves the quality and size of yield, while also reducing the carbon emission that these farms produce. Our focus has also been to make sure that the food that is available to a greater number of people were not treated with fertilizers or pesticides, are non-GMO, and are fresher and more nutritious, than those produced through normal farming methods. Our business plan is peculiar than most agricultural corporations because we don't really own any agricultural lands or cattle.

"We primarily focus on the development of technology that allows us to achieve our goal of spreading sustainable and eco-friendly agricultural practices while making sure that all walks of life get to enjoy fresh and nutritious produce. We earn by partnering with agricultural corporations, cooperatives, and family-owned farms, and lending them our technology, products and expertise, for a fee. By our existence, we hope that we not only improve, but also change, the global agricultural and environmental landscape.

"That being said, and to be upfront, we are a very young corporation that experienced tremendous growth over the last few years, and as a result, our small finance team no longer had the competence, nor the manpower, to be able to handle the monitoring and compliance of our monthly, quarterly and annual filings and compliance requirements, among others. We initially had a small law firm that assisted us in our incorporation, as well as during the initial stages of our early corporate life, but as the needs of our firm grew, we felt that the small law firm was no longer able to satisfy our requirements.

"So, we are now looking for a law firm that can help us understand all our current regulatory requirements, and help us comply with all of the said requirements, on time and as they come. On top of that, we would want your law firm to make a diagnosis on our current corporate structure and established procedures, and give us recommendations on how to improve our legal compliance positions; make our company or possible group of companies easier to manage; avail of possible tax or regulatory exceptions applicable to us; and establish protocols and contract provisions that can protect us from all possible risks in the future.

"We came to your firm because Mr. Paul, of the Roe family, had high praises for how your firm has been handling their requirements. Having known Mr. Paul for a while, and after relying on his constant guidance on how to better manage the company, I've known that he isn't the type to easily be impressed.

"That aside, we would still be mindful of the fees for the legal services, as we still would want to remain within our set budget for the year. And so, I am hoping you can also accommodate us on that front", discussed Marvin, as Stan strategized on how best to insist on their fees, while still giving them some leeway to not reject their proposals outright, due to fees.

As Marvin paused, Stan tried to formulate the right combination of words to make Marvin appreciate just how indispensable their expertise and service are for the success of their business. As Stan was about to mutter his words, Marvin cut in. "We were able to receive your list of services and fees last night, and we thank you for that. And want to discuss them one by one later in our call. But I hope you won't mind if we ask you to give us some overview of the tax, labor and other legal regulatory requirements applicable for our company and for corporations in general, so we also get to have an idea, in a way, as to which services we need to prioritize.

Slightly taken aback, but still composed, Stan replied "Sure, that won't be a problem. We do normally start off our meetings with some lecture on the legal and regulatory landscape anyway, as clients in general want to know what they are actually dealing with before moving forward".

Stan then began to lecture on the legal landscape and after some question and answer, began discussing the list of services offered and the quoted fees.

After Stan's discussion, Marvin paused before saying "thanks for the discussion. It was really insightful. Having heard about the things we need to do and the consequences should we not comply, it appears imperative that we handle these issues now, before they become bigger problems in the near future.

"Based on how our company stands right now, and given our budget limitations, is there any way for us to get all the services offered at a slightly reduced price? Now, I know your standing in the legal practice, and I also appreciate that your reputation is unparalleled, but making sure that your fees also meet our projected budget, would go a long way for us to go with you as our law firm of choice".

"So, if possible, we would like to ask for some discount on your fees", continued Marvin.

Slightly pissed but still maintaining composure, Stan answered "we understand your concerns Marvin, but I hope you understand that our fees are quite fair, for the amount of work that is required from us. It may be hard for us to further lower our fees at this time, given the already low margins we have on the fees we gave you". And Stan paused briefly, as he thinks about how best to continue, and also to gauge Marvin's reaction to what he just said.

"To be frank, we really want to work with your firm, not only because of your impressive reputation, but more importantly, because of the trust that Mr. Paul has in you. Is there a way we can explore some arrangement, wherein we can still work together but still keep things under budget?" said Marvin with a calm undertone.

"We appreciate the confidence in our capabilities, and we also want to work with your company", said Stan before pausing. "I can't give you any guarantees, but let me consult with our managing partner on this and we will try to work out the best approach to hopefully proceed with our engagement", continued Stan.

"Yes, I perfectly understand. I hope to get your feedback on this as early as possible", said Marvin.

"We will", replied Stan.

"Ok, good to hear. So, what would be our next steps?" asked Marvin.

"I will set a meeting with Mike on this today or tomorrow, then we will get back to you at the latest, by the end of the week. And we will see from there", replied Stan.

"Ok, sounds good! Will wait for your reply. Thanks for your time" replied Marvin.

"Sure. Have a great day! Goodbye!" replied Stan as he hung up the call after Marvin and Patty said their goodbyes.

After giving some instructions to Brad, he tidied himself and called Shirly's local. "What conference are we using for the partner's meeting?" asked Stan.

"Today's venue is the McArthur conference room", answered Shirly.

"Is Mike and the rest of the partner's already there?" asked Stan again.

"All the other partners are already there and I see Mike getting out of his office right now", reported Shirly.

"Ok perfect! Thanks", said Stan as he dropped the call.

Stan quickly got out of his office, and looked for Mike as he opened his door. Upon seeing him, he quickly walked towards him.

Stan was able to catch up to Mike as he waited for the elevator. "It's not like you to be late Mike", quipped Stan to a Mike who was reading emails in his phone. "Hi Stan. I can say the same about you", Mike wittingly fired back as they stepped in the elevator.

"Sharp as always. No, I just got off a call with a prospective client. The eco-friendly agricultural company Famer's Charm", discussed Stan, as they stepped out and walked towards the conference room.

"Oh, yeah! A lot of my clients, especially the younger ones, are raving about that up-and-coming start-up company. So how did the meeting go?" asked Mike, as they were getting closer to the doors of the conference room.

"The owner joined the call and was actually doing most of the talking during the call. We checked their financial statements and their current income, as well as their project growth, and the figures were very promising. Despite that however, their compliance and record keeping infrastructure needs a lot of work. And given the work my team and I currently have, I don't think it would be best for us to take on the Farmer's

Charm group, unless it came with very big returns", discussed Stan, as they were now at the door of the conference room.

As soon as Stan finished saying his last word, Mike stopped walking, and turned to face Stan. "Did they ask for a discount?" calmly asked Mike.

"Yes. They said that they were very interested in having us as their law firm of choice, but that they also wanted to make sure that they don't overstep their budget in hiring their law firm", replied Stan.

After a pause, Mike asked "So did they already reject our proposals?".

"Not yet. Marvin, the owner, asked if we can figure out an arrangement, wherein we can work within the limits of their budget, and also make sure that our work and margins are not compromised. I then told him that I'd have to consult with you first on this and get back to him afterwards", said Stan to an intently listening Mike.

"Oh, good! It's a good thing that you did not yet deny his request for a discount. Try to get in touch with him again as soon as possible, because we need to get them to sign with us. As I will discuss during our meeting shortly, the current projections of our earnings are currently in the red zone, and we need to get as much cash go in, so that we don't have to borrow to pay for our short-term expenses", discussed Mike, with some sigh of relief.

"Well, I don't mind giving them any discounts, as that has always been effective for me to close engagements these past few months. But my concern is my workload and that of my managers and staff. We are already getting slightly behind on some of our deliverables, due to the sheer number of jobs on our plate. So maybe I can transfer this engagement to Shin, or some other partner who needs the work more than I do. I already exceeded my targets by ten percent last week, and maybe this engagement can help out another partner that is falling behind his or her target", reasoned Stan.

"How exactly did this engagement get into our pipeline?" asked Mike.

"Well, Mr. Paul referred him to our firm because he was impressed with how we handled the Roe Family Group. It seems that Mr. Paul acts as a consultant or at least mentors Marvin on how to manage his business, and so they came to us because of Mr. Paul's referral", answered Stan.

"Well, in that case, it wouldn't seem ideal if we transferred the account to a different partner. More or less, it's your brand of work they are after, and we may lose their business if we gave their job to another partner. Besides, I don't think any of the partners have enough time and competence to handle this additional work.

"As I discussed with you before, we as partners support each other in times of trouble. Right now, we need to earn more for the quarter for us to maintain a healthy financial position. You are in the best position to help us get over this situation right now. And we hope that you won't shy away from the opportunity to carry us through", elaborated Mike, as he signals the other partners to settle down and get inside the conference room.

"Besides, the earnings from these new jobs get added to your end of your profit share, so it's not like you're working for peanuts right here. You are already part of the ownership, so you always get a percentage of all the fees you attract into the firm. Just try to manage the people working under these accounts and just feel free to reward them later on", discussed Mike, as both him and Stan now enter the conference room.

Stan thought about what Mike discussed as they walked towards their seats in the conference room. Before Mike could reach his seat, Stan asked "so how much discount should we give them on this? And how do I maintain my profit margins on these activities?"

"Well, I think it depends on the type of work they need and what type of services we can lump into the other jobs, or just set aside for now. We can talk about that later. What's important is that you get in touch with them as soon as possible, and possibly try to make them come to our office to meet face-to-face and try to close their accounts as soon as possible", said Mike, as he now takes a seat in front.

"Are we on the same page on that?" asked Mike. "Yup. Copy that", said Stan as he walks towards his seat while Mike signals to start the meeting.

As the meeting started, Stan got to his seat near Shin. Before Stan could sit comfortably in his chair, Shin was already leaning towards Stan. "Hey, do you know a lawyer working at the supreme court by the name of Lloyd?" whispered Shin.

"I have a law school classmate by that name who works for the supreme court. Tall skinny guy with glasses?" asked Stan. "Yup, that's the guy", answered Shin. "What about him?" asked Stan again.

"Well, a friend of mine who works at the supreme court said that your friend recently got appointed chief of staff to the incumbent house speaker in congress", explained Shin.

"Well, I never would have known that he'd go to congress after working for so long at the supreme court. Besides, he always wanted to become a judge in the later periods of his career, although getting close to the speaker of the house might actually be more strategic, if he wants to get appointed as judge someday", whispered Stan, as Shin listened on.

"But it's still surprising how things turned out, because he was always talking about staying with the supreme court as he waited for his chance to get appointed. Me frankly, I never thought he'd get hired as the chief of staff by an incumbent speaker of the house, considering that he really didn't have an assertive personality during our law school days", continued Stan, as he paused to visualize how Lloyd was able to get the chief of staff role.

"Yeah, my classmates at the supreme court were also surprised when they heard about the appointment, especially because we had classmates, whom we thought had more experience and credentials than your classmate and yet were not hired. When I heard that he came from your law school and from your batch, I had a hunch that you'd know the guy", said Shin.

"I've known him all my life. We were neighbors and we practically grew up together", answered Stan.

"But again, I'm as surprised as you are with that appointment. You can also never tell with those appointments. Trust is always an important role in selecting those positions, so we never know how the applications all went down. All I can say is that he can easily use that position to get appointed to a government post of his choice, once his speaker's tenure is ending. That's actually an impressive opportunity he just got", said Stan with a grin, as he tries to recall his school and childhood days with Llyod.

"Yup, no doubt about it. He would feast with connections while he remained chief of staff. Anyway, I'll just tell my classmates that they lost to a younger lawyer because they didn't look decent enough", sarcastically said Shin, as he laughed.

"Wow Lloyd, never knew you had it in you", said Stan to himself as he texted Lloyd to confirm the news. "He better pay for a round or two the next time we get together", said Stan to himself with a big smile. He then hid his phone and listened to Mike's discussion.

"Yup, just got the news. How did you know?" texted Llyod. "A partner here at work just told me a moment ago" replied Stan, as the meeting was still ongoing. "Anyway, congrats! You better pay for a few rounds, when the gang gets together!" texted Stan, before Lloyd could even answer.

After a few minutes, and while Stan was still in the partner's meeting, Lloyd replied "Thanks! Sure, I'll take care of a few rounds. Anyway, just thankful I was lucky enough to get the spot. Text Monica and the gang, and let's hang out this Friday. See you soon!".

Stan felt happy and proud as he looked back at how he and Lloyd overcame college and law school. And he can't help but wonder how he would fit in, if he were the one handling the chief of staff position, instead of Lloyd. But as the discussion in the partner's meeting now focused on the need for new jobs, Stan ended his visualization, and focused on the ongoing discussion.

Once the partner's meeting ended, Stan approached Mike, and they discussed further how to approach the Farmer's Charm proposals, as well as the other details on the discount they can extend. After making several computations, and after deciding on the final fees to be quoted, Stan said "ok, I guess that settles it. I asked Brad earlier to call the head of finance and get a feel of the discount that would put us over the top".

"That's good. Let's just stick with this for now. Never mind the margins for now, and just focus on closing this deal. As I've discussed earlier, ask the client to have a face-to-face meeting, whether here or in their office, just to show that we really want to have them as a client, and to show that we are taking their concerns seriously.

"In my experience, clients better trust the lawyers that they actually get to meet first hand. So, I hope you've already set a meeting with them on this. Also try to set the meeting as soon as tomorrow, if they are free, so we can demonstrate how quick our turnaround is for any of their concerns", stated Mike.

"I understand. I'll try to set a meeting as early as possible, but tomorrow might not be possible because I have a hearing in the morning, and I'm joining you in the board of director's meeting with the Rocker Group in the afternoon", said Stan.

"Don't mind the board of director's meeting in the afternoon. Shin can attend that instead of you. Our top priority for now, is getting the Farmer's Charm group on board with us on the proposals. Have Brad prepare the paperwork for Shin to take your place in the board meeting, and just focus on Marvin. Also, email me tonight the draft opinion you made, so I can study them for the afternoon board meeting", instructed Mike.

"It's best if you can already finalize by tonight our revised proposals with the new scope and fees. So, try getting that done tonight, and forward to them an advance copy for their review. When you email them the advanced copies, ask them if they are available tomorrow afternoon, so you can go there and at least be able to tell if the discount is already enough. If they are available then you need to be there, but if they are not, then you can join me instead in the director's meeting. Ok?" asked Mike. "Got it" answered Stan.

"Good! So just be ready to discuss for both meetings just in case", said Mike, as he readied to leave the office.

"Will do. Brad already called the head of finance to ask if they are available in the afternoon, and so far, their schedules, including Marvin's, seem open. But they would have to check again tomorrow morning with Marvin's secretary, if the afternoon is really vacant, and will let us know as early as possible", reported Stan, as he walks with Mike towards their elevator.

"Ok good! Now make it happen", said Mike, as he entered the elevator. Shortly before the elevator could fully close, Stan was already walking back to his office.

Early the next morning, Stan set aside his coffee in a coaster and began checking his email. In the middle part of several emails received a few minutes past midnight, he saw a reply from Marvin to their earlier email. Upon opening, it simply read:

"Hi Stan,

"Thanks for the quick turnaround on the revised quotes. We are happy to discuss the same tomorrow from 1:00pm onwards. Just look for Patty when you get to our office.

"Cheers,

"Marvin"

Stan kept reviewing the email to make sure he did not miss anything, as he thought about how to go from the courtroom to the Farmer's Charm's office, as well as what he needed to bring and read to get him ready for the afternoon meeting.

After a few more minutes of fiddling over the email, Stan emailed Mike back, and afterwards emailed Brad his instructions for their afternoon meeting with the Farmer's Charm team. After reviewing some other emails and documents in his office, he tidied himself up, and went to court.

Shortly after his hearing ended, he got a quick lunch and immediately proceeded towards the Farmer's Charm's office. As he got to the receiving area, Brad told the receptionist that they were from the same firm. After getting his visitor's pass, he sat across Brad in their receiving area, as they waited for Patty to get them.

"Did you bring the proposals I signed this morning?" asked Stan.

"Yes, I got them all here in my bag", answered Brad.

"Ok good. Do they know that we are already here?" asked Stan again.

"Yes, the receptionist already called Patty to tell them that we are here and I also texted Patty of our arrival. Patty said that she is just arranging the board room we would be using and also just waiting for Marvin to finish his call", answered Brad.

"Ok good", replied Stan after which he opened his phone and checked his emails.

After a few minutes, the office entrance opened, and a seemingly jolly woman stepped out and walked towards their direction. She approached them with some apprehension, but got close nonetheless.

"Stan and Brad?" asked the woman with a smile. "Hi! Yes, I'm Brad, and this is my boss, Stan", greeted Brad as he pointed at Stan.

"Hi, I'm Patty by the way. Glad to finally meet you in person. You guys look younger than we imagined. But that's good!" said Patty as they shook hands. "Hi Patty! Nice to finally meet you! We can also say the same about you. We thought you were a staff in your finance division because you look very young", replied Stan.

"Thanks for the compliment, but I am already in my late thirties. I'm just fortunate to have a great team working under me, so I don't get too worked up about every small detail in our job", answered Patty with a smile. "So anyway, let's go ahead to our board room", as she led them inside and towards their venue. "Marvin is just finishing up on a call abroad and will join us shortly", continued Patty.

They walked towards a vacant board room and Patty called her staff to get them some refreshments. Shortly after they got in, a bearded but unassuming man, who was probably in his early fifties, entered the room.

"Hi, I'm Marvin. Thank you for your time", greeted Marvin as Stan and Brad introduced themselves while they shook hands.

"Well, first off, we'd like to thank you for the swift and very considerate response to our request for a fee reduction. And second of all, we appreciate you taking this time from your busy schedules to visit our office and meet us personally. We do prefer meetings in the flesh, although for the most part, it's really hard to set them up because of our hectic schedule here in the office, and so we were actually relieved that our schedule this afternoon was still free", discussed Marvin as they took their seats and the refreshments arrived.

"Yes, it is our pleasure to come to your office to actually meet you and your team as well. Of course, we didn't want to take too long to give you our feedback because we understand how busy your schedules are, and how important timely feedback is, to be able to effectively manage your corporation. Especially with how hectic things might be, considering all the recent growth you've had over the last few years", answered Stan, as he looks at Marvin intently, trying to look for some twitches or sudden facial cues with every word he delivers.

"Yes, we really appreciate the consideration, and that's really one of the things we like about your firm, on top of the impeccable reputation for quality service and renown expertise, and why we really had you as our first choice to help us through this transition.

"Now, going into the revised proposals we received last night. We were able to go through them earlier today and we have also made some discussions on them this morning, and have come to some conclusions on the same. Nonetheless, we would be happy to hear from you first regarding the scope of work and the fees involved, as well as what revisions you did to the proposals, and what the next steps would be", discussed Marvin.

"We really appreciate the trust and the opportunity to help you transition towards better opportunities in your field", Stan opened. Stan then proceeded to give Marvin and Patty copies of their proposal and began discussing the salient features of the contract and the revisions they made on the same.

After going through all the areas of the contract, Stan closed "and so, that's how our thought process was in coming up with our revisions and we really see your company as a pioneer in your field and it would also be a great opportunity for our firm to walk hand-in-hand with true innovators, as you fulfill your goals as an organization.

"As to the next steps, the only thing remaining before we can formally start this partnership is for the contracts to be signed and sent back to us. Once we receive the signed contracts, that would be our cue to begin working on our engagements".

"Thank you for that discussion Stan", said Marvin before pausing to choose his words. "As I said earlier, we already had some discussions on your proposal earlier, and we really appreciate how considerate you were with your pricing to make this partnership push through.

"To be honest, your revised fees were still a bit above our planned budget, but we do understand where you are coming from. Nevertheless, as we are committed to pursuing things the right way, we understand that having a solid team to support us in our legal standing and requirements, is a must, if we want to achieve what we want to achieve, in the manner we want to achieve them. So, we made some adjustments to our budget, and I am now at liberty to approve your proposal at the provided price point", said Marvin as Stan's eyes lit up, while his face was still able to maintain its calmness.

"If you have the contracts on hand, I can sign them here now, so we can save on time and on logistical expenses", asked Marvin as he did a signing motion with his hands.

"Yes, of course. We have the signed proposals here for your signature", answered Stan as he directs Brad to get them from his folder.

"Wow, another unexpected win", thought Stan to himself, as Brad got the proposals out and laid them on the table for Marvin to review.

"For a moment, I really thought we would be going home empty handed. And now, just like in the Roe family meeting, another big contract is unexpectedly signed. Brad should learn from this experience and always bring a proposal for signature at all times, especially when he becomes a partner", Stan thought to himself as Marvin signed the proposals.

"Well, now that that's done, it would be a waste if we sent you home without giving you a tour of our workshop, don't you think? Unless of course you have pressing matters to attend to, then maybe another time?", said Marvin as Brad and Patty tidied things up with the contracts and the venue.

"We'd love to have a tour of your office. Getting to know our new clients and how they conduct their business is the most important thing for us right now, and we wouldn't want to waste the chance to get to know you and your team more", replied Stan.

"Good! Don't hesitate to ask anything about our company or point out any of our practices that we should be concerned about, okay?" said Marvin. "Of course!" replied Stan with a timid smile.

"Well, this is unexpected", Stan to himself as they waited for Patty to return from his office. "With how busy the owner should be, and how intentional he conducted the meeting, I thought he preferred to end this quickly, so that he can keep with his schedule. But I can't complain.

"As much as I want to start working on the pending tasks to at least get them down a bit, my mind is really fatigued right now. Even if I went back to the office right now, I may just end up staring at the ceiling all day and actually just slow down my progress, or worse, give crappy outputs", Stan further thought to himself.

"Are you ready?" asked Marvin after Patty entered the room. "Yeah", answered Stan. "Good. Let's go then" said Marvin, as they led Stan and Brad out of the room.

"Maybe this tour is what I need to get my mind off of work a little bit, and maybe reboot my process so I can maybe get to a level I can work effectively again", said Stan to himself as Marvin and Patty talk to the employees working just outside the boardroom, they were in.

As Marvin and Patty approached the different areas in the office, they greeted each employee by name, and each employee responded by a warm greeting. As they continued on their tour, this trend continued.

"This company may be new, but from what I saw from their records, this is still a pretty big organization compared to most. I don't know how he can still keep up with the names of all his employees, but that's impressive, considering the number of people he probably has to talk to on a daily basis", thought Stan during their tour.

As they continued with the tour, Stan noticed that despite the varied backgrounds and expertise of the different employees they talked to, they seem to be familiar with all the other employees in the other departments, and seem to have an appreciation of how hard the other department's work is, on their side of the operation.

It was astonishing for Stan to see such a familial vibe among the employees, not just among their department, but astonishingly, even across the organization. And even more astonishingly, Stan noticed that even the employees that have progressed in age, seem to have a spring in their step and a curiosity that matches, and in some cases even exceeds, that of the younger employees.

"This doesn't feel like work", said Stan to himself, as he absorbed his experience of the tour.

After going through all the departments and going around the offices, their group is now on its way to Marvin's office, as they close the tour. "I hope you enjoyed our little tour?" asked Marvin. "We really did", answered Stan.

"Good to hear. I guess the last stop for our tour would be my office over there", said Marvin as he pointed to his office. "And as has been a custom here in the office, we normally give our guests some produce we have in store that are in season. I mean, we can't be bragging about our technology and strategies in agriculture without at least letting you have a taste of some of our products. And maybe even convince you to shift to our products, once you've had a first-hand experience of what we were able to achieve in these past few years", said Marvin with a wink.

"That's perfectly understandable", answered Stan with a polite smile. "I hope you like strawberries then, because they are in season right now", answered Marvin as they entered his office.

"Patty, I already ran out of strawberries. Can you kindly ask some from the marketing division and give some to Stan and Brad?" asked Marvin. "Sure. Just give me a minute as I get in touch with marketing", answered Patty.

"Maybe Brad can give you a hand? He's on his way down anyway. I hope you won't mind if Brad goes ahead. He has an appointment he needs to attend, so he can help you pick up the strawberries and just go straight to the parking lot after that", said Stan, as he motions Brad to help out. "Wouldn't mind the help then. But it won't take long, so you can just wait here while we get the strawberries", said Patty.

"I'll stay put then", politely said Stan.

As Patty and Brad left the office, Marvin sat on his chair, and motioned Stan to sit in the chair in front of his table.

Shortly after Stan got seated, Marvin softly asked, "so what do you think of our little company?"

Slightly taken aback at the timing of the question, Stan fiddled with his thoughts and answered, "I've seen and got to work with a great range of corporations in my line of work. And I have to say, this is the first time I've seen a company with an environment like yours".

Pausing a bit to make sure he doesn't say or use any words that may offend Marvin or disclose the identity of any of their clients, Stan continued, "the environment is usually very competitive, in most of the corporations that I've handled, and the heads and even the staff in the different departments within the organization, normally have these quiet but apparent differences and rivalries happening between them. And I guess the different backgrounds and competitive nature of the people within an organization plays a part in why there is normally a tense environment in these high performing corporations. But to me, it seems as if that same competitive nature allows these corporations to excel. Although it can be a very stressful environment, I believe that environment also allows the talented and dedicated employees to rise above the rest.

"On the other hand, the environment here seems widely different from what I am accustomed to. There seems to be an apparent harmony with everyone around here", discussed Stan, while intently observing Marvin's facial expression, as he gives his assessment.

"I understand your recordkeeping and your organizational setup is still messy. But that can understandably be attributed to a lack of guidance and technical proficiency in your accounting and legal departments, and can easily be remedied with our expertise. But the culture, I believe, is something that is impressive and very hard to replicate. And considering how well your profits are, I am under the impression that despite the cozy atmosphere, are very competitive people that can constantly deliver results, with little to no supervision", said Stan, before pausing briefly when he noticed Marvin making a gentle sigh.

Unsure if he may have offended Marvin, but nonetheless compelled by genuine interest and the overall pulse of the moment, Stan asked "So, I have to ask. How do you do it?"

"You have a very keen observation, Stan. I see why Mr. Paul trusts you", Marvin said with a slight grin. "I'm happy that you felt that way about how we do things here, and I think that reinforces our belief that our strategies are leading us to the right direction", said Marvin before pausing as he ponders on Stan's question.

"It's not so much as to the 'how' and to the 'what' of what we do, but I believe more with the 'why' of what we do, that results in the culture that we have here", said Marvin, as he looked Stan in the eyes.

"We all used to work for separate corporations before, and were top engineers, scientists, and experts in various fields. By us, I mean the directors and founders of this company.

"For a great majority of our lives, we were employees working for different corporations, and we were constantly working to get to the top of our chosen fields and endeavors. Despite the success however, life never really felt complete for us. And despite the decent paychecks and constant accolades, we kept on looking for some satisfaction that always seemed to be beyond our reach.

"Now I just have to mention that we personally did not know each other then, and it was only a few years before we started the company that we actually encountered one another. Although we came from very different fields and backgrounds, to us it was apparent that our careers all had the same pattern and feel. And these shared feelings and thoughts about work, kind of made us feel connected to one another despite the differences.

"Now at the beginning, a majority of us weren't really informed about how the agricultural methods of large-scale farms were affecting our environment. But all of us did have a great sense of connection and care for the environment, from a young age. Because of this connection, the majority of the founders, myself included, attended a symposium on carbon emissions that Drake, one of the founders, helped organize.

"After hearing how severe the situation of our environment is, and after understanding how modern agriculture is affecting greenhouse gas emissions, I personally felt a subtle and yet ever constant desire to make things right. At that moment, it felt as though all my experiences, skills and education all made sense, and that I knew what I had to do with my life. As though a great weight or veil was lifted in my head, and suddenly, my head was totally clear.

"Now I don't want to sound too dramatic, but for that brief moment, it felt like the world was my compass as I stood there in stillness, and in that moment, I knew what I needed to do. To my surprise, the other founders also felt the same way. And it was at that moment that we conceptualized and started this corporation.

"Now, to circle back to your question. Having worked for very successful yet very stressful and empty careers, it became a focus for us to try and reach our goals without repeating what we felt were unfair, and impractical ways of doing things. Having this urge to do things differently from how everybody else does things, coupled with the desire to make a positive impact in our environment, gave us a great sense of purpose that convinced us to further pursue our goals.

"Having those goals and values, we put up this corporation, and we tirelessly worked to make sure that our values were reflected in how we do business. And as they say, the rest is history" discussed Marvin to a very attentive Stan.

Stan listened to Marvin as he, at times, showed some emotion as he was talking. Stan briefly motioned to speak, but hesitated a bit, before asking "were you ever afraid to pursue this path?"

Marvin smiled as he faced Stan who now was looking more intent than ever. "We did have our fears and doubts. I think it's normal to have them, no matter how strongly you feel about your goals. But I guess that's what makes these decisions, and life in general, worthwhile. Knowing that things will not always turn out the way that you planned, that gives life excitement and wonder.

"Having dedicated a good part of our lives studying our crafts and working for the organizations that had us, and limiting our encounters with other fields so that we can give more time to our paths, did put a sense of discomfort among us when we were at a crossroad between taking that big chance, or just simply staying the course.

"It wasn't an easy choice, and some of us took a long time before buying in. In our minds, we were choosing between a great path that was already set for us, and a path that can only offer us a chance to find the life that we always wanted.

"And yet despite it all, our hearts knew that despite the hard work and long hours, we were actually walking the path away from our true goals and our true selves. We also realized that for most of us, this was our only opportunity to seize the moment, seize the chance. That for the first time in our lives, we can actually go for broke and find out where it goes.

"And for people like us who stuck with the rules and followed the norm all our lives, we felt a sense of excitement and liberty that we never experienced before. For once in our lives, we get to be selfish and actually do what we wanted to do. And that experience, that freedom, is more powerful than any lecture or book can ever give you. To actually live out our calling and purpose, that is true liberty", said Marvin with a highly emotional tone, but with a surprisingly calm facial expression.

"I can't say that I understand how you feel, because to be honest, I haven't been in a situation just like yours. And as unconventional as your approach is, some part of me truly want this approach to succeed. But the more practical side of me questions if this management approach can really sustain such a big organization for a long period of time.

"I mean, I agree with your desire to create a very positive work environment for your employees, but I don't think I've encountered a company with an approach such as yours, with a competitive bottom line. And investors and even employees look at the bottom line to determine if a company is healthy, and can have a long existence", said Stan, with his head facing down as Marvin laughed when he heard the question.

"You sound just like Melissa", as Marvin laughed on, while Stan looked puzzled. "But I do know where you are coming from. Almost all of the founders used to be part of management in their respective companies, so we do understand a bit of how these things work.

"It may not sound very CEO of me, but to answer your question, we simply don't care about the bottom line. Well, not that we don't care if we meet our target income or not, because we still have to meet our targets to be able to continue doing what we want to do. But we also decided not to put income as our main focus in doing our business. To us, the bottom line can go up and down and we can still be happy, as long as our culture and identity is unchanged. We were never really organized to make money. Our goal has always been to make a positive impact in the world, and do it in a way that all stakeholders find their peace while trying to accomplish it. And although money is a means to accomplish that objective, we also understand that money is not the goal.

"Having this understanding makes our decisions easier to make. As long as we are staying true to our identity and forwarding our goals, then we push forth the needed decisions, regardless of what the short-term or long-term financial consequences, they may result. And the only thing left to do is to openly and constantly communicate this mindset with our investors, employees and other stakeholders, which we do. Whether they stay or not would be up to them. But for those who do decide to stay, at least they know what they are going into.

"From our experience thus far, this honesty has made it hard for us to find enough people that fit our culture. But at the same time, this honesty has also made sure that only those who buy-in to what we believe in, actually stay.

"I'd like to underscore though that our employees actually appreciate our honesty with our ideals and objectives, and how open we are in discussing how transient our existence is as a corporation. As one of our senior engineers once said 'at least you were brave enough to tell us that this party won't last forever, so we can at least help to keep it going, and enjoy every minute, while it lasted'.

"Besides, in this day and age, even the most senior employees in the most successful businesses don't have any guarantee that they won't be laid-off, or that their business won't just close down, or that an economic collapse won't suddenly force them out of work. And so, it's not right to give your employees the illusion that the company they're working in will operate forever.

"I could be wrong, but maybe that's just lazy management. I don't think every organization was meant to be rich and famous, and certainly no corporation was meant to live forever", discussed Marvin.

Stan listens intently, as he tries to make sense of what Marvin is saying, and tries to compare it with what he learned in his lifetime. Despite the silence, as Stan absorbs all that he heard, Marvin remained silent, while waiting for Stan to give his feelings and thoughts.

"What other goals are there than to do your best, get rich, and have a peaceful life?" asked Stan rhetorically.

"That's something only you can figure out. What I can say is, even with all the money and the power in the world, if you are living a life opposite to what you were meant to be living, then you won't be any closer to happiness then, than when you have absolutely nothing at all. And you're only left wondering, if you were really able to live a meaningful life?", answered Marvin.

Before Stan had time to respond, Patty entered the room with a few boxes of strawberries. "I hope I didn't take too much of your time while we were getting these strawberries", said Patty.

"Not at all, and thank you for taking the time to get these for me", answered Stan as he took the boxes from Patty. "I know you also have a lot of things to do, so it may be best if I also get going", said Stan with a bit of hesitation, as though waiting for Marvin to ask him to stay a bit longer.

"Well, thank you for your time then, and we look forward to working with you", said Marvin as he reached his hand to Stan. "The pleasure is ours, and we look forward to this new partnership", replied Stan, as he shook hands with Marvin and was ushered out of the room and the Farmer's Charm office by Patty.

Despite now being a few kilometers away from the Farmer's Charm office, Stan's mind could not stop thinking of Marvin's office, and the conversation they just had. Having now returned to his office with his schedule loaded, and his work piling up, somehow, in Stan's mind, none of that mattered. Despite the world still revolving, and the work kept on piling, his mind could not get past what Marvin said. And in those instances, he would remember the salaryman's question, and would ask himself, "have I been wasting my time?"

Chapter 9

Falling Pillars

Getting home from work, after staying late yet again, Stan took a shower to get some time to think. Stan still recalls his conversation with Marvin a few hours ago and how his words resemble that of the salaryman he saw at the park a few months back.

"Why can't I shake this feeling off? As much as I'd like to get some work done at the office, I can't even start, if I am not in the right frame of mind. Maybe this shower and an early sleep can allow me to properly restart", thought Stan to himself.

After taking a bath and getting into some sleeping outfit, Stan laid on his bed with the lights turned off and tried to think about what he heard from Marvin and the salaryman.

"I guess I understand where Marvin and the salaryman were coming from when they asked those questions. But I think I am also making a difference with what I am doing, and I have to stay the course and have faith in what my parents have set me to be.

"This is a lucrative career and I am very good at it. It would be a mistake if I just gave it all up just for the heck of it. Right now, I am where I am supposed to be, and right now, I am doing what I am supposed to do. And to properly show my appreciation to all that I have been blessed with, I should give a hundred and ten percent in all my effort", Stan said to himself as he nodded his head repeatedly, as though agreeing to his own conclusions.

Early the next day, Stan got up his usual early alarm, went for a jog, had a light breakfast and coffee, and went to the office early. In those moments, he was only thinking about the work that he had on his plate, and his ideas on how to complete them. In those early parts of the day, he was completing work efficiently and with ease.

"I think it's best to review the short Roswell and Lawrence case drafts this morning so I can have a thirty-minute lunch first before reviewing the large pile of documents and draft pleading on the Jackson case this whole afternoon. I better have that Jackson pleading done by tonight otherwise we may not make it for filing by tomorrow", Stan thought to himself.

"Shirly, kindly block off my whole afternoon. If there are requests for a meeting, just give them next week Friday instead", said Stan to Shirly through the phone. "Got it boss", said Shirly. "Thanks!" replied Stan. And Stan continued working on the Roswell case.

After returning from a short bathroom break and before he can begin his review on the Lawrence case, and before he can even take his seat, his office door opens.

"Stan, let's go!" said Shin as he entered Stan's office. "Go where?" asked a confused Stan. "To Mike's office. He emailed just a few minutes ago. He wants to talk about some new development before the partner's meeting this afternoon", answered Shin.

"Why the meeting all of a sudden? I don't think I have any partner's meeting in my calendar", said a still confused Stan. "Mike's emails on our meeting at his office, and the invite for the partner's meeting later, were just sent a few minutes ago. Sort of an emergency meeting. So, let's go", said Shin. And after checking his emails for the invites, Stan and Shin went to Mike's office.

"Thanks for getting here on such short notice", said Mike as he offered Stan and Shin a seat at his table. "First of all, I heard the new wins on the Farmer's Charm company. Glad you were able to get them to sign our contracts so quickly. We badly needed those acceptance fees right now so kindly send them the bill as soon as possible, so we can take care of our immediate expenses for the month", said Mike.

"Will be sending the bill on the acceptance fee today and will have Brad call their head of finance to have our bill paid as quickly as possible", reported Stan. "Ok, good!" replied Mike as he took some paper from a folder.

"Now regarding our partner's meeting this afternoon, I had that called to discuss the allocation of our target collections for this year. We understand that Stan has already reached his target collection for the year and we are just in the third quarter of the year. First of all, congratulations on already reaching your target! Well Done!" said Mike as he and Shin gave him a round of applause.

"Now unfortunately, Leo, Grace and Justin are way behind their budgets, and based on the issues they have with their clients these past few months, it is very likely that they will miss their targets by almost a third of the allocated amount.

"Now the partnership is giving a hand in trying to resolve the problems they have with their respective clients and cases, but we don't have any guarantees that things will get polished out by the end of the fiscal year. If the current projections hold and we don't find enough business to plug the gap of those lost opportunities, we will not be able to pay off all our expenses by the end of the year. So, to prepare for the worst-case scenario, we would have to ask all the partners to increase their collection targets for the year, so we can absorb any shortages in cash flow by year-end", said Mike as he pauses.

"We will discuss the details of the increased collection budgets later in our meeting, but I wanted to meet with you two first, as our youngest partners, so I can better explain these matters. Being the youngest partners, we are really expecting a lot of contribution from your part, so we can overcome this unfortunate situation.

"We noted how Stan has been able to complete his target so quickly, and are therefore expecting you to focus most of your effort this third and fourth quarter, so we can bridge the gap in the collection that we are expecting to miss this year. With that, the management committee has decided to increase Shin's target collection by twenty percent of your current target, and you Stan will increase your current collection target by forty percent of your current target budget. We are hoping for your dedication in these trying times, so we as a partnership can overcome this together," discussed Mike.

"To be honest, since I was able to complete my targets for the year, I was really hoping for me and my team, during the remainder of the third quarter and for the whole fourth quarter, to lighten our loads a bit and replenish ourselves for a new fiscal year. I was hoping I can go home and celebrate with my parents for a week or so during the third quarter and focus on some networking and marketing activities during the remaining months of the year, so I can bring more work to the firm in the long run.

"I was actually hoping to study some of our procedures and also review some topics I wanted to master and also give some lectures to the new staff so that their work might improve a bit", said Stan to himself as Mike waited for his response.

"Since we are already at this point, then we might as well earn a little more money at the end of the year. How do we intend to find the jobs we need to fill the needed profit?" asked Shin.

Mike waited a bit for Stan to give his reaction, but after a short while with no response from Stan, Mike answered "since we are pressed for time to get to the amount we need at the end of the year, the main approach we are looking at is to give significant discounts to our new clients so we can quickly get our acceptance fees.

"We are also going to be less picky with the clients we are going to market to and also be less stringent in our client due diligence, that we normally do. Of course, we are open to any suggestions, and we can further discuss that during our meeting later.

"For the possible clients we might approach, that can be further discussed later. The main thing for me is to have you on board with all this. In as much as we wanted things to be different, we are already at this point, and it can also be a good opportunity to earn a bit more".

"I appreciate the chance to pile more into my profit share at the end of the year, but it's going to be tough for my end to complete the work in time to collect the additional twenty percent, especially given the current work load of my staff and myself. Nonetheless, we will endeavor to get it done as far as humanly possible. So, you can count that we will do our best on this", answered Shin.

Stan still remained silent across these exchanges as he tried to calculate in his mind if the forty percent was achievable, and how he could make that possible. Despite Shin's commitment, Mike's gaze remained focused on Stan, as he waited for his reaction. Stan, noticing Mike's anticipation of his reply, thought of the best way to reply.

"As a partnership, we have to carry one another regardless of the situation. Given where the firm is right now, it's a given that I am going to do the best I can to meet the needed forty percent. So, let's get this done", said Stan with a stern but sad expression.

"Glad you're on board! Spoken like true partners!" said Mike with a big smile on his face. "Well then, see you later in the partner's meeting". After a few pleasantries, Shin and Stan returned to their offices.

Now sitting in his chair and still running through different scenarios in his head, Stan still could not find a situation wherein he can meet the forty percent additional collection target imposed.

"How in the world am I supposed to collect that much money at this time in the year?! Can't they give a bigger target to the older partners who have more established clients?!" said Stan to himself with some anger.

"How in the world did my carefully planned and executed year as a new partner end up with more work?! I should have been able to cruise through the second half of the year, as a reward for my diligent work during the first half?!" again said Stan to himself as he pounded his table with the bottom of his clenched fist. With his heart still pounding and his temper still flaring, he stood up to collect himself.

Looking through his window, he looked down at the street. As his gaze went from one end of the street to the other, his eyes focused on a familiar image. In the street, walking towards the park, he saw what looked like the salaryman he once talked to. Stan's eyes widened and he tried to verify if indeed the image he is seeing is the man he once talked to.

From afar, the image wasn't very clear, and so he tried to look for some clues in the overall appearance and movement of the man to know if he was indeed the salaryman he once shared a bench with. But as the person walked further, and the more he focused on the image, he knew that this wasn't the man he once talked to. With a bit of disappointment, he made a sigh, and sat again in his chair.

"Why does that salaryman's statement resonate with me so much? How can a stranger's sentiment mean anything to me?" Stan asked himself as he reflected on his actions and choices in the past, and the situation he was now in.

As he assessed his life, he felt a slight sadness creeping within him. Along with the sadness, he felt a chill coming from within. For the first time in his life, he felt a fear that he never knew he had in him.

As he transitions from reviewing his past and present, and now envisioning what his future looked like, the fear kept growing and gripping from within. And for the first time in his life, he was stumped. For the first time in his life, he had no answer. All he could do at that moment was to ask himself, "did I waste my life?"

Somehow, as the question sank deeper and deeper in his mind, it seemed as though nothing but that question mattered. It seemed as though only answering that question made sense. That the world was second priority.

Stan sat there in his chair, trying to figure out if he only walked the earth to live another person's life, or was he able to live the life he truly wanted. As seconds turned to minutes, and minutes turned to an hour, he still couldn't find the answer, and he still could not find his peace. His mind seemed clouded as though he couldn't see the light. And although he eventually took a short lunch and attended the partner's meeting, his head was never clear and his mind was never made up.

As the meeting ended and Stan faced with the work that should have been completed, but was postponed because of the afternoon meetings, he tried to force through with his tasks despite the heavy heart.

Unlike before, wherein he was always motivated and enjoyed his time figuring out his tasks, he now was doing the work only because he had to, not because he wanted to. Although he knew the deadline was almost due, he was no longer motivated by the desire to truly be of service to his clients. This time, he did the work, only because of the fear that there would be significant backlash, should he be unable to meet the set deadlines.

Despite the unforgiving situation, Stan carried on with the work, without rest, comfort or motivation, because in his mind he had to. As though a zombie walking, not because it wanted to, but only because it had to, Stan completed the review of the pleadings that they needed to file. But unlike before, wherein he was very meticulous, and wanted everything to be done perfectly for the client, he only wanted to submit what would be good enough to pass the client's needs.

Eventually, Stan was able to complete his tasks. But somehow, he knew, he no longer wanted his current situation to continue.

Chapter 10

The Fallout

A few weeks have passed since the partners' meeting wherein Stan's collection target was increased by another forty percent. Across this period, Stan continued to work, but with no clear motivation to do so other than to avoid getting reprimanded for unmet deadlines and tasks. And although Stan was still getting up in the morning to go to work, most of the time, he just wished that the weekend and holidays would come and allow him to forget about work.

On a Friday morning, more than three weeks since the partners' meeting, Stan woke up to the sound of his alarm.

"It's already seven am?" said Stan to himself as he turned off his alarm. Gingerly rising from his bed, Stan went to the bathroom to wash his face.

"Do I really need to go to the office right now? Maybe I can just call in sick today and try to get some work done here at home. Or I can just use my partner card just this one time, anyway I don't have anything to sign today and I can just ask Shin to cover for me if I need to sign anything. Besides, I took home with me the needed documents for my review. Worst case, I'll ask any of the staff to email me a scanned copy of the documents I need for my review", said Stan to himself as he stares in his reflection in the mirror.

"If me staying home today can get me energized for the hectic Monday schedule, then it would be worthwhile for me to stay home just this once", Stan said to himself as he decided to go back to bed after texting Shirly of his absence. "I'll take this leave today and just get some work done this weekend", said Stan to himself before going back to sleep.

With a ringing that echoed across the house, Stan woke up to a call from Mike. "Hi Mike. You called?" asked Stan as he answered the phone.

"Hi Stan, noticed that you weren't in your office this morning and Shirly said that you were going to work at home today. Is everything ok?" asked Mike.

"Yeah, I'm good. Just wanted to focus on some tasks I had and decided to do them at home so I can avoid the Friday traffic", replied Stan.

"Oh good! Glad you're fine. Anyway, just wanted to get an update on your latest collection targets. The third quarter is about to end and we wanted to know how far back you are on the forty percent?" asked Mike.

"Yeah, regarding that. I closed some new clients these past few weeks and based on my computations, the new accounts reduce my deficiency to thirty percent. I know I still have three more months to go, but I am not sure if I can hit the remaining thirty percent by the end of the year. Despite the discounted fees, I think clients are still preferring to work with their previous law firms despite us offering our services at the same price point as their previous firms", reported Stan.

"How much work is in your pipeline right now?" asked Mike. "If we can win all the proposals that we have already sent out to the clients, that can already exceed our collection by at least five percent of my previous budget. But frankly, I don't think we can close fifty percent of the proposals in our pipeline", answered Stan.

"Let's try further reducing our prices to below the price of their current law firms so we can get those wins. Also increase your marketing a bit more even in the last quarter, just so we have an allowance should any of our proposals not push through, or just in case any of the other partners don't reach their targets. Let's go through all your pending proposals on Monday so we can come up with ways to close them", emphasized Mike.

"Understood. But I just want to call out that my team and I may no longer be able to handle any additional work beyond what is already in the pipeline right now. As it is, the managers and staff can barely get by with the work we already have. Based on my discussion with them, we can only accommodate just the work that is in our pipeline right now, and we run the risk of not being able to perform all our contractual obligations if we add in more work at this time", reasoned Stan.

"We don't have any other choice at this point but to accept additional work to get us through. We at the management are also looking at how you can manage your team to perform beyond what they think they are capable of. As their leader, you should be able to ride their effort until we reach our goal. That's part of your obligation to the firm and to them as their mentor", sternly replied Mike.

"I get that. But any further work and their backs would break", sternly answered Stan.

"That's why you are there, to make sure that their backs don't break and still get the job done. I've seen you do it before. I'm sure you are more than capable of doing it again", Mike replied, this time with a milder tone than earlier.

"I'll try my very best. But I can't give any guarantees that we would be able to reach the targets or make sure that all our clients are fully satisfied with our service", replied Stan.

"Let's just give it our best effort. It's just going to be for another three months and we can relax after that", said Mike jokingly.

As Stan did not respond, Mike said "Ok then, I'll let you get back to your work. See you on Monday. Thanks!"

"Ok, see you on Monday", replied Stan.

As he dropped the call, Stan checked his phone's clock. "It's still just eleven am and Mike is already calling me. I guess I was really tired from last night that I slept for another three hours", Stan said to himself.

"When has the partnership ever been like this. Looking at how extravagant the way the partners lived, I thought things would be cloud nine twenty-four seven once I become a partner", thought Stan, as he got up to prepare a light breakfast.

"As an associate, all I wanted was to be a partner because I thought this would give me a happy and satisfying life. Being in this moment now, I don't even recall why I ever wanted to be a partner in the first place. All I ever knew was that reaching this point in my career should have solved all of my problems. But now being a partner, I don't even know why I am still doing this", said Stan to himself as he slowly eats his breakfast.

"If this doesn't make me happy, then what does?" he asked himself. The questions lingered in his head as he eats before he decides to let it go for a moment.

After taking a shower, he went out to get some lunch at his favorite restaurant. Upon reaching the restaurant however, he couldn't get any seat and was told that he had to wait for about an hour to be seated.

"I don't think I can wait for an hour to eat. It's been a long day so I don't think I have the patience to wait for that long", Stan told the receptionist as he returned the menu and was about to walk out of the line.

"If you have your meal for take-out, we can give it to you in under ten minutes", said the receptionist as Stan was about to walk away.

Stan turned around to look at the receptionist, as he paused for a bit to think if he would prefer to have his desired lunch but on take-out, or him looking for another place that might satisfy what he was looking for at that moment.

"Ok, I can go for take-out. But should a table open up as I wait for my take-out, can I still eat inside instead?" bargained Stan.

"Sure. We can get that done in the event that a spot frees up", replied the receptionist as she then took Stan's order.

While waiting for his order, Stan was still hopeful that he would get a seat, as he checked the tables to see if any of the diners were almost done with their meals. At the same time, Stan was preparing for the worst, as he thought of a place to have his lunch.

Barely nine minutes have passed, and Stan's name was already being called by the receptionist. With a heavy heart, he went and got his order and went to his car.

"I still wasn't able to think of a good place to have this lunch", he said to himself as he went inside his car.

Just as he was about to move his car, he stopped to let another car get past him. As the car was passing him, he was quick to notice a surfboard on top of the car.

"I always wanted to check a nearby beach around here. Brad said that there was a not so touristy beach near here that had a great sunset view. Maybe I can have lunch and hopefully catch the sunset view at that beach?" he said to himself while he paused for a moment. "Why not!" he finally decided.

After driving and getting to the beach, Stan looked at the view of the beach that he has passed by on several occasions, but has never had the chance to fully view. It was around three pm at that time and the sun was not yet setting.

Stan got to the beach with his food in his hands and he checked at how peaceful and seemingly undisturbed the beach was. There weren't any hotels around the beach and people had to walk a few meters from the parking lot to get to the actual sandy front of the beach. There were only trees that provided shade around the beach, as well as some rocks, logs and some grassy spots that can serve as sitting areas.

After walking into the sand to take in the atmosphere, Stan closed his eyes and took a sip of fresh air as he tried to absorb the moment. In his mind, he felt like a child again, seemingly unaware of the world's problems, and only able to focus on the view and the environment that was right in front of him. With the sand in his feet, the sunlight in his face, and the breeze blowing through his neck, for a moment, he forgot his fears and his hunger.

Opening his eyes, he was reminded once more of the reality he was in. But nonetheless he was thankful for that brief moment, which to him, felt like an eternity since he last had.

"Glad the restaurant didn't have any seats today", he thought to himself as he grins. He then scouted the area to look for a shaded spot where he can eat his lunch and wait for the sun to set. Finding a grass covered area that slightly plateaued the sandy beach, and seeing that it had ample shade, he walked towards the spot, and took out his lunch.

Stan consumed his lunch, while facing the sea as he savored the view and the ambience that the area provided. On top of the great view, Stan was in awe at how peaceful the area was and how at peace he was at that time. "Why can't everyday be like this?" he thought to himself as he gobbled the last bite of his dessert.

Still taking in the sun and the view, Stan's mind began to wander. "Never knew life can move so fast. One time I was just a little boy in the province playing with friends, and the next thing I know, I'm already a partner in a big law firm and people expect me to provide enough collections so we can meet our yearly targets. Since when did my transition begin?" thought Stan as he recalled his early years.

"I guess I never really had a set goal to begin with, other than to just have a decent career that can earn me enough money to get what I needed", he said to himself as he thought hard about how he got to his current situation.

"I appreciate my parents for pushing me to take up law, since the practice of law has been a pleasant profession to be part of, and because it has given me a solid position to be financially stable. Besides, it wasn't like I had any immediate plans after I graduated from college, other than to get a job and try to save enough to hopefully have a decent retirement.

"But from elementary until now, the plan has always been to be able to enjoy myself in every activity that I am doing. And although it didn't seem apparent to me before, but I guess the way I approached school, my extra-curricular activities, and work, have always been as a means of developing myself as a person, while at the same time making sure that I am always having an enjoyable time while doing whatever activity I was involved in.

"I guess that was always how I approached things since before. But somehow, for the first time in my life, I have not been able to find joy and fun in what I do anymore. And I can't figure out why", said Stan as he continued to analyze his life. "What changed?" he asked himself.

As he stared at the leaves and branches that gave him shade, as the sunlight tried to pass through it, he thought long and hard to find the answer to his question.

He remembered how much he had a great time with all the sports activities he was involved with, wherein he pushed himself to train and compete for them to win each game. He realized how fond he was of those memories regardless of the game's outcome.

He also looked back at his school days wherein his diligent studying and methodical approach to studying, allowed him to dominate all his classes. And how fond he was of getting validation of his sacrifices at the yearly school ranking.

He also remembered all the events he organized and the leadership roles he took on during his school days, and how much fun those days were. He also recalled several instances wherein he and his friends skipped classes or studying, but still got away with it somehow.

Yet somehow, as he looked at his current career, something no longer seemed the same. Somehow, it was not as competitive or as fun as before. And despite a promising career set before him, somehow, he was not sure if that was the same path he still wanted to pursue.

"I have a great and promising career ahead of me and I am very grateful for the opportunity before me. At the very least, that fact is not lost on me. But why has this life become so hard to live?" he thought to himself.

"I've given this time to pass, as this may just be a phase that I am going through. But even time was not able to cure whatever it is that I am feeling. Time may have even made these feelings grow even more", he thought as he sat upright to face the sea yet again.

"Can I just continue to live my life without a sense of direction and reason? I may be able to perform my tasks despite my unsettled motivations, but do I really want to? Do my clients and firm deserve to keep paying me money without actually getting the best of me? And is this really all the excitement that life can give me?" he continually asked himself as he wallowed in frustration.

"This indecision, about what I'm supposed to do with my life, seems to have lingered and has weighed heavily in my life for a long time now. If I don't find an answer, it seems like it's going to linger even more and completely smother my energy and motivation.

"I guess I had it easy back in the day, because my objectives and the rules in my activities were always set, and all we had to do was try to accomplish the tasks in the best way possible, while following the rules. Now with work, and with life, nothing seems to be set, and everybody can do his or her thing, and find success even in the most unconventional way. And as far as career and life goes, rules have constantly been written and rewritten every time", he said to himself as he smiles.

"With no right or wrong answer, and with no standards set to guide me anymore, how am I supposed to continue? Should I stay, or should I go?" he asked himself as he took a moment to reflect on the question.

"Best sunset view in town", said a familiar voice, as Stan turned his head towards the direction of the voice. When his gaze fell upon the source of the voice, he was surprised to see a familiar figure in a dress and flip flops, holding a bottle of water and a foldable chair.

"Didn't know you'd stalk me until here. Had I known; I would have brought a few cans of beer instead", said the familiar voice.

"Stop insisting that I have a crush on you Monica. That joke stopped being funny way before we graduated law school", replied Stan with a smile.

As he waited for Monica to reach his spot, he returned his gaze to the original direction it faced before he was interrupted. Upon him facing the sea view, he was immediately in awe at the mellow but beautiful sunset view before his very eyes.

"What a view! I can't believe I didn't realize just how perfect of a sunset was already there in front of me, until now", he said to himself as he was still surprised of the view that he only just noticed.

"It gets better in just a short while", said Monica as she placed her foldable chair beside Stan's sitting spot.

"So, something this perfect still has a better version?" said Stan jokingly. "Anyway, what the heck are you doing here?" he continued.

“I should ask you the same thing. How in the world did you know my secret unwinding place? And you’re in my favorite sitting spot, of all places” jokingly said Monica.

“I don’t see your name written on any signboard! And I certainly didn’t see your name in the parking lot either! So, this spot should still be fair game!” said Stan emphatically.

“Alright, take it easy Mr. Grumpy”, replied Monica with a smile.

“But seriously, what brings you to this spot? Isn’t this far from your office?” asked Stan.

“Well yeah, this is far. But I had a court hearing nearby, so I decided to come here after work to take a break. I might not be able to swim right now, but at the very least, I can soak up some sunset view and a little sea breeze. Plus, I get to avoid the Friday traffic at this moment, so this made sense.

“Just in case you were wondering, I heard about this place from Lloyd so I checked it out a year ago. When I saw the sunset here, I tried to come here as much as possible whenever I am in town and whenever the schedule permits. How about you, what are you doing here in this perfect Friday sunset? Don’t you have checks to collect or something?” sarcastically said Monica.

“To be honest, I’m also not sure what I’m doing here, but I sure am glad I got here”, Stan said as he looked at the view with a smile. Monica noticed Stan’s smile and looked at him for a while.

Noticing Monica’s silence, Stan jokingly said “I had a day off at work and decided to have lunch at this popular restaurant near here. Unfortunately, there were no longer any seats available at that time so I just had my food for take-out.

“Also having heard great things about this place from Lloyd and from an associate at the office, I decided, what the hell. Might as well check the place out while I eat my lunch. As for your sitting spot, this was the spot with the best shade and had an elevated spot for my backside so here we are. Besides, I already called dibs”.

“Fine, I’ll let you have that spot for now. But don’t be so sure that spot will be available the next time you’re around”, replied Monica as they both laughed and stared at the sunset once more.

“Can I ask you a more serious question?” asked Stan. “Sure, as you can see, I’m not doing anything at the moment”, replied Monica as she tried to lighten the mood.

“Were you always so sure about becoming a lawyer?” asked Stan.

Monica paused for a bit as she thought about the question that Stan asked. After collecting her thoughts, she answered “I always admired the passion that my parents had for their careers as lawyers. Having seen how happy they were doing what they were doing, I guess it also made me happy to be able to pursue the same passion that my parents had. So that was kind of my motivation as I took up law and across my years in law school.

“But after doing this activity for a while now, I got a better appreciation of the profession and how much we impact the lives of a lot of people who come to us for our capabilities and guidance. And to have the chance to serve in the same capacity that my parents also serve, gives me pride and joy each day I go to work. So, I guess you can say that I have always wanted to be a lawyer, but now, more than before, I am happy being a lawyer, more than anything else in the world”.

"Wow, never knew you felt that way about our profession. I always thought you just liked coming in second, that's why you worked so hard in our exams", sarcastically replied Stan.

"Oh, shut the heck up. You just got lucky! And you were only ahead by a very small percentage. A few correct answers here and there would have made me the top of the class!" energetically replied Monica as Stan laughed.

"But seriously, if you didn't have such a strong feeling about our profession, would you still continue on, or would you look for what truly makes you happy and leave this life behind?" asked Stan as he intently checked Monica's reaction to his question, and tried to anticipate her response.

"Where are you coming from, with that question? Is everything ok?" said Monica, with her expression becoming serious.

"Well, first of all, I'm feeling ok. And I guess, I just feel like I'm at a crossroads in my life at this point. Not that I am depressed or anything, or at least that's what I believe to be the case. But I guess, I am really just curious about how this all works. How life in general works, and how I should approach it to get the best of this limited opportunity and time on earth that I have", said Stan as he pauses to properly put to order his words.

"Don't get me wrong, I think I've lived a very blessed life and I wouldn't change anything, if I had to do it all over again. I guess I'm just at a point wherein I feel like I've followed the script more than enough. And I'm happy that my parents and the academic institutions I attended, guided me to be the best person that I can be, and I will never take that for granted. But having followed the rules and standards set upon me, I feel that at the very least, I deserve to follow my own choices just this once. That from now on until my demise, I should at least get to choose how I get to live my life. Is that too big of an ask?" said Stan with sadness in his voice.

Noticing the disturbance in Stan's voice, Monica cautiously asked "I may not completely understand where you are coming from, but I understand your sentiments. But I think the only thing that matters now is what you want to do? What I've realized these past few years is that we should also give emphasis on living, and not just focus on staying alive."

Pausing to think about what Monica just asked, Stan tried to dig deep in his heart to know what he really wants.

"As of right now, I really don't know what I want to do for the rest of my life. I guess I really haven't asked that question until recently. It's not that I hate where I am right now, but I guess it's more of me realizing that I may actually want goals of my own.

"That somehow somewhere, there is a path for me to take that will give me purpose and direction, the more I pursue it. A career or life that would make my life meaningful. Just like your track in the legal profession.

"I guess I just realized that this path I am on now, may not be the path I was supposed to travel. That maybe there is another path that was set for me. And now I am stuck in a position wherein I have to choose between continuing the current path that I am now in, so that all my years of hard work will fully be rewarded, or scrap all the positioning and network that I accumulated all these years, and look for the path I was supposed to have taken.

"As these choices lie before me, I feel shackled by the indecision. My plans, expectations, and even happiness seem to hinge on this decision. And not having any decision has limited my enjoyment of each passing moment. Like being stuck in quicksand, I feel like before I can make a decision, I'll continually struggle to no end, as my body continually sinks deeper and deeper, until I am completely submerged and gasping for air, only desiring to break free even at the expense of the career I spent my whole life building.

"So, what I want right now is to be able to make the best decision, and continue to go on with my life", explained Stan as he sighs.

Monica paused for a moment, then asked "do you still have it in you to continue on with the role you currently have, should you choose to carry on with this path?"

In his mind, Stan took a step back from himself, so he can have a better perspective of his situation. Coming to a conclusion, he answered "I guess even if I chose to stay, I think it would only be a matter of time before my desire to follow what I truly want catches up to me and forces me to retire from the firm. So, I guess the best thing to do for me is to leave the firm to look for what it really is, that I want to do for my life".

As he said those words, Stan was able to picture himself leaving the firm. And in that moment, as he knew he had come to a conclusion, it felt like the world just opened. Like any hindrance for him to fully appreciate all the things around him, was actually removed. That at long last, after a long time, he knew what he needed to do and how he wanted to do it.

"Then I hope that settles it", calmly said Monica. "It does. Thanks for making me understand" said Stan as he looked deeply into Monica's eyes with joy and appreciation.

"Anytime Mr. Bigshot!" replied Monica as she tried to lighten the mood.

"So, what now?" curiously asked Monica.

"I guess now I resign and get as much back from my capitalization and profit share, and try to minimize my spending, so my money can last me until I figure out what I really want to do with my life. But I think I'd hold off on telling my parents about this sudden move, just so they don't worry about me", replied Stan.

"How do you plan on finding the track you want to pursue?" asked Monica again.

"I am not quite sure as to how. But I think I'll rest for a few months as I meditate on what I really want to do with my life. I will probably be travelling here and there, and try to experience new things along the way", said Stan as he envisions what his next months would be like.

After visualizing some details in his possible travels, Stan's eyes shifted from looking far away, to looking at Monica. And with a grin he said "since you convinced me to follow my dreams, whatever that may be, you'd need to join me in all my coming trips".

"Now wait a minute! It's not like I can just leave work like you, to go off some trip every now and then", replied Monica.

"Come on, when was the last time you took a vacation. Besides, you're due for some mandatory leaves. Just say you went abroad to unwind or something. You at least owe me a trip abroad, as my companion. I'll pay for the fare and the accommodation. But you pay for your own meals and for your shopping", said Stan very persuasively.

Hesitating at first, Monica eventually accepted the offer. "I'll accept, as long as you make all the reservations and planning", said Monica. "Sure, I'll take care of it! It's settled then", said Stan while feeling proud of himself.

The two friends chatted more until the night, before eventually going their separate ways. The next day, Stan called Mike and Shin, and told them about his decision to retire. The two were shocked at his decision, and tried to persuade him to reconsider. As Stan's mind was already made up, he insisted on his retirement, and was able to withdraw from the firm.

ACT II

Chapter 11

Clean Slate

After several weeks of back-breaking work and very long hours, Stan was finally able to complete all his remaining tasks, and was even able to collect the additional forty percent collection target. Yet despite the busy weeks, this was the first time in a long while that Stan knew he was alive and had purpose. Despite the stacked work, he was again moving with identity and direction. And he was able to pursue his tasks with vigor and bravery, knowing for the first time in a long while, that in a few more days, he was nearing the light at the end of the tunnel.

With sunlight beaming through his bedroom window, Stan opened his eyes to a room already brimming with the day's sunlight. "What time is it?" he asked himself. Checking his phone that was beside his bed, he saw that it was already eight in the morning. "How long did I sleep?" he asked himself again.

After pausing to think, he thought to himself, "This would have normally been a very late time for me to wake up. But maybe this is still early for some?" he said again as he raised himself and sat at the edge of his bed. "Regardless, I'm already up", he said as he walked towards his kitchen.

Taking bread from his refrigerator along with a bottle of fruit juice, Stan sat down at his table, and consumed the cold bread and the half-empty bottle of fruit juice. "I guess this is how I start the first day of unemployment", he thought to himself as he consumed his breakfast, while he looked back at the things that lead to where he was now.

"For the first time in forever, I actually don't know what I'd do today. I can go on a jog, or do a full workout, since I have the time. Or I can go have lunch in any of the popular restaurants around, that always had long lines. It Would be nice to go there earlier than most, since I don't have any deadlines to follow today", he thought to himself, as he slowly finished the stale bread.

"Or maybe I can try and look for a job with less pressure, but with good enough pay, so I can make do with my monthly amortization on this house. It also won't hurt if I can get a steady source of income, as I try and figure out what it is that I really want to do from now on. But the work should be one that won't encroach on my time beyond the hours required per day", he thought to himself as he washed his glass and plate.

After a few back and forths in his head, he thought "I think at this point, it would be best to look for a role that doesn't eat up much of me, just to get paid. Something that at least allows me to focus more on my hobbies and passions while I work, or at least doesn't demand my free time for me to provide excellent work.

"Maybe I can start a business that I really have a strong connection with, and spend time on it after office hours and during weekends", he said to himself, as he imagines the type of work that might fit his criteria. "Anyway, the next job might just be a temporary stop, as I sort things out with myself", he finally said to himself before taking a shower.

After taking a bath, he put on some comfortable clothes and just sat on his couch. "I wonder what happens if I suddenly had a medical emergency? Can I actually find a decent job that can pay for my mortgage?" he asked himself.

"All I want right now more than anything is rest. But I never knew how much uncertainty there was, in being unemployed. Should I already scramble to find another job?" he said to himself with a soft frown.

After taking a short while to think of his priorities and objectives, his mind finally calmed down and settled. "Despite the uncertainties, I guess the primary objective for me right now is to try and get my joy, my energy, and my passion in life back. Everything should come second to that", he thought.

"And despite this overwhelming sensation of uncertainty, surprisingly, I'm unafraid. Despite a lot of people not prescribing, just resigning without a sure job waiting, who would have thought that this feeling of not knowing where I would get my next paycheck, can be refreshing and liberating. I guess part of the adventure of life, that a lot may no longer be familiar with, is the thrill of not knowing where life can lead you", he said with a subtle smile. "Maybe I really needed to go down this road more than anything else", he said to himself with slightly moist eyes.

"I guess the first thing for me to do then, is to take my time and fully recover. I'm already unemployed with no deadlines in the near future. Might as well enjoy this before I start needing to work again", he said to himself as he nods his head.

Having resolved the crisis in his mind, he began executing this plan to relax and take a step back from life. He lifted his feet up, opened his television, and started watching whatever interesting was on.

After a few hours of watching, and not finding any show that was compelling, he turned off the television and opened his tablet. He checked for any interesting videos or blogs on the internet to pass the time. As he was browsing the internet, he saw a blog about the top ten best cities in the world worth visiting. As he checked the list, he saw the city that he was in, was part of the list. Checking the blogger's description of his city, he was surprised at how many interesting places and activities were within his driving range.

"It's been several years now since I studied and worked here, coming from my small town. I was able to go to some of the places mentioned in the blog, but I'm not sure if I have ever been able to fully explore all the best places this city has to offer? I guess I was mostly too preoccupied with trying to maximize the potential that everyone was convinced I had, and wasn't able to explore the great things that were so near me" he said to himself as he tried to recall the popular spots in the city he was able to visit. "I guess, if anything, I can at least try to check the best spots in the city before I start getting busy again", he said to himself.

Checking the time in his tablet, Stan saw that it was already eleven thirty am. To be able to plan out how long he needed to travel and the type of food that was most intriguing to him at that time, he checked the internet once more to see which of the popular restaurants were nearby and what type of food they were offering.

"With the way I woke up, I kind of feel heavy and flat right now. I just had a glass of red wine last night, but somehow it feels like I drank a few bottles", he said to himself with a smile.

"That being said, I am craving for a place that serves hot soup that can maybe get me out of this weird hangover", he continued to say to himself as he browsed the internet for recommended restaurants that were near his house.

Seeing a restaurant that had a dish he missed and can actually quench his cravings, he clicked at the name of the restaurant and browsed at the review page and menu.

"Heard a lot of good things about this ramen shop from some of the associates at the office and the reviews are incredible. The price is a bit higher than most, but for the reviews that it's getting, this seems like a good enough deal. They do seem to specialize only in ramen, so it must be that good, if this is the only product they are offering and yet they are still in business. And it's only a fifteen-minute drive, so that's a big plus. But given the time, I'd have to get going if I want to avoid a long line for this kind of establishment", he said to himself as he hurried to his room to get dressed and got his keys and wallet as he went.

"Well, at least this ramen shop doesn't need a reservation", he said to himself as he went inside his car and drove to the nearest parking area near the ramen shop.

After parking, he immediately looked for the ramen shop using his phone. Having figured out the location, he walked there for a few minutes. As he was nearing the ramen shop, he checked his watch and saw that it was already eleven fifty-two am.

"I hope the line is not that long yet", he said to himself. Turning a corner as he neared the ramen shop, he immediately saw a long line out the door of a shop with oriental decorations. "This must be it", he said to himself as he confirmed with the last person in the line that it was indeed the shop he was looking for.

"It's not yet twelve, but there are at least forty people in line. Ramen must be good", he said to himself as he sizes up the people eating inside the establishment, and trying to get a feel of the system for getting a bowl of the sought-after noodle and soup.

"When was the last time I had to fall in a line this long, just to get a meal?" he wondered. "Regardless how long it's been, I'm just glad I at least have enough free time to wait for this line to free up, so I can get what I came here for", he said to himself with a small grin.

"Better make this trip worthwhile I guess", he said, as he scans the menu on his phone to try and get the best ramen and side dishes, to try and satisfy his cravings.

Having picked out the ramen and sides that he wanted, and moving with the line as he does, he looked at the line and saw how quickly the line shortened. Seeing how quickly the staff cooked and served the meals, he had a sense of relief knowing that despite the long line of people, he wouldn't have to wait that long for him to get the satisfaction he had to travel for.

With the line quickly dwindling, Stan was now at the front of the line and waiting for the waiter to clear the table he would be given. As he was escorted to his seat, he had a great sense of relief knowing that his travel was not in vain. And as his order was being prepared, he waited with great anticipation for something more than just a meal.

Despite his hunger, his being there seemed more than just partaking in a meal that would quell a hunger that his body keeps reminding him at that moment. More than that, it seemed to him that he wanted to also feel the dedication and passion that the creators of the dish had, when they started doing the business. He wanted to be touched by the level of craftsmanship and hard work that the creators of the ramen placed on their dish.

He understood that all he was paying for was ramen, and all he was ever going to get were noodles in a broth, but somehow at that moment, he was looking forward to indulging in the ramen creator's care for their customers, which should somehow translate in their food. He knew that was a tough thing to ask from a bowl of noodles, but with the things he read and the reputation that the establishment seemed to have, that seemed to him to be the difference between him leaving unfulfilled, or being completely satisfied.

As he saw a staff carrying a bowl of ramen with the sides that resembled the ones he ordered, and the staff going his direction, he was in eager anticipation of the type of meal he was going to get. With the staff placing the great smelling and great looking ramen and sides on his table, his heart was slightly racing, as he was now before a meal that, to him, could either make him happy or sad for the rest of the day.

"So far so good with the presentation and smell. But the proof is in the pudding I guess", he said to himself as he starts off by tasting the broth.

Having the broth and being satisfied, he then proceeded to consume the noodles along with the broth. As he partakes of the ramen, he also consumes the highly recommended side dishes that the shop offers. Savoring his meal and also trying to avoid taking too long to finish his meal, he consumed his meal with gusto.

"I can't say if this is the best ramen I've ever had, but this meal really hit the spot for me", he said to himself with a smile, as he checked his plates to make sure that he consumed everything. "That was a wonderful meal! I'll definitely come back again. But I'll probably come a little early, to avoid the line", he said to himself as he paid for his meal and left the shop.

"Just what the doctor ordered", he said with a smirk. "Wonder what I do next?" he asked himself as he checked the area. Looking around and noticing a cafe across from the ramen shop, he thought "since I'm already here, and it may take a while before I come by again, might as well check out the desserts in this area".

He then crossed the street and had some coffee and pastry inside the café. As he slowly enjoyed his dessert, he kept looking at salarymen and executives alike, walking past the big glass window of the café.

As he was seated right beside the window, he couldn't help but notice how preoccupied and bothered all the men and women's faces were, as they passed by the café on their way back to work. He also noticed some salarymen with jobs indicating that they work more with their hands, passing by the café.

Surprisingly, Stan noticed that most if not all of the laborer's faces had brighter expressions on their faces, compared to the facial expression of the suit and tie guys and gals that passed by the café.

"That's odd. I thought the people in the financial and professional fields had it easy compared to the people who do things with their hands", he wondered. "Weren't we supposed to get better grades and have better paying jobs so that life gets easier? Then why do the people, who were supposed to be having the harder time, feel like they are having a better time than those who were supposed to be paid more?" he ponders as he consumes his dessert.

Still not able to comprehend what he just noticed, and still watching closely more people who passed by, he didn't notice that he already ate up the dessert and fully drank his coffee. Paying for his meal and walking to his car, he still couldn't understand what he observed.

As he was walking to his car, he checked his watch for the time. "It's still only two pm. Maybe I can do some other chores since I'm already out of the house", he asked himself as he thought of ways to get his chores done.

"I don't feel like going out of the house tomorrow, and maybe I can get my laundry done and get the house clean. I also want to try cooking a pasta and chicken recipe that I saw on the internet", he said to himself as he paused to organize his upcoming activities. "Since I'm already out, might as well do my grocery for the week", he said as enters his car and drove off to the nearest grocery.

With his focus shifted, Stan made mental notes of the things he needed to buy in the grocery as he drove there. Reaching the grocery, he walked around the store, making sure not to miss any aisle, like a kid walking in a zoo, making sure to get a glimpse of each cage that was there.

Although he had a planned set of things he wanted to buy, he thought that it wouldn't hurt if he checked all the things in the shop, just in case he encountered something that he may not have included in his initial list, but were needed by his new lifestyle. And as he roamed the aisles, he was engaged in the activity, and found amusement in finding the best product among the available choices in the store.

As he drove home, he was already visualizing the dishes he would cook using the things that he just bought. He also had a few items that he was excited to open, and thought of the spaces to store them in the meantime, as he waits for the opportune moment to use them in the future. After parking, he stored the things that he bought with excitement.

"This is the first time since I moved to this house that I was actually able to buy some stuff for it. The house has never been cluttered, and I don't want to start cluttering the house now. So, I got to put all the stuff I just bought in the most efficient manner possible, for an easier life, I guess," he said as he looked at some of the things he just bought.

Scanning the stuff he just bought, that were now at his table, he made a mental list of where each item should be placed, as he looked at them. He then proceeded to place them in the most ideal drawer available, each time making sure to put the things with the same use or frequency of use, in the same container.

Finally finishing storing the things he bought, including the food items and fruits, he checked his hamper to see if it was full. "Wow, almost overflowing with clothes", he said to himself as he opened the hamper. "Do I have time?" he said as he checked his watch.

Seeing that it was already seven pm, he hesitated for a moment and then thought to himself with a sigh “I'd like to start making dinner, but best get this over with tonight so we can have a clean house before my first day of unemployment ends, I guess”.

Taking the hamper to his washing machine, he poured the clothes in, placed detergent, and started the machine. After hearing the machine working, he went back to the kitchen and prepared a quick dinner for himself.

After he finished cooking his dinner, he first took his clothes from the dryer, before he had his meal. He had a few glasses of red wine, and chased it with some sweets he got from the grocery, and sat at his balcony as he stared at the people and cars that passed by his house.

“It's been a while since I did all my chores in one day”, he said with a smile. “I would have cursed these chores before, because they interrupted my work hours during the week. And yet, for the first time in a long while, doing all these things felt more like a treat than a chore. It's been a while since these activities actually entertained me. Who would have thought a day like this would come!” he said to himself as he laughed.

Chapter 12

Get Together

Three weeks quickly passed since the first day of Stan's unemployment. During this time, he normally stayed at home watching shows on the television or online, or busied himself reading articles or books. When he saw an interesting activity or restaurant online, he would visit the said establishment and savor the experience. In all these instances, he preferred to go alone, so that he didn't have to entertain another person, and be able to fully immerse himself in the activity or food that he was partaking in.

Although he twice had lunch with a partner or two in the three-week period, he tried to avoid any dragging activities with them. He was open to having the two lunches because he knew, with how busy the partners were, they only had time for lunch, and cannot stay long due to work. To Stan, it was ideal because he was able to catch up on their lives and also relieve any worry that the other partners in the firm might have about his well-being.

He avoided making his interactions with them longer than necessary, because he knew how busy their schedules were, and he did not want to take too much of their time. More importantly, Stan refrained from long lunches because he wanted to have as much alone time as possible, at that juncture.

During this period, he received invitations from friends and partners in other firms to join them as partner in their practice. He tried to be as polite as possible by entertaining them up front, and tried to relay to them that he was thankful for the consideration, but wanted to take his time as of the moment, to think and plan out how he wanted to proceed with his career.

Some friends and partners understood his desires, and gave him space to think about his next move, and told him to just get in touch with them should he feel that he was willing to work in their firm. Others were pushier in trying to get him to join their practice, arguing that he needed to take the opportunity they were providing while he was young, and while the spot was still available, and have a meeting with them asap, to have him join their practice.

Although in all instances, Stan kept polite in explaining that he was not yet ready to work, there were some partners and friends who still insisted that he should come to their offices and allow them to present to them what they had to offer.

As much as Stan didn't want to waste the time of these partners and friends, and also not to waste his time, he still went to some of the meetings that were set-up for him, simply because of how hard they insisted that it wouldn't be a bother to them, and that he didn't have any obligation to accept their invitation, but only had to hear them out.

In these meetings, he felt flattered, knowing that people were giving him attention and time to invite him to their practice, and excited, knowing that maybe one of the inviting firms can provide a situation for him wherein he can find the work experience that he wanted. But after seeing the offices and understanding what was going to be asked of him, despite the persuasive insistence of the inviters, he politely said no.

After understanding how similar his responsibilities would be in the offered job and his previous role, he knew it would not be wise to leave his previous situation, just to end up in a similar position, only in a different office. At least, not at this time in his life. That to him did not seem logical, nor practical.

In the subsequent weeks, he tried as much as possible to distance himself from any work, or work-related activities, and also tried to avoid invites regarding possible work or business opportunities that he knew would preoccupy his mind. He understood that for the time being, all he wanted was to be left alone, just relaxing and replenishing.

This became his game plan, because he understood that diligence has always been his way of doing things. He only needed to find what he really wanted to do, and he knew for sure that the tough grinds would follow, because that is what he does whenever he finds something to pursue. And he wanted to be fresh enough and replenished enough to go for it, when the perfect job comes.

So, although he kept himself available, he also tried to keep his profile low. All he wanted at that time was to enjoy his time alone, enjoying the little things that he was not able to enjoy before.

A few more weeks passed and Stan was now able to just shut the outside world temporarily. All he did was work out, cook and eat healthy, visit the places in his city that he wanted to visit, and enjoy the voice of his own thoughts as he tried to understand who he was, and what was really important to him.

In this same period, there were a few calls that he received from head hunters, asking if he was interested in some position that they needed to fill. Knowing his focus now, he was more meticulous and upfront in expressing his unavailability or lack of interest in the position offered.

His initial reason for foregoing hiring invitations was to avoid wasting his time, and that of the job hunter. But as time passed on, he understood why he was so indifferent to these calls or meetings with HR. In his heart he knew that he was no longer interested in talking about his motivations in work and in life with complete strangers, because he felt that none of these strangers would understand where he was coming from. Or at least, he knew that none of these strangers actually wanted to focus on his motivations, but just wanted to check or cross out his credentials and previous work description, against a checklist of descriptions that they think would fit the candidate they were looking for, regardless of his actual work happiness and motivation.

With an alarm beeping, Stan woke up to a cold and rainy day. Turning the alarm off, he immediately got up and did some push-ups and curl-ups while still in his bedroom.

"Well, now my body is awake", he said to himself as he ended his quick routine. "So, it's already seven am. Time to lose some weight", he said to himself as he checked the weather through his window.

"Or maybe not", he said to himself, as he saw the rain through his window. "I can just work out at home with some of my equipment then", he decided, after seeing the bad weather.

As he went to a room in their house with his workout equipment, he checked his phone to see if he received any email from prospective employers and firms that he had an interest in. As he opened his email inbox, he saw that it had one new message. With some excitement, he opened his inbox to see what the email was about.

Upon opening, he saw a lone message coming from an unknown email, with the title indicating a job position he never applied for. Reading the email, he understood that it came from a headhunter, expressing interest in his profile and work experience, and asking if the sender can call Stan to further discuss the offered position.

"I don't want to be rude to any of these headhunters who are just doing their roles, but at the same time, I don't want to waste their time in an interview with me, when I already know that I don't fit in the position that they are offering. So best just reply to the email and tell her that the role does not fit, but would be willing to talk in case a more senior role is available", he said to himself as he drafted and sent a short email reply.

Putting his phone down, he stepped on a treadmill and began his workout. While he was doing his workout on the treadmill, Stan looked back at his previous experience of interviews with headhunters, as they tried to ask about his work experience and motivations. And although they were professional, and tried to make the calls as less stressful as possible, all of them nonetheless, proved draining and distasteful somehow.

"Since when did I stop liking having a conversation with a professional?" he asked himself with a smile, as he increased the treadmill's speed for a few minutes before turning it back down again.

"When I was trying to get more clients to engage us for any work, it was almost every day that I had a call or meeting with a stranger, just to present what we can do, and convince them that we were their best chance at solving any of their issues. Now for some reason, I don't even want to start a discussion?!" he said with a laugh, as he now jogged at a slower pace. After a few more minutes in the machine, he stopped his workout and drank water as he rested.

"Maybe I just got used to not having any lengthy or considerable conversations with anyone these past few weeks. Or maybe I'm enjoying the silence of these past few days" he said with a smile, as he cools down from his workout.

"Well, to be fair, most of my conversations before were about work. Although I have to admit, even then, the discussions I had with clients, potential clients, staff, and even colleagues in the socio civil clubs I was involved in, tried to insert some marketing and networking aspect as subtly as possible, and try to sell myself as a respectable person worthy of trust and capable of finishing jobs", he said to himself as he pauses to remember how those conversations generally looked like.

"I guess now I see why I prefer this silence. Even during the social events, it was always a battle of wits, composure and the ability to use and comply with the norms in civilized interaction, so that you can get the answers and response that fit your strategic requirements at that time. Like constantly going to a battle with cocktails and fancy wardrobes, but every person methodical in their appearance, gestures and dialogue, so as to avoid any pitfalls, and be able to maneuver yourself to the promised land", he said with a sigh, while still recalling those moments. "I feel tired and stressed out, just thinking about it", he said with a laugh.

"But considering the status I already established for myself, I guess even the more informal interactions felt more tedious than they were supposed to. I guess having to become a representative of our firm, and having established an impeccable reputation that goes with the position, I always had to carry myself well in all situations, so that I not only embarrass myself, but more importantly, so I can always bring up the reputation of my firm.

"So, I guess in this aspect, even in my personal life and personal interactions, I was still working. And I guess I never really understood how draining that aspect of my life was, until now that I was able to have a cleanse of sorts with life's constant interactions", he said to himself, as he looked back at his life.

"When have conversations become such tedious tasks?" he asked himself.

Reflecting on his casual conversations and interactions, he thought "come to think of it, to a degree, even the way I handle myself among my peers, now seem tedious and straining".

"I may not have complained about it before, nor notice how much attention and concentration it took for me just to present and carry myself and my conversations well, even on the most informal of settings such as a party or a basketball game", he thought.

"Even during family occasions or school reunions, I was required by the norm to talk to people and socialize, lest I be tagged as anti-social. Somehow, if you don't talk to people, the world thinks there is something wrong with you. And I kind of get it to an extent, but why should I be required to talk to a cousin of mine who only talked about fish all the time?" he said to himself with a laugh.

"But honestly, even the most casual events required a certain way of dealing with others. Even talking to colleagues, or workmates requires that I be careful not to offend others, and try to make sure that I respond, one way or another, and on occasion try to make a joke, just to get a leg up in life. Although I feel like I've had great success in this requirement of society, I have to admit, it also takes a lot of my energy to try and be at my game all the time. Like having a job, within a job" he said with a sigh.

"I guess, this unintended fast from having to comply with society's requirements, was also something that I needed. To just be able to retreat from the world for a moment, and focus only on my thoughts and myself, seemed to be more important to me, than all the sleep in the world", he thought.

As he felt his body completely cooled down, he took his phone and went to his room to shower. As he placed his phone beside his bed, it suddenly made a beep. Hesitant to answer, thinking it may just be the headhunter, he nonetheless checked the message.

"Hey Mr. Big Time, are you by any chance free tonight?" said that message that came from Lloyd. As he read the message, his face brightened and he was excited for a moment.

"Of course! What's the occasion?" he quickly replied. After sending his message, he decided to wait for a moment, just in case Lloyd calls.

A minute later, his phone again beeped. "Well, it's been long overdue since our schedules didn't match the last time around. But just wanted to treat you for a few rounds to celebrate my appointment as the chief of staff in congress. It's not like I had much of a choice but to treat you guys. I'll never hear the end of it from Mary. You know how it is. lol" said the message. With a big smile, Stan replied "lol. Wouldn't miss it for the world. Just let me know the time and place. See you later Mr. Chief of Staff!"

As he placed his phone back beside his bed, he once again looked back at his earlier conversation with himself. After a brief pause, he thought "I guess conversations with friends are different. To be with people you can truly be yourself around, takes away the pressure and just leaves the fun in the conversations.

"I guess in those moments with friends, I just get to relax and be myself, and in a way, retreat for a moment from the needed conversations I would need to have again, once my short moment with friends eventually ends. And I guess, in this demanding and controlling world, time with friends does provide an important refuge that I think everyone needs."

Stan then proceeded to take a bath and prepare for his day. After getting the venue for their get together, Stan made preparations and when the time came, he was on his way.

Arriving in an upscale restaurant that also served beer, Stan asked for the reserved table for their group. Being the earliest in the group to arrive, he got all their orders so he could already have them cooked while they were on their way.

As Stan waited for his friends to arrive, he looked around the establishment to get a feel of the crowd present at that time. "I don't see anyone familiar", he said to himself with some relief. "Good. Because I am not really in a mood to have any awkward conversations about some people from my office, or a client. And although I do have some planned answers just in case, I'd rather not have to use them at this moment", he thought to himself.

"So far, I only see some groups of associate lawyers, a table with possibly a head of finance guy, and a few dining couples. Good enough crowd for us to also be rowdy", he said to himself with a smile.

From the door, Stan saw a familiar face entering and coming closer to their table. When the waiter at the establishment pointed to their table, Stan waved, and they smiled at each other from afar.

"Hey Mr. Big Shot! How have you been?" asked Jen as she got near their table. "Couldn't be any better", replied Stan, as they exchanged pleasantries.

"I heard from Monica that you resigned. What happened there?" asked Jen as she sat down.

"Well, first of all, I am still amazed at how news travels so quickly. I mean I tried to keep the resignation as low key as possible, but here we are", said Stan jokingly, as he tries to lighten the mood.

"Well, to be honest, it was really a spur of the moment idea for me to resign. But I thought about it for a long time before I eventually put those thoughts into action", said Stan as he realized at that moment, that he was deviating from his planned response to the topic, but nonetheless did not bother to stick with his script.

"It's Jen. It's them. I don't think it would hurt to give them an unfiltered narration of what happened. They would probably notice if I was restrictive with my details and actions anyway, so might as well tell it to them straight-up. Besides, it might be better for them to hear the details, and get their perspective on things", he thought to himself as he paused momentarily to structure his words.

"Anyway…" said Stan, before his thoughts got cut when he saw two more familiar faces entering the door. As Stan waved back at Mary and Monica, Jen turned around and also waved at them. They exchanged pleasantries once more and the two sat down.

"Where did you two come from?" asked Stan. "We both had hearings on the same court so we just decided to share the cab here", answered Mary.

"So, what's up with you Mr. Big Shot? What's with the sudden resignation?" asked Mary.

"Until when will I have to endure that nickname? For crying out loud, I already resigned! Can we dial that down already", said Stan jokingly.

"Nope. I am still having fun with the nickname. Especially now that I know it bothers you that I use this nickname", replied Mary as the group laughed.

"But seriously, why the sudden resignation?" asked Mary, now with a more serious expression.

"Well, it was supposed to be a secret, to begin with, so that no one would have to worry about this phase of mine", said Stan as he looked at Monica.

"Hey, you didn't tell me this was supposed to be a secret! Besides, it's not like I told everyone I know about it. I just told the guys about it, so don't look at me like I committed a felony or something", said Monica, half-jokingly, as the group again laughed.

As the laughter settled down, Stan continued "anyway, what's here is here. As I was saying to Jen, and as discussed with Monica, this was really an unexpected decision, even for me. But nonetheless, I've had time to think it through, and for me, resigning was the best thing to do, at this stage".

Pausing for a bit to construct his thoughts, Stan continued "as to why I resigned, well, I guess I figured out that, of all the possible things I should be doing in the world right now, this wasn't one of them. And I guess, that's ultimately the reason why I resigned".

Looking straight at his face and listening intently at the pitch of his voice, or for any hints of lying or hesitation, and not detecting any, Mary paused for a moment to think of Stan's answer and asked "then what do you want to do with your life?"

"I haven't figured that part out yet. All I was sure of, at that moment, was that I wasn't where I was supposed to be. And I guess that was more than enough for me to decide to let go and change direction, whichever direction this decision leads me to", said Stan with a more serious note.

Still looking at Stan's body language and overall emotional tone, and convinced that he firmly believed his decision was the right one to make, Mary replied "well, as long as you're settled with that, then that's that. All we can do now is eat some good food and have cabs take us home drunk!"

"I won't object to that!" shouted Jen, as she raises a beer bottle, as she motions for a cheer. "Sustained!" said Monica whimsically, as they chugged a bit of the beer that was just delivered to their table.

After things settled, Mary said "anyway, if you're interested in more intellectual property rights practice, I can refer you to our partner. I'm sure they'd take you in a heartbeat".

“Thanks! I’d definitely remember your offer. But I guess for now, the most important thing for me is just to get some rest and relaxation. Just to recalibrate and get my mind right, before I take on the next stage of my life” replied Stan.

“Of course. Take your time. Just let me know if you are ever interested”, said Mary, as they chugged their beers a second time.

“I kind of expected some form of intervention from these guys, and I secretly knew it was coming at any time during this dinner. Not that I mind. But I actually thought there would be a longer, sadder, and less relaxed tone once that discussion comes.

“Never knew they’d easily agree with me. I at least thought Mary would get mad at me or feel bad about the opportunity I am letting go in my resignation, considering that she aims to be a partner in their firm as well. Maybe my well-being matters to them more”, thought Stan, as he paused a bit at the realization, but tried to avoid them noticing his emotions.

Finding a reason to rub his eyes, to conceal them slightly being teary, they talked, drank and laughed some more, while waiting for their food and companions. Shortly after, and as their food was served, Lloyd, Ben and Jason came into the restaurant, one after the other.

“What took you so long?” asked Jen. “Well, traffic and more traffic”, replied Ben, as the group laughed.

“So how is our new Mr. Chief of Staff?”, asked Stan.

“Doing as well as you’d expect. And thankful that I had enough leeway today to make it here”, replied Lloyd with a sigh of relief.

“Congrats by the way on the appointment! That’s a really big position you got! Hope you still remember us when you get appointed to a bigger position after that”, half-jokingly said Stan, as the other boys jokingly echoed the sentiment.

“I sure hope I can maximize this situation going forward, because to tell you the truth, the job is really high pressure 24/7”, said Lloyd, with a sad smile.

“You’ll come out of there on top. You always do. Just hang in there while there is still some term left for your house speaker. But I suggest you already make moves to secure your next role. You got this, buddy! With you already being there, half the battle’s been won” encouraged Jason.

“Yeah, I got it already. And thanks for the congratulations! Just to be clear, I’m only paying for two rounds, got it?!” said Lloyd, as the group jokingly bargained for more free rounds.

“Anyway, thanks for making it here and celebrating this milestone with me! I’m sure the beer was not your only motivation for coming, right?” sarcastically asked Lloyd, as the group laughed.

“But more importantly, how have you been Stan? We were really surprised when we heard you resigned. I mean, wasn’t that supposed to be the dream. To become partner one day. To be the boss, and to be the man” asked Lloyd.

Stan smiled slightly, as he paused to answer, while the rest of the group intently awaited his reply. As his face lit up, he replied "I also thought that was the dream. But after all the work and sacrifice, I guess I can now say that it really wasn't. I'm just glad I was able to figure that part out while my legs can still carry me places".

Looking intently at Stan as he said his reply, and looking up, as he took a deep breath once he heard Stan's reply, Lloyd said "well as long as you're settled with your decision, then I guess we have no reason to worry. You, of all people, can definitely figure it out and come out on top".

"Of course, he will. I told you there was nothing to worry about. It's Stan after all! He probably has a plan right now to come out on top. Right?" asked Jason.

Stan pauses, and with a sheepish smile he said "actually, I really haven't even thought about my next move after this. I've just been relaxing all this time. The plan however is for me to replenish my mind, body and soul during this period, so that when the time comes to work again, I'd be set to go".

"Well, that's one way of doing it. Or you can already start looking for the next big job while you rest. I mean, it wouldn't be that hard, and with your credentials, I'm sure there are a lot of firms and companies that can easily offer big bucks to hire you. Right?" eagerly asked Jason, as Stan tries to find the right response.

"I think Stan just wants to take his time right now and try to figure things out before committing to anything again. Stan has always been focused more on the long game in any of his endeavors, so just take your time before you make your next step", said Ben with a smile of assurance.

Taken aback with Ben's statement, and realizing that he may have stepped out of bound, Jason replied "of course! Don't think about these things for now. Work will always be available, especially for you. Just try and focus on what you really want right now, and push forward once things get sorted out".

Pausing for a moment as Stan smiled and nodded at him, Jason inserted "but just in case you are interested in practicing criminal law, just give me a heads-up. I'm sure our firm will be more than welcome to have you".

"Of course. If I were to practice criminal law, I'd rather work with you than be on the opposing side of the case. I don't want to keep treating you to drinks every time I beat you, you know", jokingly replied Stan, as he tries to lighten the mood.

"Smart-ass! Despite how good you are in law school; I have more experience in criminal law practice than you. So, you'd be fortunate to have me on your side if you want to win", proudly replied Jason, as the group burst into laughter.

Once they settled down, Lloyd motioned that they start eating while the food was still hot, which was seconded by Ben. As they were half-way through their meals, Lloyd suddenly remembered something, and asked "by the way, what did your parents say when you told them you quit?"

"They didn't say anything. Well at least not yet", Stan replied with a sheepish smile. "What?! So, you still haven't told them?" replied Lloyd.

"Yes. I thought I'd rather not worry them with these things for the moment. Anyway, I still have some cash to carry me through, as I figure these things out on my own. But I do plan to tell them, as soon as I start working again. At least they don't have to worry about anything by that time", replied Stan with a smile.

Thinking for a moment about Stan's plan, Lloyd replied "I don't think that's fair for them to find out later, or worse, find out from someone else, that you already resigned. Better just be upfront with them, as early as possible and get it over with already.

"I don't think you'll worry them that much, since you do still have some money to carry you for a long time, and I don't think you'll have any problem looking for another job. Besides, you can also take this time to spend more time with them, since you are not doing anything at the moment. I'm sure they'll appreciate it".

Stan stopped eating as Lloyd was talking, and looked at him intently, as he sensed some concealed motive in Lloyd's statements and action. Looking back at Lloyd's statements and reactions, and analyzing what they all could mean, Stan suddenly felt a sudden fear creep within him.

"You already told your parents that I resigned, haven't you?!" said Stan. Ashamed at what he did, Lloyd replied "Yes, I told them when they asked how you were doing".

"When did you tell them?" asked Stan, as calmed down a bit and tried to analyze the situation. "Just last week when they called", replied Lloyd.

Stan paused as he thought about the best- and worst-case scenarios that could happen and how he can best play his options.

Noticing that the group was looking at him, as Lloyd kept apologizing, he looked at Lloyd and said "don't worry about it. They were bound to know sooner or later. The world has become smaller after all. It's also my mistake for not asking you to keep it a secret, so I share the blame. Anyway, just glad you told me now. I think I still have some time to tell them myself before your parents have the chance to speak to them".

"Yeah. I don't think my parents have already told them about it. They probably would have kept that to themselves for the moment, considering how sensitive that matter is. Anyway, how do you plan to tell them?" asked Lloyd.

"I am still not sure how. But considering how long it would take for me to travel there, I'm thinking of just calling them", replied Stan.

"Maybe it's best if you talk to them in person. I think they'll appreciate the face-to-face honesty. Besides, you visiting them would be a good enough treat to lighten the mood before you tell them your decision, don't you think", said Monica.

Looking at Monica, Stan thought for a moment about her suggestion. "That would be the best thing to do. But considering that a week has already lapsed, giving them a call tonight or tomorrow would be the quickest way to tell them, before they hear about it from anyone else", counter proposed Stan.

"I suggest you send them a text, hinting of your move, to at least ease them up to your revelation", suggested Jen.

"Or you can just initially text them some bad or sad news, so that the call regarding your resignation becomes the better news", suggested Mary.

"And what bad news would that be?!" asked Lloyd. "I don't know. That Stan knocked a girl up in a one-night-stand and is now forced to marry her?!" replied Mary.

"I don't think they'll believe that! Besides, if they hear that Stan will get married and can give them a grandchild, they will most likely consider that good news instead of bad news!" replied Lloyd. As he said that, the group paused, looked at each other, and laughed.

"Yeah, I don't think my parents would buy that, nor be sad about that news", said Stan as they now settled down a bit from the laughing. "But I liked the creativity and enthusiasm there", said Stan, as they laughed again.

"Anyway, I'll figure it out. I'm a big boy. I'll try to gauge them first, and try to see if they already have an idea of me resigning, and just adjust my moves from there. Anyway, let's not get too carried away with that, and just enjoy our friend's appointment. Cheers!" said Stan, as he raised his bottle and the group in unison said "Cheers!".

Chapter 13

The Call

The group continued to celebrate Lloyd's appointment and Stan's new path in life. After a few more beers, they went their separate ways.

Although a bit tipsy, Stan was still lucid enough to give instructions to the cab driver. As he looked out the window of the cab, he remembered once more his parents, and the situation he was now faced with.

"It's already too late, so I'll just call them in the morning. Maybe I'll call around lunch or dinner so I can be sure that they would both be at home. Yeah, probably during lunch", Stan concluded to himself.

After getting home, Stan quickly got ready for bed. Although fleeting, due to the alcohol and his sleepiness, his potential conversation with his parents once more popped in his head. And he thought for a moment about how the call would play out. But as he imagined the conversation, his thoughts weighed down, and before he knew it, he was asleep.

As the beams of light hit Stan's eyes through his window, Stan woke up to an already late morning. "What time is it? And how much did I drink last night? I knew for sure I took my beer in moderation", he thought, as he paused for a moment to recall how many he drank.

"I don't recall drinking that much. Must be lacking practice, I guess. Can't believe how sleepy I was, after only a few bottles", he thought to himself as he got up and went to the bathroom.

Coming back to his bedroom, Stan checked his phone and saw that it was already ten forty-eight in the morning. "Wow, last night's sleep must have been a personal best. Never knew I could sleep that long", he said to himself as he smiled.

Thinking back to his final thoughts before he was fast asleep, Stan recalled the need to call his parents. "Do I really need to tell them?" he thought to himself with a sigh.

"Wouldn't this just upset or worry my parents? I've already resigned, so there is no turning back from that. But do I really need to tell them that news, right now? Would that really help?" Stan asked himself, as he thinks of the pros and cons of telling his parents about his departure from the firm.

"Oh yeah, I forgot, Lloyd already told his parents. I guess it's only a matter of time before my parents find out. Better tell them before they find it out from someone else", he thought, as he went to his refrigerator and drank some water.

Sitting on a table by his kitchen, Stan searched for his father's number in his phone. After finding his father's number, he placed his phone on the table, while looking at the "Dad" tag on the number in his phone.

"Is this the right time to call?" he thought to himself, as he continued to stare at his phone. "Maybe calling later would be a better idea because by then they would already have settled down while having lunch", he thought, as he imagined that scenario. "But then again, I'd be ruining their rest time. I guess it's still best to call them now, while I have the chance to tell them before anyone else", he thought, as he fiddled with the phone.

"How do I even start?" he asked himself, as he recalls how his parents normally talk to him. He recalls how insistent his parents were that he always had good grades in school, and that he took up law. He also remembers how much they monitored his grades and his behavior in school, to make sure that he was not only complying with the grade requirements, but was also showing good behavior.

"Well, it was not like it only ended in school", Stan said with a smile. "Now that I look back, the standards imposed on me were even applicable at home and during social occasions when I had to be courteous and polite every single time, lest my parents be criticized for raising an animal. I guess I had to be Mr. Perfect for as long as I remember", he thought to himself, as he recalled his childhood.

"Not that I'm complaining or anything. The practice I had in carrying myself among other people, helped not only in school, but even in work, since for the most part, work constantly asked me to deal with different types of people, under different types of situations, and expecting me to carry myself in the best way possible in all those situations, so that we can eventually get what we wanted every time.

"And to have lived under that pressure, that microscope, at a very early age, and to make it look easy, did give me a sense of confidence and calmness, regardless of the situation presented. I guess I could say that with the various social situations I've been through, at this point, I've seen and done it all, relatively speaking.

"Although I did enjoy learning the ways of society and competing to stay ahead of my peers, I guess only now do I realize how straining all that work was. And because I never wanted my parents to look bad in the eyes of other people, and also to make sure I give them as much honor as they deserve, I never acted out and even volunteered to take on those challenges consistently, without complaint and with a smile.

"I did want to be Mr. Perfect, so that they wouldn't have to worry about me, and have them entrust me with their goals and aspirations. They deserved that and more, and I was always happy to live out that Mr. Perfect life, as my way of showing my appreciation. I therefore didn't have any option other than to succeed, and succeed without supervision and fuss, so that my story can validate how well they raised me as a person. I wanted that more than anything. And I guess because of that, I rarely allowed myself any rest. Through time however, I may have become too proud to show my parents, or anyone, that I too get tired, just like everyone else, which could have added to all this fatigue.

"Regardless, it is not lost on me how better my life has been because I had their guidance. Some of my contemporaries, as talented as they were, ended up with bad vices, bad friends, and bad reputations, and eventually got into all sorts of trouble with the law and with their family, just because they did not have parents to move them across this tedious life. Besides, it's not like I had any concrete plans when I was younger, other than to complete the latest anime episodes and what not.

"But I guess, eventually, the constant expectations and requirements of life caught up to me. And all I need right now, at this stage, more than anything, is just some rest. Rest from work, and rest from the hustle of life", he thought, as he stared blankly in the direction of his wall.

"Maybe now that I've at least amounted to something, and Gram and I already have stable financial positions, I can try to rest a while and eventually go after something that would deeply make me happy", he thought as he again looked at his phone.

Taking a moment to collect himself and consolidate what he just meditated upon, he then settled down, and was now focused on figuring out how best to express these thoughts to his parents, during his call.

"Best start by asking them how the weather is in the province, and how well Dad's crops have grown this season. And probably just start with Lloyd's appointment, so I can use that as a pretense in calling, and try to figure out if they already talked with Lloyd's parents", he thought, as he paused to think if that introduction would work. "Yeah, I think that would work!" he proudly said to himself.

"If they did already talk to Lloyd's parents, then maybe it's also best for me to just come out and tell them. Maybe I can just go ahead and say 'not sure if you already heard, but I called to tell you about a big decision I just made a few months ago'", he thought, as he paused again to play out that situation in his head. "I think that would work", he convinced himself.

As he imagines himself saying that he resigned from his work and stepped down from partnership, he pictures his Dad becoming disappointed at him for giving up on something that he already worked hard on, for such a long time. He also sees his mother becoming worried about him because a decision like this would not have been made by him unless something terrible happened, thus forcing him to resign. With this, he tried to modify some of his statements and tried to imagine different scenarios that could happen, and the various questions that his parents could potentially raise.

His mind wandered and got stuck again on the images that may become, and he was unable to do anything other than stare blankly, for a brief moment. Realizing that it was already twelve ten in the afternoon, he immediately got a jolt of electricity with the urgency to call his parents before their lunch time was over.

"How time flies. It's best to just call them now, regardless of what could happen, lest I lose the opportunity to come out and tell them before someone else does", he thought, as he pressed his dad's phone number to start a call. "Hope it goes well", he thought to himself with a lot of worry, as his dad's phone was now ringing.

"Hey Stan, how have you been?" said Gary, Stan's dad. "I'm doing fine, dad. How about you, are you and mom doing fine?" asked Stan.

"Yeah, never better. We've been busy lately with the farm, so we do get some exercise despite being retired", Gary joked.

"Great! That's good to know. You both look a bit thinner in your pictures. But still, it's great that you're getting exercise, so your hearts are healthier!" replied Stan.

"Of course. By the way, your mom and I are just about to have lunch. We just cooked some of the vegetables we harvested on the farm", Gary said as another voice joined the conversation.

"How about you Stan, have you had your lunch?" asked Martha, Stan's mother.

"Not yet mom, but will have lunch shortly. By the way, are we on speaker phone now?" asked Stan.

"Yes. I have it in speaker so we can talk while we eat", said Gary.

"Oh, good. Just go ahead and eat then, since it's already lunch time", replied Stan.

"Don't delay your meals too much. You could get sick if you delay your meals for too long" warned Martha.

"Yes mom, I'll quickly fix a meal in my kitchen shortly", obeyed Stan.

As he hears the sound of utensils clanging, Stan continued, "by the way, how is the weather there? Have you already planted your crops?"

"It's been raining here for some days now, and that's good because now we can plant our crops", Gary replied.

"Oh, good. Glad you were able to plant on time" replied Stan, as he scrambles to think of his next line.

"By the way, have you heard about Lloyd's appointment as chief of staff to the speaker of the house?" Stan asked in panic, as he listened intently to his dad's reply.

"Yeah, we heard from Rick, just the other day. You know Rick, right? The one who comes to our house all the time. Always with the shaved head", Gary asked.

"Yes, I remember him. How is he anyway?" Stan replied, as he tries to fish for any clue if his parents already know about his resignation.

"He is doing fine. Just planted his crops yesterday" replied Gary.

"Not sure if they have any idea about my resignation. They already know about Lloyd's appointment, but they heard it from Rick instead of Lloyd's parents. Nonetheless, with how things work in our small town, if the news on Lloyd's appointment already reached my parents, there is a great chance they already know about my resignation", Stan thought to himself before making a sigh.

"Is everything ok?" asked Gary when he heard Stan's sigh. "Ah yes, everything's ok", he replied, as he was in a split-second indecision on whether or not he should just go out with his news or not.

Taking a deep breath, Stan said "I'm not sure if you already heard, but I just called to let you know about a decision I made a few months ago".

"What decision?" Gary asked.

Gasping for air, as though his body forgot how to breathe, Stan's mind raced to find the right words to start his confession. "You see dad, last month, I decided to resign from work", softly said Stan, as he paused to wait for his parent's response.

Taking a moment, Gary responded "yes, we already heard. Rick told us, saying Kevin, Lloyd's dad told him about it and tried to check on us about the news".

A bit shocked that his parents already knew about his decision, Stan didn't know what to say next. Eventually he was able to find his bearings, and softly asked "I hope I did not worry you?"

"Of course, you didn't. We just wanted you to be ready to tell us yourself. Even at an early age, we always knew that regardless of the situation, you always had a plan. So, we knew this wasn't any different. And maybe the resignation was just part of a greater plan of yours moving forward" calmly said Gary.

"Maybe you just wanted, or needed a change of pace. Although you were having great success with your highly competitive and fast paced career, to be honest, we were a bit worried at how stressed and drained you were because of work. Despite our concerns, we wanted you to pursue what you felt suited you best. Anyway, we're already retired and stable financially, so we just wanted you to focus on what you feel is best for you", said Martha.

Still in disbelief at the reaction he got from his parents, Stan wasn't able to speak for a moment. In his mind, was sure that this conversation would have played differently. And yet, for all the doubt and fear he once felt, he was now struck with regret that he did not tell them sooner. He was also in awe at how full the support was from his parents, despite a decision that to him, seemed illogical and misguided.

His heart felt like it expanded, and although a river of happiness swelled within him, his eyes could not help but cry. He sobbed as he absorbed his parent's support and trust in him, despite what he had just done. Although it made no sense to him how much they believed in him, he knew more than anything that he was happy to have been given such trust.

"Sorry mom, dad, that I didn't tell you sooner", said Stan as he sobbed.

"It's okay son. We understand. It's just part of life", said Gary, reassuringly. "It's just part of growing up. You're still alive and well, and that's more important now. You can always work again and make a new opportunity for yourself. You're still young", said Martha, comfortingly.

As Stan's feelings began to settle down, he tried to regain his composure and give a better picture of his situation to his parents. "To be honest, I really don't have a plan right now on what to do next.

"I really just got to a point in work wherein I no longer had any motivation or passion to work. Like what I was doing there was pointless, at least for me. And the only thing I knew for sure was that I didn't want to continue there any longer. But I don't know yet what I want to do following my resignation. That's something I'm still trying to figure out", humbly said Stan.

Gary listened carefully at what Stan said, and after collecting his thoughts said "it's perfectly ok what you did. I really wouldn't blame you. We may not look it, but went through a similar situation back in our youth, regarding choices that did eventually result in the lives we have today.

"We too have had a moment wherein we had to choose between increasing our activities to further our careers, or take a different route, to be able to prioritize other things that we deemed important. And in those moments, we had to face who we were and what we really wanted, and come to a decision on how we want our lives to proceed.

"Although I have to be honest, I am a bit frustrated that you left the lucrative job that you already have, and already work so hard for. I am disappointed not because I think what you did was wrong, I guess I just wanted you to continue with the current career you had, because as a father, I wanted you to have the abundant life you were guaranteed in your previous job.

"But seeing how sure you are of your decision, then I have no objections whatsoever on this path you want to take. Anyway, I think the point of life is to continue living without losing excitement and passion, while ever so slightly, getting older and wiser as time moves on. As the saying goes 'for what shall it profit a man, if he gains the whole world, but loses his soul', right?

"So never underestimate the value of your heart. Although it may not be the wiser, I do believe that only by living it's truest and purest desires, can we actually have a life worth living. And maybe, just maybe, that's the way for us to live a life free from regret.

"I've been rambling a bit, but I guess, all I want to say is that it's okay for you to follow your passion, even without a plan. A lot of people have succeeded by following what they truly wanted for their lives. And resigning from your previous job isn't the end of the world.

"A lot of people found success through very diverse paths. You really don't know where life will eventually take you. Besides, some of life's most defining moments happen, while we are detracted from life's usual plans.

"So, just live the most while you can. And always know that not everything in life revolves around the world's concept of 'winning'".

A bit astounded at how his normally silent dad offered a lot of advice, and swelling with appreciation for the words he heard them say, Stan replied "more than anything, I am truly happy that you understand. I really needed to hear those things from both of you. Mom and dad, thank you for everything. I love you both".

As he said those words, his heart swelled and he was again in tears. Once again, his parents began consoling him, as he tried to regain his composure. After that, they discussed other topics as they tried to once again lighten the mood. As they discussed Lloyd's appointment, Martha inserted "so as you rest for now, do you have any plans of coming home for a vacation?"

Noticing the short pause from Stan, Martha said "of course you don't need to visit if you still have things to complete there. Just come visit if it's already convenient".

"I was actually thinking it would be good for me to go home a few weeks from now. It may help me figure things out if I stay there for a few weeks. Besides, I think the fresh air back home can really improve my health", replied Stan.

"Of course, just come when you are ready", Gary replied. "I'm just going to fix a few things here and go home by next week. If next week is okay with you?" asked Stan.

"Of course! Your room is always ready so just come home anytime you want", replied Martha.

"Okay, that's good to know. I'll make the arrangements and tell you when I'm on my way home", said Stan.

After a few more pleasantries, they said their goodbyes and ended the call. Still happy about how the conversation went, Stan was excited to go home. He thought about the things that he needed to prepare, as well as the gift he intends to bring home from the city.

As he visualized his plans, he thought about how he was going to travel back home. "Should I take a plane home, which will take me just over an hour of flight, and have dad pick me up, or should I go travel by car instead, with about a day of travel across the country?" Stan asked himself.

"Normally I would take the plane home to save time, because I normally had a busy schedule. But as I'm no longer on any deadline, maybe I'll drive home just this once. That would also make sure that I have my car available while in the province, since dad still is very strict about me borrowing his car", Stan said with a smile.

"Besides, driving home through the country will also give me time to visit some scenic views and popular local destinations. I can even try some popular attractions and food along the way. That sounds like a once in a lifetime adventure I'd like to take on just this once. Or twice, since I'm probably also going back to the city using the same car", he said as he tries to figure out how he is going to complete this adventure.

"But it would be dangerous to drive alone without someone to take over the wheel while travelling. It would also be livelier if I had someone to join me as I go home", he thought. "But who can accompany me home on such short notice?" he asked himself, as he thought of the possible candidates to join him in his expedition across the country.

"Monica!" he thought, with a eureka expression on his face. "She did convince me to resign. And she already committed to joining me on a trip", Stan said to himself.

"It's settled then. Guess all that's left now is to let Monica know about the discussion and the verdict!" he said with a sheepish look.

Stan then proceeded to call Monica and tell her about the possible trip home, with her as the driving partner. She was surprised to hear that they were going to Stan's hometown, instead of abroad. She hesitated for a moment, considering the work that was still on her plate, and how sudden the travel would be. But after Stan said that he would help Monica in her cases, and after figuring out the other details, she agreed to come along.

Chapter 14

Road Trip Home

Fastening their seat belts, Stan and Monica are now set to drive back to Stan's hometown. After stocking up on supplies, and with Stan's gift for his parents already in the car, they were now set for the long drive.

"It's still just six am", said Monica, when Stan motioned for the time. "Good! We can still avoid some traffic. By the way, how was your trip coming here?" asked Stan, who was now slowly driving away from his house.

"I didn't have any problems coming here since it was still so early. Still pretty sleepy though, but the coffee helped. But I still haven't had a proper breakfast, so if we can pass by a drive-through, I'd appreciate it. And for making me come this early, you should be paying", said Monica with a frown.

Stan looked briefly at Monica's facial expression as she talked, to check if she was telling the truth. "Quit fooling around. It was necessary that we left early otherwise we would be stuck in traffic. Friday is still a workday, so you know how it is. But since you got here on time, I'll take care of the breakfast", said Stan, as he was able to get a glimpse of Monica's face lighting up.

"Great! Let's look for a great place to eat then", said Monica, as she browses her phone. "Not sure what choices are available at this hour, but hope we pass by somewhere tasty", said Stan with excitement.

"I'll make sure we find a tasty spot. Especially since you're paying. So just leave it to me", confidently said Monica. "Just in case I don't find a decent drive-through, are you open to stopping by an open restaurant along the way?" asked Monica.

"Well, there are a few tasty restaurants along the way, but I don't know what time they open. If you can find an open restaurant that can serve us a meal before you become a cannibal, then I don't mind stopping by", said Stan, as they now enter the main road.

"Found one!" quickly replied Monica. "Franko's is open by seven am, and it's about an hour and a half away from here. I can wait an hour and a half for a good breakfast. Especially since you're paying", said Monica, with a big smile.

"Oh good! It's been a while since I ate there. I used to drive there on weekends just to have breakfast. They have a great full breakfast meal there with coffee. But my favorite order there is their bagel. You should try it" said Stan with excitement.

"Okay, I'll get the bagel. But I'll have that along with the full breakfast. I am kind of hungry you know", sheepishly said Monica.

Looking blankly at Monica for a split second, Stan said "oh what the heck! Have the full breakfast and also get the bagel. I owe you that much!"

"You bet!" replied Monica. "But seriously, try the bagel. It's really good" said Stan as he briefly looks at Monica, before quickly looking back at the road.

"I know this was a sudden and random thing that I asked you. So, thank you. I really appreciate you coming to this trip with me", calmly said Stan.

"Why the sudden seriousness?", sarcastically asked Monica. "You know I already committed to you before, so shut up already and just pay for my breakfast of champions", jokingly said Monica, as they laughed.

"Although, it just occurred to me, but wouldn't your parents think it's odd that you'd bring me along with you on this road trip?" curiously asked Monica.

"To be honest, I don't remember telling them that I was driving with anyone. Not that they asked. After our call last week, I just messaged them a few days back that I was going home tomorrow night. And then they just said okay. So, I guess the topic never came up", said Stan as he notices some concern from Monica.

"But I understand your concern. I guess to avoid any misunderstanding, I'll just tell them that you are a law school classmate of mine and a very close friend who was the only one available, among our friends, to join me as I drive home", said Stan, as he tries to gauge Monica's reaction.

"Well, I think that could work. Just wanted to avoid any misunderstanding from your parents about our relationship, and possibly avoid any weirdness along the way", defensively said Monica.

"Yeah, don't worry about it. They are cool about that sort of thing. They'll understand. And if they act funny, just tell me, so I can set things straight", confidently said Stan. "Glad we're on the same page with that", said Monica, as she looks away.

After over an hour of driving, they were already out of the city and could see some country scenery. Checking the time, Monica asked "how long till we reach Franko's?"

"We're almost there. Probably another ten minutes and we would be there. If you can't take the hunger any longer, there is bread and some water in the back", replied Stan.

"It's ok. I can still wait a while longer. I don't want to spoil my appetite before we have breakfast, so I'll endure this", jokingly said Monica.

"Quit being so dramatic. Just have some bread if you really can't take the hunger any longer", replied Stan.

Driving a few minutes more, Stan said "there it is. I already saw the sign for Franko's. You'll live!"

"Just in time! Any longer and I would have resorted to cannibalism!" jokingly replied Monica.

Still joking around, Stan slowly changed lanes to his right and slowed down as he approached the entrance to Franko's parking lot. A few meters away from the entrance, a Porsche dangerously cut him off and drove past him, as Stan was barely able to maneuver himself out of a collision.

"Jerk!" said Stan, as he blew his horn at the Porsche that was now far away. "What a prick!" said Monica as she follows the direction of the Porsche.

"Did they hit us?" asked Monica. "Fortunately, I was able to veer away from him. But they really almost hit us", said a pissed Stan.

Surprised and a bit disoriented at what happened, Stan slowly moved his car to the parking lot, while trying to follow the direction of the Porsche. As they entered the parking lot, they saw the Porsche speeding to an open parking spot with a sedan already signaling and backing up to park on the open slot.

Before the sedan was able to park, the Porsche quickly raced inside the lines of the parking slot from the opposite direction of the parking space. Surprised and disgruntled, the driver in the sedan honked a few minutes, but to no avail. As the sedan honked, the driver of the Porsche remained inside without even flinching. Frustrated, the sedan just drove away from the parking space to look for another place to park.

"What a jerk!" angrily said Monica, as they looked for a space to park. Shortly after the sedan drove away, they saw the driver of the Porsche step out of the car. Out from the Porsche was an out of shape man in his early forties, but wore a brightly colored shirt, hippy pants, and high-end basketball shoes. He was alone, but had with him an Hermes bag with a chihuahua head popping from the top of the bag.

As they examined the expensive watch and jewelry that the man had on, Monica said "seems like a genuine rich prick we got here. Over the top, but a rich prick nonetheless."

As they were now backing up to park, Stan replied "probably overcompensating for something". The two looked at each other blankly for a second, and burst to laughter. "Yup, probably the case", emphatically said Monica, as they burst in laughter again.

With a lighter mood, they proceeded to the entrance of Franko's. "Let's try to sit away from that prick", said Monica. "Yeah, let's do that", agreed Stan.

As they entered the restaurant, they both scanned for the available seats in the restaurant, as well as the seat of the Porsche driver. They immediately saw the Porsche driver, but tried to act normal, so that the Porsche driver wouldn't know that they were the ones he just cut off by the entrance.

"He acts as though he doesn't care about the other people around him, but he somehow seems to be super sensitive about how others are secretly looking at him. A peculiar situation, especially for someone who wears a shirt as bright as that", Stan thought to himself, with a smile.

Having located the person they wanted to sit as far away from, they walked further inside to look for the farthest away seat from the Porsche driver. Unfortunately however, the only available table at that time was the one right in front of the Porsche driver.

"Maybe we should find another place to eat? I can just have some of the bread that you bought while we drive to the next open restaurant", said Monica.

"Let's just stay. We're already here, and you and I are both hungry, so might as well eat breakfast before we go. And why do we have to go, when we did nothing wrong anyway?" said Stan as he looked at Monica. "Besides, the full breakfast is really good here and I really kind of missed it", continued Stan with a smile.

"Well, if you say so. Then let's stay. Anyway, you're the one paying, so if you say so, then so be it", playfully said Monica with some hand gestures as though taking an order from a king.

They walked towards the empty table in front of the Porsche owner, but tried to act as normal as possible, to avoid giving away themselves as witnesses to a great wrong. Fortunately, the Porsche owner was busy using his phone, so they were able to take their seats without much incident.

Their table was parallel to the table of the Porsche owner, with Stan sitting on the seat across the chair in front of the Porsche driver, so he had a better view of the Porsche owner with his peripheral view than Monica. Stan however tried to focus more his attention on Monica who was sitting in front of him, so that he didn't have to look at the Porsche owner.

Checking the menu and eventually giving their orders, they were both more focused now on the breakfast they would soon be enjoying.

"I really hope the breakfast here is as good as you say. And I am trusting you with the bagel as well, so if our order isn't that good, you're still paying for our next meal", said Monica.

"Just wait for the food. You'll like it", confidently said Stan.

After a few minutes, their order was delivered. In almost the same moment, the Porsche's meal was also delivered, albeit a few seconds later than the delivery of their orders. Stan noticed the timing of the meal, as well as the irate expression from the Porsche driver when he saw that their meal was given ahead of his.

"Well, I guess the world can even things out sometimes", Stan said to himself with a smile. "But so much for that. Time to focus on my meal. I've been craving this for a while, so better take the little wins as much as I can", he again said to himself as he surveyed his plate to find the best place to begin.

"I think I'll start with the sausages", thought Stan. At that same moment, he also noticed that his order and that of the Porsche driver were the same. "Well, can't be helped because this is their most popular dish", he again said to himself.

But just at that moment, Stan saw that the Porsche owner's chihuahua was eating the sausages in his plate, while he was busy talking with someone on the phone. He thought about signaling the Porsche owner about what his dog was doing, but before he could do anything, the dog had already eaten the two sausages that were on his plate. Right after the dog ate the sausages, it immediately withdrew its head inside the bag, just as the Porsche owner ended his call and looked at his plate.

Unsure if he should say something, Stan decided to just keep to himself what he saw. "I don't think this prick deserves my help, but I think even if I helped, this prick would just take my help the wrong way. I think the dog is free from any rabies or any disease considering that this dude can afford an Hermes to carry his pet around. Besides, at this point, I think the dog's saliva may actually be safer than that of its owner's saliva", he said to himself as he kept on smiling.

"Well, you're right. The food here is great", said Monica after consuming a portion of his full breakfast. Looking at Stan as he said that, and noticing Stan's expression, Monica asked "you haven't touched your food yet so I don't understand why you're already smirking so much".

"Oh, sorry about that. I just saw something funny", said Stan in a whisper. "I don't get it" replied Monica. "I'll explain to you later", said Stan as he signals with his eyes while trying to control his laughter.

"Hey waiter! Come over here!" yelled a voice that can be heard across the restaurant. Surprised at the yelling, Stan and Monica followed the direction of the sound and saw that it came from non-other than the person across their table.

"Why is there no sausage on my plate?! I expressly ordered the full breakfast! So, why isn't there any sausage on my plate?!" said the Porsche owner in a loud voice, even before the waiter got near his table.

Before the waiter could respond, the Porsche owner yelled again "where is your manager? I don't want to talk with you! Give me your manager!"

Unsure what to do, the waiter went to his manager, who was an older gentleman, probably fifty years old. As the manager and waiter were walking towards the Porsche owner's table, the waiter whispered his account of the incident to the manager. Once the manager and the waiter were within shouting distance, the Porsche owner yelled again "is this how you treat your customers around here?! Are you trying to cheat me?!"

"No sir, we mean no disrespect, and we would never try to cheat our patrons", calmly said the manager.

"Then how do you explain a full meal without a sausage! I paid for a full breakfast, and yet, you're not giving me what I paid for! That's cheating! You're shortchanging me here with your service!" again said the Porsche owner at the top of his voice.

"We would never try to do that sir", said the manager, still in a calm voice. "Then you're saying I'm lying?! Who do you think I am! What kind of customer service is that?!" the Porsche owner continued to yell.

"Of course not, sir. We would never call you a liar. But I do want to understand what happened here, so we can make the necessary corrections, sir. And maybe we can just cool ourselves first, and try to calmly figure out what happened", calmly continued the manager.

"This is unacceptable! No! I won't cool down for you! You disrespect me and now you expect me to cooperate?! What kind of establishment is this?!" loudly continued the Porsche owner.

"Excuse me sir, but I think there is a misunderstanding", abruptly but courteously interjected Stan.

"Mind your own business Mr.!" yelled the Porsche owner, but in a curiously lower tone when he saw Stan and Monica.

"I saw what happened from my table as I was eating and it wasn't the waiter's fault", continued Stan as he ignored the Porsche owner. "The full breakfast plate had two customary sausages on them, but as soon as they were placed on the table, the chihuahua in that bag ate them", quickly continued Stan, before the Porsche owner can react, and at the same time pointing at the dog in the bag.

"That's impossible! I was here all along, so I would have noticed if my dog ate the sausages" replied the Porsche owner, but now in a calmer voice.

"Yes sir, but you were on your phone a few minutes ago, and were distracted just enough, for your dog to quickly sneak in and eat the sausages without you noticing", explained Stan, with a very cool but firm voice.

A bit flustered at what Stan said, and feeling the stares and some giggles from the people eavesdropping, the Porsche owner doubled down on his stance. "I don't care what you say! I don't believe my dog ate the sausages! This is bad service, and I won't pay for this!" loudly said the Porsche owner to the manager, as he tilts his body away from Stan and avoids any eye contact with them.

"That wouldn't be fair, good sir. They gave you a full plate, sausage and all, and your dog already ate a portion of what they gave you. It would therefore be unfair if you just left without paying even for the sausages at the very least", Stan explained.

As Stan was saying this, the Porsche owner listened and moved his eyes to look at Stan, but his body remained facing the manager and the waiter. After Stan's explanation, the Porsche owner returned his gaze on the manager and waiter, as he continued to face them, and said "I don't care what you say. Bad service is bad service. I'm not paying for this."

After saying this, the Porsche owner quickly took hold of his dog bag, and stood up to leave. "Sir, you should pay before leaving", calmly said Stan, before the Porsche owner can make another step. The Porsche owner quickly glared at Stan and shouted "so sue me!", before storming off.

Having anticipated the reaction from the Porsche owner, Stan darted forward and reached his hand to grab the Porsche owner. But before his hand could reach the back of the Porsche owner's back, the manager inserted his hand between Stan and the Porsche owner, to signal Stan to stop.

A bit confused, but convinced by the composed expression of the manager, Stan stopped his action, and just watched the Porsche owner storm out of the restaurant with his dog barking.

"Let's just let them go, sir. Don't worry about that and just enjoy your meal", said the manager with a smile.

"But that's just so arrogant of the man to come here, disturb the peace, and just walk away without even paying, despite being wrong. He can't even give an apology. That's just disrespectful", exclaimed Stan in frustration.

"Don't worry about it, sir. What's important is that no further incident ensued, so we can still be happy about that", said the manager with a smile.

"But even a child would know that he needed to apologize in that situation. That's just totally uncalled for what he did to your staff. And now he gets to leave as the waiter pays for the sausage after taking some words from him. That's just unacceptable sir, and I'm more than willing to help you out to get back at that arrogant prick", ranted Stan.

"Let's just let it go, Stan. We don't have to ruin our day for jerks like that", said Monica as she tries to pacify an enraged Stan. As Stan calms down a bit, his eyes gazes at the waiter slightly before looking back at the manager and Monica.

Noticing the pity in Stan's eyes when he checked on the waiter, the manager explained "you don't have to worry about that. We won't deduct that from the waiter's salary. We'll just charge it to marketing or something".

Looking at the manager's face and noticing some deception, Stan asks "I'll calm down if you tell me honestly who will shoulder that unpaid plate?"

With some hesitation, as the manager tries to pick the right words, he responded "don't worry about the waiter, you were able to explain what actually happened so he is off the hook. And I thank you for that.

"As for the meal, since it still has to get paid, then I'll take care of that. I'll just consider that a treat to myself for being able to properly control the situation. Besides, I'd honestly prefer paying for that, than having this incident turn into a lawsuit for us. So, don't worry about that, and we really appreciate your help there."

"But that was really unfair what he did to you and your staff. And injustice should always get punished if we really want to make our society work", explained Stan to the manager.

"I thank you for your concern. But I guess not all instances deserve the full extent of the law. And I believe this instance is one of those instances wherein it's better if we just let it go. But make no mistake, if the stakes involved were higher, you best believe that I wouldn't let it go, and make sure we get what we deserve", said the manager.

Still frustrated and angry, but slightly pacified by the manager's explanation, Stan just gave the manager his card and offered to help them for free, should the Porsche owner ever decide to give them trouble for the incident.

"Let's just ignore that jerk. He's gone now anyway, and I do hope he gets a scratch on that Porsche on his way out", jokingly said Monica, as he tries to make Stan laugh.

"Yeah, hope he gets a big and long scratch on his Porsche", replied Stan with a smile.

"That's the spirit! Now let's try to enjoy the full breakfast and bagel that you highly recommended! Hope this blows me away as you said" said Monica aloud.

"Oh, shut up and just eat already!" replied Stan with a slight smile, as he put his attention on the plate before him.

"What kind of prick does that anyway! I can't believe pricks like that get to enjoy good things in life! People like them should seriously be disciplined and taught a lesson so that the world would be a better place!" Stan keeps thinking to himself as he takes in his breakfast.

Monica, noticing that Stan was a bit more quiet than normal, and was less ecstatic with his food now than he was a few minutes ago, tried to change the mood of the table. "This is really some good sausages. I get why the dog just ate it and why the prick got mad that he wasn't getting any of it. This thing is divine! Good call and thank goodness you're paying", enthusiastically said Monica.

"Yup, that's why I wanted you to try this place", replied Stan as he ate on without any further reaction.

"You know, I took a look at that man's plate, and I saw that some of the hash brown had some bite marks on them", interjected the manager, as he offers them some hot sauce.

A bit surprised at the manager being there, and confused about the question, Stan asked "what do you mean? Sorry, I don't follow".

"Well, I'm just saying, if you think about it, the Porsche owner took a bite at some of those hash browns that are normally platted beside the sausages", said the manager. "So?" curiously asked Stan.

"Well, if I were in his shoes, I'd also be pissed if I knew that I ate a hash brown that was soaking in the chihuahua's saliva. It's like I French kissed my own chihuahua in that sequence. And I don't know about you, but I'm not really a cat or dog person, so French kissing my dog really doesn't sit well with me", said the manager in a calm and serious tone.

In a brief moment, as they all absorbed the situation described by the manager, they looked at each other momentarily, then immediately burst into laughter. "Come to think of it, I did see a lot of drool coming from the chihuahua when it took the sausages", said Stan, before again laughing hard.

"He probably thought the saliva was just oil dripping from the hash browns!" said Monica, as they kept laughing.

"So, you see sir, we did get our justice in that scuffle. It may not look like the justice we read in our textbooks, but for me, that was good enough retribution or reparation for this situation", said the manager as he smiles and looks at Stan.

"Besides, we may just be walking into their web if we get involved with them any further. Oftentimes, people like that have warped their lives into something that's unbearable for themselves and the people around them, only to get their way in life. And as financially and materially well-endowed that life may be, having pushed your friends and family away, will probably still feel lonely, regardless of how strong willed a person can be.

"I don't care who you are, or how strong you think you are, but everyone feels lonely. That's probably just how we are programmed. And people like that would probably prefer to engage with other people, even as enemies, just to avoid that loneliness.

"So maybe in this case, the justice that we deserve, is to simply be able to continue on with our lives, and just allow him to continue wallowing in his self-inflicted misery. Besides, I don't think I'd particularly enjoy dumping my current life right now, and strive to get rich or powerful, just to get revenge on a guy like that. That would be a waste of time, and a waste of my life", continued the manager.

After reflecting on the things, the manager said, Stan makes a big sigh. "You're right. We did get our justice in the end. Thanks for the wise words", said Stan as he gave the manager a warm smile.

"Happy to have helped! Hope you enjoy your meal!" warmly replied the manager as he went away, while Stan resumed eating, but this time livelier and chattier.

"That was a great meal! Glad I had the bagel. Never knew bagel that simple can taste that good", said Monica, as she asks for the check.

"It has always been good. That's why I've craved for this place for a long time", seriously said Stan.

"What's your deal?" said a slightly pissed Monica.

"Ah, no, I wasn't trying to make fun of you or anything. I guess I am just thankful for you and the manager's words, that I was able to enjoy the food right in front of me. I really needed a taste of that warm and comforting meal again. And I probably would not have been able to enjoy it, had my thoughts lingered more than it should have, on the events a few minutes back", said Stan with a quiet smile.

"So, thanks for joining me in this selfish trip of mine", continued Stan as he smiles at Monica.

"Hey, don't start crying on me now. I did owe you this, as you consistently insist. So, don't sweat it. Besides, we never know. Maybe I also needed this trip, just as much as you, so we're even", said Monica with a subtle smile.

Feeling a bit awkward at their exchange, Monica jokingly quipped, "besides, you're paying for this meal and for my vacation. So, it's not like it's a bad deal".

"Well, you do have a point there. I mean, I would also find it hard to say no if you invited me to a vacation with you paying for the whole trip", seriously said Stan, before they looked each other in the eyes and burst into laughter.

After paying for their meal and saying their goodbye to the manager, the two went back to their car, and continued with their trip. As Monica insisted that she now take the wheel as she was bored, the two went on with Monica driving.

As they travelled, they continually changed places driving. As they went through the countryside, they were again reminded how beautiful the countryside can be. They were constantly in awe and intrigued with the sights they passed by along the way. On their mutual decision to keep their speed slow and safe, the one-day drive home turned into a day and a half of driving. But as they weren't in a rush, they were able to have a good time.

On their way home, they stopped by some historical and popular tourist attractions that although Stan was able to pass by before, he never had time to visit. On several occasions that they were too tired to drive, they would park along the road and both take a nap. There were also instances when they had to go to the bathroom or wanted to buy some interesting souvenirs or street food along the way. In these instances, they would either make a stop, or make a quick detour.

Several more hours away from Stan's hometown, and as they were driving on a road at the side of a mountain, Monica was looking at the cliff side of the road. After they passed through some trees, the cliff side of the road cleared from any tree. As the view unfolds, Monica was immediately in awe at the sight she saw.

"Wow!" said Monica in a deep and prolonged tone. "What happened?" asked Stan, as he drove the car. "Is there a place to stop the car?" asked Monica. "We're on a cliff right now, but let me see what I can do", replied Stan. "There, I see a clear space over there!", said Monica in excitement, as she points at a spot.

Without hesitation and with full trust in Monica, Stan slowed down the car and parked in an open space on the mountain side of the road. After locking their doors, the two crossed the road and went on the cliff side of the road.

The cliff side of the road did not have any observation deck of any sort, but only had a railing to stop any car from falling down the cliff, should it ever lose control. As that portion of the road was near the top of the mountain, Stan didn't understand why they needed to stop to check it out. In his mind, he thought "it's a nice sunny day, so maybe Monica wants to have a great view of the sky". But as they reached the edge of the railing, Stan slowly understood.

"Wow, that's a great view", he said in a low and prolonged tone, as Monica was also mesmerized at the view before them. With the gentle sunlight on their head and a steady yet cool breeze crashing with their skins, they were lost for words at the panoramic view of the side of the green mountain that stretches down into a scenic beach front with majestic blue waves crashing on large black rocks that open into a vast blue sea.

"I really wasn't sure it was that good a view at first. But when I got a few glimpses of the beach, I wanted to see the rest", said Monica, while still enjoying the view.

"Yes, I've never seen this view before. But not for a lack of trying", replied Stan, as he was also mesmerized at the view.

"But that beach doesn't appear in any of the listings online, nor on any blogs that I've read", Stan continued.

"Maybe that's still an undeveloped beach, that's why it's not on any website", said Monica.

"Probably so", agreed Stan.

"I hope no one discovers it, so it can stay that way forever", said Monica.

"I sure hope so", replied Stan.

"I'm glad we stopped when we had the chance. Living in the city all my life, I guess I forget how beautiful life and the world still was", thought Stan, as he continued to enjoy the view.

"Who knew such a simple and breathtaking surprise can be found in this unassuming location. I probably would have missed it if Monica did not join me on my trip", Stan said to himself, as he subtly peeks at Monica, who was still in awe at the view.

"I'm glad she joined me on my trip. It probably wouldn't have been an enjoyable drive home, if she didn't come along", Stan thought to himself, as he recalls the laughter and enjoyable back and forth between her and Monica, during their drive.

Noticing that Stan was looking in her direction, Monica asked "is there anything wrong? Do I have something in my hair?"

"Ah, no. There's nothing on your hair. I just wanted to check if you were having as good a time as me during our trip", seriously said Stan.

"Of course, I do. It's you, and it's me. We go way back, so of course I'd have a blast on this trip", said a slightly startled Monica.

"Thanks nonetheless", said Stan as he smiled at Monica. "Don't sweat it", said Monica, as she smiles back at Stan.

After a few more minutes, they went back to their car and were on their way, with Monica driving. After a few hours, and with Stan now driving, their car reached the border of Stan's hometown. It was almost sunset at that moment, and the sun gave a silhouette of the countryside as they travelled along.

"Wow, what a nice sunset" exclaimed Monica. "Yes, I really missed those sunsets", replied Stan with joyful eyes.

"Life here was always simple. Nothing too fancy, and nothing too complicated. Just simple and honest people, trying to live out their lives to the best that they can", said Stan with some passion.

"I'm not sure why, but whenever I come home, I feel like time moves slower, and the days get longer", said Stan with a smile.

As they get closer to Stan's home, Stan points to some of the establishments familiar to him, and he tells his childhood memories about them. They eventually got off the main highway, and entered a residential area of the town. As they went further in the residential area, Stan drove silently, while Monica observed the area around her.

Stopping in front of his childhood home, Stan could not help but recall all the good memories he had as a child. Despite going home on a yearly basis, this trip home seemed more special than the ones before.

As he looked at his childhood home, he remembered the chores that he did to maintain the house, as well as the games they played inside it. As Stan checked their neighbor's houses, he noticed how most of the houses remained the same, with only a few changes since his childhood days.

"We did play a lot of games with the neighbors back in the day. I wonder how they are doing now", Stan thought to himself.

After parking the car, Stan and Monica got out of the car and walked to the entrance. With Stan slowly moving close to the door, he remembered once more how it felt like to be a child running home after a long day of school. As he knocked on the door, he felt once more the warmth and assurance that this place represented. And he thought to himself with gratefulness, "I'm home".

Chapter 15

Hometown

Shortly after Stan knocked, steps were heard from the kitchen and as Gary peaked from the window he said "oh it's you Stan. Come in, the door is open. Got your message earlier about your time of arrival, so me and your mother are in the kitchen preparing dinner". After Gary said this, Stan and Monica got in, dropped their bags and immediately went to the kitchen to greet Gary and Martha.

"Glad you were able to make it before dinner. But uhm, I never knew you had company. I think the food we prepared would be enough, but had we known you were going to bring someone special, then we would have gotten some pastries or cakes at the store", said Gary with a big smile on his face.

"Oh, it's not what you think dad", quickly replied Stan. But before Stan can explain, Gary excitedly calls Martha. "Hon, Stan is here, and he brought a special someone!" called Gary.

Quickly, Martha got out of the kitchen and with a big smile, said "oh Stan, why didn't you say you were bringing your special someone home. Had we known, we'd have bought some dessert from the store".

"It's not what you think. And by the way, this is Monica, she is also a lawyer and a classmate of mine in law school. I think you can remember her as the second rank in our graduating class?" said Stan, as Monica and Martha exchanged pleasantries.

"Oh yeah, I remember her. We had the chance to talk with her parents during the ceremony. And we always thought she was a lovely girl, and would really love for her to be part of the family, once you both decide to tie the knot", said Martha, as she and Gary exchanged smiles.

"It's not like that mom. As I was about to tell dad, me and Monica are good friends, and since I needed someone to alternate driving with me, I asked her to come. As she was on leave, and wanted to check out some of the beaches here, she went along", defensively said Stan.

"Of course, we understand Stan", said Gary with a sly wink.

"Why are you winking?! I hope you don't get the wrong idea. We are good friends since way back, but we are not in any relationship whatsoever", again defended Stan, as Monica silently listens.

"Well, maybe we don't know how things work between young people these days, but can we ask you Monica, if you are currently in a relationship right now?" said Gary, as she asks Monica.

"Well, I don't have any relationship right now. But we are just friends, Stan and I" said Monica in a very polite way.

"And how about you Stan, are you currently in any relationship?" again asked Gary. "Well, I don't have any relationship as of the moment, but just because we are both single, doesn't follow that us travelling together makes us a couple", defended Stan.

"But on your way here, how did you spend the night? I don't suppose you spent the night in the car?" curiously asked Martha.

"Well, actually we did just take naps on occasion, just inside the car, whenever we both feel too sleepy to drive", said Monica.

"That's no way to treat a guest, Stan. You should have just stayed in a hotel along the way if you needed a nap. I'm sorry about that Monica. My son can be rude at times", said Gary.

"Oh, don't worry. I didn't mind at all. It would have been a waste of money and time if we checked into a hotel during our trip. We wanted to check out the tourist attractions along the way so taking a nap along the way made sense.

"We were also able to brush our teeth and use the toilets of the restaurants that we passed, so there really wasn't any more need for checking in. But I really was hoping to take a shower once we got here", said Monica in a shy way.

"Of course! Where are our manners?! You can take a shower while we finish cooking our dinner. I'm sure you're tired and worn out as well, so we can just continue our discussion during dinner. I'll show you to the bathroom", said Martha as she leads Monica to the bathroom.

"Well, I guess that settles that. Now let me just change so I can help out in the kitchen", said Stan.

"Well, there is still one concern", sternly said Gary, as Martha and Monica paused, to hear what Gary's concern was. "Are you going to be sharing a bed tonight? I mean we won't mind, but as we may not know how things work between 'friends' these days, might as well ask upfront, so we can make the necessary arrangements in your bedroom", said Gary with a smile.

"Let it go already dad, sheesh!" quickly said Stan with embarrassment. "I apologize for my parent's behavior. They don't have guests very often, so they are like this. But they are decent most of the time", apologizes Stan.

"Well, we do have guests, but this is the first time that Stan has brought a girl over for dinner. And so abruptly, and a bit secretively if I may add. So, we really don't know how to interpret it", said Martha with a smile.

"No need to apologize. I guess I understand a bit where you are coming from. But I think it's Stan's call where we will be sleeping and how to proceed. Now won't you explain Stan?", said Monica with a coy expression.

"Thanks for the help Monica", said Stan with sarcasm. "But as I've already said, we are good friends, but we are not dating. So, we'll sleep in different bedrooms. She can sleep in Gram's room, while I sleep in my room. So, mom and dad, please cut it out already. And stop acting like you don't understand how these things work, already. It was funny the first time, but it's no longer cute", said Stan with some annoyance.

"Okay, we get it. Stop being so defensive, Stan. We were just trying to entertain our guests here. I think she gets it, right?" said Gary with a big grin as Monica nods. This prompted Gary, Martha and Monica to laugh, while Stan was irritated.

"Well, let's get you settled in already. Now come Monica, I'll show you to your bedroom and the shower. As for you Stan, better take a shower yourself before you change clothes and have dinner. We'll take care of the cooking. It's almost done anyway. I'll just see if I can get some cake from the nearby café", said Martha.

"Oh, I forgot. We bought muffins from the city, so you don't have to get any cake. I'll take them out so you can serve them later", said Stan. "Oh, great! Get them out first so we can ready them for later", said Gary.

Shortly after, Stan gave the muffins to Gary. After taking a shower, Stan and Monica had dinner with Gary and Martha. As they enjoyed their meal, they exchanged stories and updates, with Gary and Martha subtly trying to get to know Monica more.

After their meal, Stan volunteered to wash the dishes, as was the tradition in their house, and especially because he wasn't able to help in the cooking. Trying to avoid being left with Gary and Martha, and also wanting to be helpful, Monica also volunteered to help with the dishes. After Monica and Stan were done, they checked their phones a bit, but eventually went to sleep.

Because they slept earlier than usual, Stan woke up early. It was still that moment in the morning, when the sun could barely rise up. But being fully awake, and unable to go back to sleep, Stan got up and went to sit on the chair by the front porch.

Sitting as he stared at a beautiful sunrise, he thought to himself, "it's been a while since I've seen this view. I guess there really is no place like home".

Looking at the other houses and how some people have already come out to exercise, go to work, or go to the market, Stan smiled and thought, "dad really loves hanging out here. And I can see why. The breeze always seems great, the sunset is extraordinary, and from this vantage point, you can watch as the world moves, and be thankful you're still part of its movement. This spot, in a way, allows me to see just how beautiful the world continues to be, and see the faces of the people who keep this play moving".

"Life is such a beautiful thing to have, if only life were simpler and more abundant for all. Then maybe, everyone can just step out of work more often, and just enjoy the life that everyone has been given", said Stan to himself, as he sighs.

"Maybe that's the greatest tragedy man has had to deal with. To be given life in a magnificent world, and have that world right in front of you, but still be unable to enjoy it, just because of all the responsibilities put on each and every person, from birth until eventual passing", Stan continued to ponder.

"I have been fortunate to have some savings that allow me this time to ponder about the world. But sooner or later, I would again have to do things that are outside my character, just so I can continue living", he thought, as he continued to stare as the neighborhood came to life.

"But I guess I can't fight how things work as I am. It's simply the way it has been, and maybe for good reason. I guess the best thing for me now is to simply enjoy the rest, that my savings will allow me to enjoy. And maybe just try and squeeze out the most fun that this limited time can afford me", he said to himself with a smile.

"Good morning!", said a voice from behind Stan. "Oh, it's you. Good morning!" replied Stan after seeing Monica walking towards him.

"Why are you up so early?" asked Monica. "We slept early last night, so I woke up early. Also went out to check the sunrise. How about you, why are you up so early?" asked Stan.

"You're right. What a lovely sunrise!" replied Monica as she stares at the view while Stan continues to look at her intently. "Anyway, I normally wake up early to take a jog and start my day early. I guess my body clock woke me up early. So, here we are", said Monica, as she smiles at Stan.

"By the way, I enjoyed our trip and I also enjoyed dinner last night. I can understand why you decided to go home. It feels very cozy and laid back here in your house. And I'm not sure if it's just the fresh air talking, but I have to admit, this trip may not have been the vacation that I imagined having, but somehow someway, this trip is turning out to be the vacation that I've been needing", said Monica, with a serious undertone. "Thanks for inviting me to join you", she continued.

Sensing the seriousness in Monica's voice, Stan replied, "don't mention it. I also enjoyed the company. I probably would have gotten lost or have gotten into trouble if you didn't join me on the trip", said Stan with a warm smile.

Seeing a warm smile from Monica, Stan felt happy. But after realizing that things might escalate and make things awkward between the two of them, Stan quickly added "also appreciate when you sing along to the stereo. Your singing was definitely better at keeping me awake, than any coffee I've ever had".

"Oh, shut up! Just be glad that you had the pleasure to hear my renditions", countered Monica. "Oh, so that's what those high pitch screeches were called?" jokingly replied Stan. "Shut up already?!" as they both laughed.

After they settled down, Stan remembered something, and said "hey, do you know how to cook breakfast?"

Monica initially looked puzzled, but eventually replied "I can handle myself in the kitchen, but I don't have a lot of breakfast recipes in my arsenal. Why? Where are you going with this?".

"Well, I just thought that since we got up early and all, and since mom and dad prepared our dinner last night, maybe we can cook breakfast for them this morning", said Stan with some excitement.

"Of course! I'm a hundred percent game with that plan. It's the least we can do", excitedly replied Monica.

"Are there any open establishments at this early in the morning?" asked Monica.

"I think the market is already open, and it's really nearby. We can get the ingredients we need and quickly whip up a breakfast, before they wake up", replied Stan.

"By the way, before we get the ingredients, let's get some bread from a bakeshop near here. Ever since we were little, we always got our bread from that shop. So much so that the taste of their bread became synonymous to breakfast and home, so you have to try them as well", excitedly said Stan.

"Sure! I'm game. Probably one of the best breads around here, so I definitely have to try it", replied Monica.

With some awkwardness, Stan replied, "well, not really the best bread around".

"If it isn't the best bread around, then why do you keep buying it?" curiously asked Monica.

"Well, the taste is not that bad, but there are better breads around. And yet because of how often we had it for breakfast, we can't think of breakfast without remembering that bread", said Stan with some shyness.

"If it's not the best bread, why keep buying it?" asked Monica.

Taking some moment to think for the reason, Stan eventually replies "well, for one thing, the bread is very affordable. But I guess more than anything, we keep buying it because the bread is already available early in the morning, and it's always hot and fresh".

"I guess I can understand that. So, let's go get that bread of your childhood already", replied Monica, as they both went to their rooms to quickly change.

After they parked, the two walked towards a brick walled establishment that seemed to be the brightest structure around. In a bright yellow neon light atop the establishment wrote a sign which read "Roy's Bread".

As they got near the shop, they saw the busy line at the front, all waiting to order bread that early in the morning. Although there was a small place wherein people can stay and eat bread and the other products of the establishment, there was also a small window by the side wherein people can get their bread for take-out. And a great majority of the people were lining up for take-out, than the ones eating inside.

"Wow, never knew it would be this busy, this early in the morning!" a surprised Monica said.

"Yeah, I remember going here as a kid, lining up, just so we can have the freshest bread available. They have several varieties of bread that we normally have, but the ones they sell in the morning are the freshest around. And people like to have their bread fresh around here", proudly shared Stan.

"Must be a proud tradition around here", sarcastically said Monica.

"As a matter of fact, it is. See, the people around here have been having the bread here since they were kids. This is the first bakeshop that opened in our town, so a lot of people have a lot of fond memories of this place. That's probably the greatest reason why a lot of people line up this early, just to get a taste of their youth again", said Stan with a smile.

Seeing how unrestricted Stan's smile was, Monica could not help but smile as well. Slowly, the two fell in line and as they waited their turn, the sun slowly began to rise.

"Hey Stan, how far away is the market from here?" asked Monica. "Not that far. Probably a few meters from here. Why'd you ask?" answered Stan.

"Well, I understand how important it is to get the bread here for breakfast, but just want to make sure we have enough time to prepare breakfast before your parents wake up", said a slightly concerned Monica.

"I think it'll take ten to twenty minutes more before it's our turn. And my parents would probably wake up an hour from now", said Stan, who now also shared Monica's concern.

"Maybe we can split up. You can wait for the bread, while I already start buying some ingredients from the market. What do you think?" asked Monica.

"Well, I wanted to give you a tour of the market since you're my guest and all, but maybe we can do that another time. Yeah, you can go ahead and get some of the ingredients to make breakfast", said Stan.

"Sure. Which direction is the market, and what do you want me to buy for you?" asked a pumped Monica.

"Wait, maybe it's better if I go to the market instead, since I'm more familiar with it and I can more quickly get the stuff we need. Plus, I know some good vendors who sell the best ingredients around. You can just wait for me here as I get the ingredients?" said Stan.

"Sure, that makes more sense. So, what do I buy here, and how much?" asked Monica.

"Just the popular bread in the picture up there", said Stan, as he pointed to the picture of the bread the people were lining up for.

"By how much? Not sure. Maybe two dozen? You decide", said an unsure Stan. "Or maybe we can wait five more minutes and try to see if the line picks up? If the line is still that long, then we can go split up", continued Stan.

"Then what is it? Should we split up, or wait another five minutes?" asked a confused Monica.

Pausing to think about the options, Stan answers "let's just wait another five minutes. The line kind of picked up, and I also don't want to leave you here alone. It just doesn't sit well with me leaving my guest here on an errand", said a slightly frustrated Stan.

"Okay, so we wait then", said Monica with a smile.

"Gorilla-hands Stan?! Is that you?" said a voice from behind Stan. A bit unsure as to who the voice belongs to, but at the same time trying to remember who among his friends have called him "Gorilla-hands", Stan turns back towards the source of the voice.

"Sheen? Hey, how have you been?!" said a slightly surprised Stan, once he saw the face of his old playmate.

"Doing fine, same as always!" replied Sheen.

"Wow, it's been a while since we last saw each other! You haven't been attending our class reunions since you started studying in the city. How have you been?!" said Sheen.

"Well, I'm still the same old me. But look at you. You look more muscular than before. Heard you married Julie. How is the wife?"

"Well, can't complain man. I'm living the dream. But look at you. Heard from Gram that you're a lawyer now. Who would have thought that the guy who was so fond of climbing trees, would someday be appearing in court? Am I right?" condescendingly said Sheen.

"Well, guess I just got lucky", answered Stan with an awkward smile.

"How is Gram doing, by the way?" asked Sheen.

"He's doing okay. He's still working for the government, and happily married. His wife is currently pregnant, and they are expecting a baby boy", happily reported Stan.

"Wow, who would've thought the crybaby Gram is now expecting a baby? Time flew so fast, huh", said Sheen.

"Yeah, it really did", Stan said as he recalled how Sheen was before and compared it to the one in front of him.

"Sheen looks like he's aged more quickly than the rest of us, for some reason. We have lost touch, so I'm not sure what happened to him. Although he does seem to have his usual confidence, so he is probably doing fine", Stan thought to himself as he continued to chat with Sheen. Then, remembering something, Stan quickly inserted, "oh sorry I forgot. Sheen, this is my friend Monica. She was a classmate of mine in law school, and she is also a great lawyer", as he smiled sheepishly at Monica.

"Where are your manners, Stan. How could you forget to introduce your fiancé! Hi, I'm Sheen. Pleasure to meet you, and I hope you forgive this friend of mine. He can be a prick sometimes", said Sheen.

"Nice to meet you Sheen! Oh, I don't mind that. He does that sometimes", said Monica with a polite smile.

"Sorry about that! But just to be clear, she is not my fiancé. She is a good friend, and she is joining me on vacation", said Stan.

"So, you and your classmates are on vacation in our little town?" asked Sheen.

"Well, just Monica", answered Stan in a low voice.

"So, just the two of you are on vacation?" asked a more confused Sheen.

"Yup", replied Stan.

"But you're not in a relationship?" clarified Sheen.

"Yes", answered Stan.

"Why?" loudly asked Sheen.

"Sorry I don't follow", answered a confused Stan.

"Well, Monica is a very lovely girl, maybe the most beautiful girl I've seen, outside of my lovely wife. She seems like a great girl. And you are a single guy, and also of age. So, I don't understand how the two of you can go on a vacation without being in a relationship?!" exclaimed Sheen.

"Can't two friends of opposite sex go on a vacation together?" rhetorically asked Stan, as she tries not to look at Monica as he answered.

"Well, you can. But at the same time, since you're already spending so much time together, then why not be in a relationship?! She's a very pretty lady, Stan. You can't find another girl like her man!" jokingly exclaimed Sheen.

"Let it go, Sheen. We've always been friends, so stop trying to make it weird", jokingly replied Stan.

After looking intently at Stan and Monica for a brief moment, Sheen answered "well, if you say so. But I'm just saying, you're just wasting your window, if you're not going to take your friendship to the next level". As Sheen frowned, the three of them laughed.

"Anyway, what brings you two to my territory?" asked Sheen. "Your what?" asked a confused Stan.

"I work here. I'm one of the two bakers that make sure everyone in town gets their bread fresh everyday", proudly said Sheen.

After checking Sheen's facial expression, and having the impression that he was being truthful, Stan replied "since when have you worked here as a baker? Weren't you studying engineering before? Why the shift all of a sudden?"

"Yup, I used to study engineering in the nearby college. But the course never really spoke to me. It didn't seem like the thing for me. I eventually shifted courses a few times, but nothing really stood out to me as my calling. Until I saw a few documentaries online about the art of breadmaking. And it just hit me.

"So, I left college and pursued this career. The rest, as they say, is history", said Sheen with a deep smile.

"Good for you", Stan said, with some reservation. "What did Lloyd and Gram say when you said you were going to pursue baking? I never heard them bring it up", asked a concerned Stan.

"Well, I just decided on my own. You and Lloyd were doing your law school thing in the city, while Gram was also preoccupied with her relationship at the time. Besides, this was the perfect situation for me. I couldn't ask for a better situation than what I have right now.

"First of all, I get to work with my hands, which is actually enlightening. And second, I get to practice the craft that I like, and actually get paid while I continue to perfect it. So, everybody wins in this situation, right?!" said Sheen with a big smile.

"Of course. That's the life a lot of people back in the city want to achieve, to be honest", said Stan with a reserved smile.

"Yup, and I get to stay here in our hometown and just watch my kids grow", said Sheen.

"Although it wouldn't kill you if you visited more often Gorilla-hands! Our reunion is only once a year, you know!" jokingly said Sheen.

"Yeah, sorry about that. I'll make sure to attend every year from now on", sincerely said Stan.

"Good! You're treating me for beer every time you don't attend, you understand", jokingly said Sheen.

"Yeah, that's a deal", sincerely replied Stan, as the two friends understood how serious those promises were.

"Anyway, as I was asking earlier, what brings you two to my territory?" asked Sheen.

"Well, we came to get some bread because we wanted to prepare breakfast before mom and dad woke up", answered Stan.

"Don't they wake up in about an hour? Is this the only thing you need to prepare breakfast?" asked a concerned Sheen.

"Well, not exactly. We still have to go to the market after here", said Stan.

"With this line, you might not have enough time to make breakfast for your parents. Good thing I was able to see you as I came back from my coffee break. How much bread do you need? I can go directly to the oven and get you your bread", proudly said Sheen.

"Really?!" said an excited Stan. "But we don't want to impose on you if it might get you into trouble", said Stan.

"Nonsense. I have free access to the oven and my workshop. Besides, what are they going to do, stop me from making more bread?" said Sheen with a proud laugh.

"I guess you're right. We do need to go quickly to the market, if we want to finish cooking before my parents wake up", said Stan, while thinking about the things that they still need to do.

"Can you get us two dozen bread? How much is it?" asked Stan, as he gets his wallet from his pocket

"Don't be silly. I'll take care of the bread. It's not very often that one of my buddies come visit", proudly said Sheen.

"Are you sure?" asked Stan.

"Of course. It's part of the perks of the job. Just give me a minute", assured Sheen, as he went inside the shop and shortly came back with a bag of bread.

"I added a few pieces there. Send my regards to your mom and dad will you", said Sheen.

"Thanks a lot Sheen. I owe you one", said Stan.

"Don't mention it. It's no big deal. You can just take care of my beer the next time we hang out, okay?" replied Sheen.

"Definitely. I'll tell mom and dad you said hi", said Stan, as he and Monica hurried to the market.

Once they got to the market, the two quickly went to the places that sold the ingredients they needed, with Stan also telling Monica the popular products in the market, and where best to get them. With efficiency and hast, the two were able to buy the products that they needed and were shortly on their way home.

In the car, and with Monica focused on the meal she was intending to prepare, Stan's mind wandered while he was driving.

"I can't believe it's been that long since I last saw Sheen. Between the busy schedule, the great distance, and us hanging out with different people when we get older, I guess the remaining chance for us to get together is only during our homecoming. We did hang out a lot when we were kids because he always biked to our house a lot, despite him living far away from us. But I guess, with me studying in the city, we never had the chance to hang out during my breaks", Stan thought.

As they parked the car and went inside the kitchen to prepare breakfast, Stan still could not stop recalling his conversation with Sheen. Despite Sheen seeming happy and satisfied with his life, Stan could not understand why he felt sad about his childhood friend. But as time was quickly running out before his parents woke up, he and Monica quickly teamed up and finished their dishes.

"What's this about?" asked Gary, when he saw the spread on the table.

"Oh, good morning! How was your sleep?" cheerfully greeted Monica.

A bit confused at the response, but smiling nonetheless, Gary answered "Good morning to you too! I had a great six hours of sleep, as always. Thank you for asking. But again, I ask, what is this spread on the table?"

"Good morning dad! Well, since you and mom cooked dinner for us last night, and me and Monica woke up very early, we decided to return the favor and cook a simple breakfast for you and mom. We even got fresh bread from the market", answered Stan, as he came out of the kitchen, just in time to answer Gary.

"Wait, so you two went to the market early in the morning? Wow, never knew you still had it in you to go to a market. I thought city boys only dine-in or order take-out food, whenever you get hungry", jokingly said Gary.

"Very funny dad. Of course, I know how to do these things. I was always the assistant for you and mom, whenever we needed to prepare dishes for a gathering here at home", quickly replied Stan.

"I actually had a good time going to the market to get the ingredients and prepare this simple spread. Besides, it's the least we can do, after you prepared the great dinner last night", replied Monica.

"That's sweet of you to get us breakfast! Good morning!" said Martha, as she entered the dining area.

"Good morning!" replied Stan and Monica in unison.

"Monica prepared a breakfast recipe that they commonly prepare at home, so please have a seat and let's have breakfast and coffee", said Stan, as he motions for Martha, Gary and Monica to take a seat. And in a few minutes, the four had breakfast.

"Well, I am impressed. This is a very lovely and tasty spread you two have prepared for us. So, thank you!" said Martha.

"I have to agree. This was a very satisfying treat, and we appreciate you two going out to get the ingredients and the fresh bread, to prepare this breakfast. Thank you very much!" said Gary.

"Glad you liked it", said Monica with a timid smile.

"Welcome. Glad you enjoyed it. And glad we were able to get this done before any of you woke up. I know if dad saw us in the kitchen, he would likely have helped out. And that would have ruined our effort to surprise you two", jokingly said Stan as the group laughed.

"You know dad, we probably wouldn't have been able to prepare all this in time, if we didn't bump into Sheen at the bakeshop", said Stan, with a keen intention to get some information from his parents.

"Oh, yeah, Sheen has been working there for quite some time now. We bump into him every now and then when we get bread", fondly said Gary. "He seems happy working there", chimed Martha.

"Yes, he did seem happy. Although, I was really surprised to see him there. I mean, he was a smart kid, and he was always very confident, so I thought he would have gotten a degree in college and got an office job. And if I'm not mistaken, his parents can afford to send him to college. So, I am still not sure how he ended up working in the bakeshop", said Stan with concern.

Martha and Gary looked at each other, as though discussing with their eyes, how to reply. With a sigh, Gary said "well, to be honest, we thought you had an idea. You were really close growing up, and Sheen and Gram were constantly in touch, so I thought Gram would have mentioned it".

"Anyway, regarding Sheen, it's true that his parents can afford to send him to college, and for a moment, Sheen attended a college nearby. Despite you, Lloyd and Gram going to the city to study, Sheen studied nearby so he can help out in his dad's business.

"Sheen's dad told us a while back that despite his confidence around you guys, Sheen found it hard to adapt in college. For some reason, he wasn't able to connect with any of his classmates in college, and he was alone and aloof most of the time.

"I guess, because college wasn't a great environment for him, his grades declined, which probably got him depressed even more. And I guess, that caused him to spiral down, and probably caused him to quit college altogether", said Gary, as he noticed a more concerned look on Stan's face.

“He wasn’t suicidal or anything however, and he still remained a sweet kid”, said Gary, as he tries to reassure Stan.

“He used to hang around with Gram during breaks, and the two would hang out a lot. I think they got even closer after Sheen quit college and I think he really was only comfortable hanging out with your group”, continued Gary.

“So, what has he been doing since he quit college?” asked Stan.

“His mom said that he helped out in their business, but after business hours, he usually just stays in his room playing video games or reading comics. He never really went out to meet other people his age, and tried to avoid social gatherings as much as possible”, said Martha.

“Didn’t his parents talk to him about how he was spending his time, or at least encourage him to try college again?” said Stan in a sad tone.

“They did. Several times. But they never really got through to him. Although you and Gram could probably have gotten through to him if tried, but I guess that’s neither here nor there”, said Gary in a sad tone.

“Maybe we could have talked to him at that time”, said Stan with a sigh. After a brief moment of pause, Stan said “but I am really happy now that Sheen seems to have found something he really wants to do”.

“Yes, Sheen seems happier now more than ever”, agreed Martha.

Pausing for a minute, Stan asks “but I am curious why he chose working at the bakeshop? Did his parents ever tell you?”

“They never discussed that with us. They are just happy that Sheen has decided to spend more time outside his room”, said Martha.

“I guess if anyone could understand his decision, it would probably be you guys. Or just ask him why, when you guys hang out”, said Gary with a smile.

“I guess you’re right. I’m just glad it worked out”, answered Stan with a smile.

“Anyway, let me take care of the dishes. You go ahead and relax, and Monica, you can go ahead and take a shower, so I can give you a tour of the town”, said Stan, as he started cleaning the table.

“Oh, so the treat isn’t over?! Well, don’t mind if I relax some more”, said Gary. “Okay sure”, said Martha. “Copy”, said Monica.

Stan cleaned the table and took a shower afterwards. But as he cleaned and while taking a shower, he still thought about the things that happened to Sheen. He tried to reflect on the things that happened, and how that applied to him and his current struggles.

After getting dressed, Stan went and opened the door of his room. As he opened his door, the door to Gram’s room, which was right in front of Stan’s room, also opened, with both Stan and Monica getting surprised.

"You almost gave me a heart attack there!", jokingly said Stan.

"Maybe you shouldn't have drank that much coffee", jokingly replied Monica, as they both laughed.

"Anyway, are you ready?" asked Stan. "Yeah, was just about to go down", replied Monica. "Good! Let's go down, then", replied Stan, as the two went down.

After the two told Gary and Martha that they were going out, they got in the car, and were on their way.

"We have some beautiful beaches around here, and also some historic landmarks. I could also take you to my alma mater first, and give you a tour of our school grounds. What do you think?" asked Stan.

"You decide. We do have some time, so I'm not in any rush to go to the beach just yet. So, I am at your disposal, your majesty", jokingly said Monica, as he gestured with her hands, as though she was talking to a king.

"Well, it's a school tour then", replied Stan, as the two laughed.

On their way to the school, the two picked on each other and had a few laughs. As he was driving, Stan looked at Monica, and was happy she was there with him.

"Maybe it was for the best to visit home, as I try and figure things out with myself", said Stan, after a brief moment of pause.

"I think the plan has always been for me to take some time off, and try to figure out what I really wanted to do with my life. But to be honest, in these past few months, with me just relaxing and not having anyone to answer to, I actually forgot the reason I decided to quit work in the first place. That is, to figure myself out.

"After overcoming some initial fear of not having any work, I immediately accepted the dynamics of not having a job. Once I figured out how great it was to just sit back and relax, I guess I realized just how much I was missing out this whole time. Realizing how much I've missed out, I guess something in me just decided to rebel and not care about life anymore. To just continue living a free life, without worry and without responsibilities.

"The more I was doing nothing, the more I wanted to do nothing. It was like getting hooked on a narcotic drug. And I guess I just kept one excuse after another, just so I won't have to pursue anything, or get stressed about anything. With the lifestyle, I guess I just forgot the initial reason why I decided to stop working. With all the mind-numbing digital stimuli and the convenience that the world had to offer, I really did forget the point of me quitting work.

"I guess I just convinced myself that I didn't really need to look for myself, and that self-realization would just come to me in time. But having bumped into Sheen earlier, and knowing him so well, I think at one point, Sheen just realized that his sulking could not get him out of his condition. No matter how convenient and comfortable his retreat became, that same retreat continued to lead him farther and farther from happiness. And despite taking a while before realizing it, at one point, he probably understood that he needed to do something.

"As inconvenient or time consuming the task of self-realization is, just like Sheen, I guess I too need to get off my ass and actually start doing something", said Stan with a short laugh.

"Why so deep all of a sudden", curiously asked Monica, as the two seriously looked at each other for a moment. "Oh, shut up!" replied Stan, as the two of them laughed.

"I guess I really needed this trip so I can get away from the nest that I built myself back home. Although I am happy to be left alone to reflect and spend time with myself, it actually got to a point wherein I just simply gave up on life and on living. Not that I'm suicidal or anything, but just felt tired of all the little things, despite me needing them. You get what I'm saying?", Stan said with a laugh.

"I think, I do", replied Monica.

After pausing for a bit as Stan tries to read Monica's body language and facial expression, Stan said with a smile "what am I rambling about? And why aren't you stopping me from rambling?!"

"Well, first off, you were having a moment, so it wouldn't have been right if I just cut you off like that. And second, I was actually trying to see how long you were going to keep on going before you noticed that you were rambling", said Monica with a laugh.

Pissed a bit, but eventually laughing, Stan replied "you know, I still don't understand why I keep you as a friend. You are kind of a mean person; you know that right?" before the two burst into laughter.

"You can be dramatic sometimes. But hey, even the dramatic ones need friends, right?" sarcastically replied Monica.

After a brief pause Stan replied "I guess what I was trying to say was that I really needed this trip home. And I really appreciate you coming on this trip with me".

"Don't mention it. I'm also enjoying our trip", replied Monica with a smile.

With both sensing that the moment got too serious for their taste, they scrambled to change the topic.

"Well now that you are home, what's the plan Mr. Bigshot?" said Monica.

Frowning on the nickname used by Monica, Stan jokingly replied, "well first priority is to get my friends to stop calling me Mr. Bigshot. I mean I quit my job already, so you can stop calling me that. And the second agenda would probably be to give you a tour of my hometown. What do you think?".

"Sounds good to me", replied Monica, as the two continued on their way to Stan's former school.

"I guess other than relaxing some more and spending time with my parents, I really wanted to come back home because I wanted to remember what my earlier motivations in life were and try to figure out how I ended on this path", said Stan.

"I wanted to reconnect with my past in the hope that it can tell me what I really wanted to be", he continued as he parked the car.

"Well, maybe a good place for that would be for you to give me a tour of your old school. It can remind you of how things were when you were young, and at the same time, I get to feel like a tourist", sarcastically said Monica, with a wink.

"Of course. I wouldn't want you reporting to anyone that I wasn't a great host", snobbishly replied Stan, as they laughed. After getting out of the car, the two went on to tour the school. They then went to see some of the museums in the town, before going home to rest.

Chapter 16

Alma Mater

A few more days passed, and Stan and Monica were able to go around Stan's hometown and visit the popular beaches and tourist destinations there. In an effort to reconnect with Sheen, Stan and Monica invited him and his wife over for dinner and the four went to one of the popular beach destinations near them.

They drove to the beach and camped along the coast, while drinking a few beers and cooking fresh fish in a grill. And somehow in those moments, Stan was not the uptight partner that the world depended on for wise counsel and quick recommendation. In those moments, Stan was a kid again, without worry and without fear. Only concerned about cooking the food that they were going to be having and the amount of beer that was available, as they stared at the stars through the nightlight. Even Monica in those brief moments, forgot how prominent and fierce she was on her side of the country.

"Oh, how great to forget. Oh, how great to reset," thought a slightly tipsy Stan, as he and Monica lay face up on the same cloth spread through the sand, as they stared at the sky.

"That was some great barbeque, man. Never knew you could cook!" said a slightly tipsy Sheen.

"Glad you enjoyed it. Probably just beginner's luck", replied Stan, as he drank another can of beer.

"Regardless, I enjoyed it. Thanks for the meal. And thanks for the invite", said Sheen, with a sincere smile.

Sensing Sheen's emotions, and trying to stop his own emotional outburst, Stan quipped "hey man, I said I'd treat you to a few rounds of beer. So here we are".

Getting a bit teary eyed, but able to control himself, Sheen replied, "thanks anyway. This was fun. Cheers!"

"Cheers!" replied Stan, as the group lifted their cans before chugging them dry.

"Well, I guess that'll be our last chug", said Julie, as she notices how wasted her husband was. "You two just go on, while the stars are still bright. As for us, I'll tuck Sheen into our tent and call it a night", said Julie, as she helps Sheen into their tent as they begin to sleep.

"That was a fun day. And what a beautiful beach", said a slightly tipsy Monica.

"Completely agree", said Stan with a smile.

“We used to enjoy going out to the beach when we were kids, and this place was our favorite. We even agreed back then to come visit this place every year until we got old. How ironic”, said Stan with a sad smile.

“What’s ironic?” asked Monica, as they both laid down on their backs while watching the stars.

“It’s ironic that we were actually able to fulfill those promises back then, despite not having a cent to our names, unlike now, who couldn’t even attend a single homecoming, despite having some pretty penny in the bank. It’s also ironic how brave children can be with their promises and outlook compared to the adults, who couldn’t even commit to a simple social activity without getting anxious and jittery”, said Stan with a sigh.

“But here you are, on your favorite beach, having the time of your life with your friends, as you fulfill your childhood promises. So, I wouldn’t consider you a lost cause just yet”, said Monica with a sincere smile.

Rotating his head so he can check Monica’s expression as she stares at the stars, Stan confirms how sincere she was. Rotating his head back to face the stars, Stan replies “I’m not sure if you’re just mocking me or not, but thanks. I needed to hear that”.

With smiles on their faces, they continued to stare at the stars before they eventually called it a night, and went to their separate tents.

“Good morning!” greeted Julie to a just awoken Stan, as he got out of his tent.

“Good morning!” replied Stan, as he looked around while clutching his head.

“Bad hangover?” greeted Monica, as she drank a coffee after munching some bread. “Hear, have some coffee. Julie and Sheen got these for us this morning at a nearby store”, said Monica as she pointed at a take-out coffee and bread.

“How’s the hangover, buddy. Must have drank some more after we hit the tent last night, huh?” said Sheen with a smirk.

“Yeah, hit some more cans before going to sleep. But I have to tell you, it doesn’t feel like it used to back in the day. There used to be a point when I can chug a whole lot of booze and still go to class the next day. But I don’t think that’s possible anytime soon. Man, my head is killing me!” said Stan, as the group laughed.

“Have a coffee already, you crybaby. It’s just beer”, said Sheen as the group laughed again.

“Anyway, what are your plans now that you quit being a partner?” sincerely asked Sheen.

Pausing to think while sipping his coffee, he replied “I have been thinking a bit since I got home, and I was planning on checking the firms in the city who had different specializations of law in their practice, and try to see if there is any field out there that I wanted to specialize in. I really don’t know right now what path is best for me, but I think sitting idly would not get me where I really want to be. So maybe it’s best right now to simply explore the possibilities out there, and see where life leads me”.

“That sounds like a reasonable plan. Any particular field you’re drawn into just the top of your head?” asked Sheen.

“Ever since I talked to a client of mine who wants to make modern agriculture efficient and eco-friendly, I developed a greater interest in the field. So, I am looking for any firm that specializes in that practice”, seriously replied Stan.

“That is a very limited practice, and I'm not sure if there are any firms out there in the city that specialize in that. But I'll ask around if any of the firms on my side of town has that practice”, interjected Monica.

“Yeah, thanks for that. Hope this episode of my life pans out well”, said Stan, with a dry laugh.

“I'm sure it will. You're the best damn lawyer I know. Plus, your gorilla hands can always come handy, if you guys are ever in a pickle”, joked Sheen.

After a few back and forth between the two, Julie remembered something and curiously asked “by the way, when are you going back to the city?”.

“Well, if I really wanted to get serious looking for the practice that I like, I probably should leave for the city in two to three weeks from now. Plus, Monica probably needs a ride home, so I guess two weeks?” said Stan, as he looks for some clue from Monica, of how long she was going to stay.

“You don't have to worry about me, you know. I can always take the plane”, replied Monica.

“But how long can you stay?” asked Sheen, with some curiosity.

“I still got two weeks in my leave, so I guess two weeks?” hesitatingly answered Monica.

“Good to know. Then I guess, two more weeks for me”, jokingly said Stan.

“Why did you ask Julie?” asked Stan.

“Well, I just remembered the send-off and brief lecture being organized by our alma mater, for its first batch of bar taker this year. And they were looking for a speaker to give tips on taking the bar and lecture on how to approach the actual day of the exam. They had initially invited a speaker from the city, but the speaker could not make it at the last minute. So, I just thought that since you had high school at SC, and you are one of the best lawyers available, then maybe you can speak to them, instead”, discussed Julie.

“Wait, our SC, you mean Stevenson College, our SC, now has a law degree?” asked a surprised Stan.

“Yup, best believe it buddy. They started a law course there at the same time that Julie started teaching biology. And how time flies, now they have their first batch to take on the bar”, discussed Sheen, with a nostalgic tone.

“Wow, never knew our little school could actually evolve to teach law. I'm really impressed and proud”, said Stan.

“One of the organizers is a friend of mine, and they really need someone to give that lecturer, so I hope you're free”, discussed Julie with visible enthusiasm.

“So, what do you say?” eagerly asked Sheen. “Well, if they haven't found a replacement speaker yet, then I'd be honored to do this for my SC”, said Stan, with a big smile on his face.

"Great, then it's done. I'll call my friend right now, and have you included in the lecture", said Julie, as she took her phone from her pocket.

"By the way, when would this lecture be scheduled?" eagerly asked Stan.

"Oh, right, it's in five days. Are you ok with that?" Asked Julie. "Oh, good. Yeah, I'm ok with that. Just wanted to make sure it won't conflict with our travel home to the city.

"Wow, the prodigal son comes back home to his alma mater!" teasingly said Monica.

"More like the chosen son comes back home, if you ask me. The school loved this guy, that's why he always had top honors", said Sheen.

"Actually, they had no choice but to like me, after I gave them some good grades", corrected Stan.

"Whatever. Same thing", jokingly replied Sheen.

"Oh, by the way... ", asked Stan. "Yup, there is a pay for your one-hour lecture", Julie quickly replied.

"Oh, ok. I'd like that. But what I wanted to ask is if I can bring Monica to the lecture? I mean she is my guest on this trip, and I'd hate to leave her home. Unless Monica wants to stay home, then I guess that's ok", awkwardly replied Stan.

"Well, if you must ask, I'd be happy to join you at your alma mater. As long as the school allows it, that is", awkwardly said Monica.

"I'll check with my friend", said Julie, as she stood up and went a few meters away as she discussed with her friend.

"Huh, never knew I'd get the opportunity to talk with the first batch of law graduates from SC. Hope my lecture can be of use as they go on their paths", rhetorically said Stan.

"I'm sure it will. After all that you've seen and done, they'd be lucky to hear your experiences and thoughts", sincerely said Sheen.

Looking at Sheen, and seeing hope and confidence in his eyes, Stan eventually believed that he can make a difference. Smiling as he reflected Sheen's confidence back at him, Stan replied "thanks, I'll make sure of that".

No sooner did the two friends express their confidence, Julie came back. "Well, it's done. You'll be lecturing the first batch of bar takers in five days. I'll give you my friend's number so you can ask about the details. By the way, I asked, and she said that it's fine for Monica to tag along", gleefully reported Julie.

"Thanks. Wouldn't miss it for the world", said Monica with a smile.

"Oh, by the way, I told them about who you are and about your current lack of employment, and they asked if you were somehow interested in teaching law at SC. Well, nothing is set in stone and it would probably depend on how well you do in the lecture, but my friend mentioned that they have some openings for a full-time professor, and if you are ever interested, you can apply", narrated Julie.

"I can actually imagine you being one of the professors at SC", jokingly said Sheen.

"I have to agree. Stan does have that professor vibe going for him", jokingly chimed Monica, as they laughed.

"So how about it? Have you ever considered becoming a professor and working in your hometown, instead of the big city?" eagerly asked Sheen.

"Teaching actually never crossed my mind as a career path. So, I'm really not sure how I feel about the idea of me being a professor. I guess I'll have a feel for it during the lecture and see what I think about it. So don't get your hopes up, just yet", sincerely said Stan.

After their light breakfast, the group packed up and travelled back home. As they drove through the countryside, Stan called Julie's friends for further details on the lecture and on the possible teaching position. Stan also asked Julie and Sheen about the status of law school at SC and other updates about SC. And after a few more stopovers and snacks, they were already back home.

After taking a bath and getting into something comfortable, the two joined Gary and Martha on the table for dinner.

"Mom, did you know that SC now has a law degree?" curiously asked Stan as the group was eating.

"Yeah, I heard that the first batch of graduates will be taking the bar this year. Time goes quick, huh?" answered Martha.

"I heard that they hired a prominent lawyer from the city to be the head of the law degree. He did his practice outside of town, but I was told that he actually grew around here but eventually studied and practiced in the city", Gary chimed in.

"Good to know. I asked because Julie's friend asked me to give a one-hour lecture to the graduating class. She also told me that they're looking for a professor and that I can have the job if I wanted", casually said Stan.

A bit surprised by the news, but still remaining calm, Gary said "that's good news. I think the graduates can learn a thing or two from you. So, when will your lecture be?"

"It's in five days from now", replied Stan.

"Good. What about the teaching position, have you thought about applying?" gently asked Gary.

"I'm excited about lecturing to the graduates, but to be honest, I'm not yet sure about pursuing a teaching career, just yet. It feels like a big change of scenery and pace for me, and although I like the change, maybe it's not yet the time for me fully take a step back on the fast-paced world of law", said an unsure Stan.

"What do you mean by fully taking a step back? Wasn't that supposed to be your plan?" again asked Gary.

"To be honest, I resigned because I thought that I was not going to be happy in the direction I had with the firm. And although I took a step back from that fast-paced world, I'd like to believe that I only did so in the hopes that I can figure myself out and find the practice that I'd like to devote the rest of my life to. Although I haven't found that practice just yet, I'd like to think that I can still find it if I tried looking a little more", said Stan with a calm but sincere tone.

Satisfied with his answer, Gary and Martha no longer asked questions, as the group continued to have dinner.

On the days that followed, Stan continued to drive Monica to the popular places nearby during the day, while he diligently researched and prepared the topics for his lecture in the evenings. He also asked for ideas from Monica as they were sight-seeing, and kept asking for feedback on his topics. Despite tireless nights preparing for a one-hour lecture, Stan somehow felt more energized than drained, as he continued to put in the work. And just like that, five days passed and the two friends were now at the SC grounds as they wait for Stan's turn to lecture.

Stan was scheduled to be the last lecturer of the day, and while the other lecturers were seated at the front of the lecture hall, Stan and Monica stayed at the back to get a feel of the general mood of the bar takers. This was also a ploy by Stan to temporarily avoid further discussion with Dean Fiona of the law college, and served as a chance for him to quietly run down his lecture in his mind.

With Monica seemingly interested on the topics being discussed, Stan was able to run down in his mind, the lecture he was about to give, and tried to foresee any potential issues that could arise. After getting through the outline of his lecture, he paused for a moment and calmed himself.

As he looked at the attendees, he remembered his time in this hall as a young kid with dreams as big as the world, and with a vision of an abundant life, that he was brave enough to believe at that time. He remembered his last days of law school and during the review, and how single minded and focused he was in achieving his goals. Somehow, back then, it felt like passing the bar was the only thing that mattered, and doing so would bring him and his family, both money and glory. And for a time, he was sure it would. And for a time, it was worth it. But then the rest of his life continued, and it was then that he realized, that the expected money and glory, was not how it was advertised to be.

"To discuss about the best approaches and possible pitfalls while taking the bar, please welcome our last lecturer and one of the brightest graduates of SC, Stan", stated Dean Fiona, after a brief discussion of Stan's credentials and achievements.

"Hey Stan, you're up!" said Monica with a slight nudge on Stan's shoulder.

Caught by surprise, as he was in a trance like state, Stan composed himself and gingerly walked towards the front of the audience. As he approached the front, he was able to catch a glimpse of the focused and hopeful eyes of the bar takers. And somehow, he felt a deep compassion and admiration towards the new bar takers, and at that moment he felt a great desire to make sure that his lecture would make a positive impact in helping the hopefuls to not only pass the bar, but become passionate and impactful advocates of the law.

"Did I also imbibe the same passion and energy before? Somehow, I can't help but see myself in each and every one of them. And as helpful for exam the practical tips I've prepared, maybe I can even teach them something more?", he thought as he looks back at the hopeful bar takers.

Standing at the podium, he sighs to relax and before starting his lecture, he looked at the hopeful eyes of the bar takers, and finally thought "maybe I can even teach them about life".

With a mild but snarky joke, Stan started his discussion, just so he can relax and engage his audience. He tried to make sure that he was as engaged, if not more than engaged than his audience, as he tried to pass on what he knows.

In his lecture, Stan was lively, energetic, informative, relatable, and had a deep connection with the audience. But more than anything, in that moment, Stan was the happiest he has ever been. And Monica was sure of that, as she stared at the joy and passion in Stan's eyes.

As the lecture went on and the time continued to move, eventually the one-hour period lapsed. With some sincere reminders and a few words of encouragement, he ended his lecture to cheering attendees.

After his time, and as Dean Fiona gave her brief closing remarks, the bar takers thanked Stan for his lecture as he passed by them. A few even approached him to ask for some tips on how to deal with some issues or nagging questions they had, and thanked him for giving them his time.

Walking to the back of the hall, he slowly looked for Monica on the seats they had at the back. Finally seeing Monica, he smiled back at her happy expression.

"Congratulations. That was probably the best lecture I've ever attended", sincerely said Monica.

"Thanks. That means a lot. I just really hope that I at least helped them pass the bar and do good in their practice, later on", said Stan.

"You did great, and I'm sure your lecture will go a long way in changing their lives", said Monica with a sincere smile.

"Excuse me, Stan", inserted a female voice from behind, as Stan looks back.

"I'm glad I was able to catch up to you before you could leave the campus", said Dean Fiona.

"Oh, hi Dean Fiona. What seems to be the problem?" curiously asked Stan, as he looks at a slightly out of breath Dean Fiona.

"Oh, no problem at all. I was just impressed with the lecture you gave just now and I'm very impressed with your credentials. And I really wanted to talk to you about any inclination you have whatsoever about teaching here at the university", said Dean Fiona as she composes herself.

"I'm not quite sure what you're asking Dean, but I'd be more than happy to discuss it with you", said Stan with a smile.

"Well, to put it simply, I would really like you to join us in the faculty. It's not the highest paying job in the world, but being able to instruct the new generation, does offer an intangible income that even money can't afford. And I really believe that you can help a great deal in raising great lawyers from our little college", sincerely said Dean Fiona.

"Thank you for the generous offer Dean Fiona. I'm both honored and humbled. As much as I would like to give you an answer right now, if you would admit, I'd like to ask for some time to decide, because I still have some unresolved matters in the city, and I can't tell right now if I can resolve all of it before the start of the schoolyear", regretfully said Stan.

"Of course. I wouldn't expect you to give me an answer that fast, so please take all the time you need to decide. Just tell me when you're ready, and the job is yours", said Dean Fiona with a warm smile before saying goodbye. Shortly after, Monica and Stan went to their car, and slowly drove off.

"Well?" Monica asked, as they were now a few meters outside of the campus.

"Well, what?" curiously asked Stan, while driving the car.

"Are you going to give SC Law a shot?" coyly asked Monica.

Quickly looking at Monica to see if she was just teasing, and returning his gaze back on the road, Stan replied "to be honest, I'm seriously considering teaching there".

"Well, good! I do think that you'll be happy there", said Monica with a smile.

Without even gazing at Monica, but understanding her sentiments, Stan smiled and replied "I think so too".

ACT III

Chapter 17

The Offer

It was six in the evening when Stan and Monica got home. As a treat because of the successful lecture, Stan got take-out food for their dinner. The two changed clothes, as Gary prepared the dining table for their dinner.

In his room, and just after he changed, he was in a good enough mood to check his emails. As he browsed his inbox, he was surprised to see an unexpected email from an unexpected sender. He was not sure at first, if the email was real, but after reading the sender and the subject three times, he was at least sure that he received one. Whether or not it contained what he thought it contained, was another thing altogether, he thought.

Hesitant as he put the arrow on top of the message, he thought "I don't think this could mean anything other than a possible query about one of my previous opinions, right? Good news or bad, might as well get this over with".

As he opened the email, he remained skeptical about what it contained. Once the message opened, he quickly noticed that it was sent by the president of Marcus Columbus Group, the highest valued listed company in the Forbes 500 list of companies. Going through the list of copied individuals, he was sure that the email copied all the biggest executives in Marcus Columbus Group.

"I've met and worked with some of these executives before, and as far as I can remember, they have always been upfront with everything and were always serious about MCG matters", he thought, as he intentionally delayed reading the email's contents, fearing he was going to get disappointed. Slowly however, Stan continued to scroll down the message. The email wrote:

> Stan,
>
> The MCG's Global Head of Legal position has recently become vacant, and our group is in need of a young and dedicated lawyer to fill the VP position. Having gone through a handful of potential

candidates, the board and I are convinced that your credentials and your extraordinary work with us these past years, make you the best choice to take on the role of Global Head for Legal.

I'll be sending through a separate email, the job description and compensation package for the position, for your review and reference. We would be glad to discuss the details further, should you have concerns. But as we are looking to fill this position by the end of business day next week, we hope to hear from you as soon as possible.

Regards,

Tristan

Stan, still in disbelief at the once in a lifetime opportunity set before him, tried to figure out how his name even got considered for the position, given that he never applied for, nor even heard of the vacancy.

"Could either be the headhunter or Megan, their VP for finance", thought Stan. "This is a very big role with some pretty big expectations to constantly meet. I've worked with their previous Global Head for Legal, and with all the pressure of the job, I wasn't sure how that guy could even sleep at night", thought Stan.

"I think I actually asked him how he could sleep at night, that one time", Stan recalled, as he paused to recall the VP's answer to him. Thinking harder, he eventually recalled him saying "'I rest by drinking myself to sleep with an expensive single malt whiskey'".

"Must have been an extravagant life. For better or worse", he thought, as he visualized himself taking on the role. Looking back on his impression of their work conditions, and recollecting the things he heard about the role, he could not help but dread at how that life might look like. Nonetheless, as he closed the message, he quickly noticed a second email from Tristan, just above the email he just read.

"These guys may be stressed, but I have never heard anyone complain about the pay. But still, after leaving that world behind, is this really the direction I want to be heading, at this point in my life? Knowing what is expected in this job, should I even give this a shot?", he thought, as he placed the cursor on top of the second email, while his insides could not decide whether to open or not.

"Would seeing the pay change anything?" he thought, before finally opening the email.

Reading the job description and the compensation package, he quickly understood how much the role could take a toll on himself. Nonetheless, he understood that the compensation package more than make up for the life that he was exchanging.

"Even as a partner, the benefits I had then couldn't even compare to what MCG is offering. This can easily cover my mortgages, and then some. They also have a car package that can easily get me a Lamborghini, on top of the other benefits. Can anyone really turn down an offer like this?" he seriously wondered.

"But is this right for me?" he thought, as he visualized the possible pitfalls as well as the advantages of the position.

"Even the more senior partners at the firm would not think twice about this offer. Not only is the compensation hefty, but the company and their legal team are highly regarded globally. Senior partners across the country can only dream of getting shortlisted for the role. And now I'm being asked to be their

Global Head of Legal? No one in their right mind will pass on this", he thought, as he drafts a reply to the email.

"I'm still young, and not everyone is given this kind of opportunity. The money is more than enough to compensate for the stress this role involves, and this role really opens a lot of opportunities, should I ever decide to leave MCG", he thought, before stopping to wonder.

"That's right, I'm still very young, so even if I don't like it there, I can try out the role while improving my credentials, and still have enough youth to start over. That seems logical and practical, I guess", he thought, with more confidence and conviction.

Now settled in his decision, he completed his email, and clicked "send". He then went down to join Gary, Martha and Monica, who waited for Stan before they started eating.

"What took you so long?" asked a slightly irritated Monica. "We have been waiting for you for half an hour, and the food has gone cold", continued Monica, as she felt bad that they kept Martha and Gary waiting.

"Really sorry about that. I just had to reply to an urgent email I just got. I'll take care of the dishes tonight and make breakfast tomorrow, so I hope you can forgive me", said Stan when he realized how long he made them wait.

"Don't worry about it. As you probably noticed, in this household, we always prefer to eat together. Makes the food taste better, I think. Anyway, I'm sure that was an important email, so we understand if you had to reply", calmly said Gary.

"Very sorry dad. Still, I'll take care of the dishes tonight and the breakfast tomorrow, so don't worry about it", apologetically said Stan.

Settling down and saying grace, they slowly started eating. During the meal, Monica continued to share with Gary and Martha what happened during the lecture and how great a teacher Stan would be, if he took the teaching position at SC. Stan however was undecided how he should share the MCG offer.

"I'm glad you had fun at SC, and happy to know that they offered you a teaching position. I know you'd make a great professor. Anyway, what was the urgent email about?" innocently asked Martha.

Unsure if it was the perfect time to share the news, but eventually believing there was no better time, Stan opened up.

"Sorry about that, I should have told you to eat ahead of me, had I known I'd take long. Anyway, I received an invitation to be the new Marcus Columbus Group Head of Legal, after the position got vacant. It took me a while to decide if I should take the position, which is why I took so long to join you", calmly said Stan, although eagerly expecting some violent reactions from both his parents and Monica.

"You mean the Marcus Columbus Group, the biggest company in the country and probably the world, and makes a lot of the things we use on a day-to-day basis? You mean that company? You get to be part of their legal team?" said Martha, with some confusion and excitement.

"That same company mom. But not just part of the legal team. They actually invited me to be the Vice President for Legal and be the Global Head for Legal", said Stan with a big smile, while trying hard to sound humble.

"Wow, sounds like a big opportunity son. Are you sure you're comfortable taking on the role?" an excited but worried query from Gary.

"To be honest, I thoroughly reviewed the job description first before anything, and I'm confident that my training and experience has more than equipped me to take on the job. So, I think I have it covered, jobwise", said Stan, as he reassures his parents.

"But I don't expect the role to be easy. I called one of the VPs there that I worked with in the past, and he told me that the role is quite stressful and demanding. He narrated all the work I needed to do and all the expectations that come with the position. To say that the role would take a lot out of me, would probably be an understatement", said Stan, as he again noticed his parents' worried expressions.

Scrambling to lighten the mood, and in an effort to get his parents to side with his decision, Stan said "but I do believe that the stress and pressure is not greater than that of my previous employment, so I'm confident I can handle it. Not to mention that the role is highly regarded, and taking on the role boosts my credentials. More importantly, the pay is more than enough to compensate for the workload they are expecting from me, so at least they are considerate in that regard".

Not sure how to respond, and vaguely smiling to show support for Stan's decision, Martha, Gary and Martha just looked at each other but remained silent.

"I think you would agree that it makes sense to at least give this new role a try, right?" Stan asked Monica, as he tried to find someone to back him up.

"Well, I agree that this is a rare and grand opportunity being offered to Stan. I mean senior partners in prominent law firms try to land the job, but can't even get shortlisted, much less get picked for the position. Not to mention that Stan would probably be the youngest to ever take that role. And I've heard a lot about how well they pay their employees and how fair they are to them, so there's nothing bad I can say about MCG.

"It's not like Stan would do all of the work, because he would probably be surrounded by a team composed of the best lawyers the country has to offer, on top of the best consultants that money can afford, so that can help make things more manageable. But more importantly, I'm a witness of how great Stan works, and how well he can handle stressful situations, so I don't think you have anything to worry about", Monica narrated, but lacking her usual enthusiasm.

"I understand how great an opportunity this is, and believe me when I say how happy and proud we are of you. I guess we just worry a little with you taking on this new role, given your recent resignation from your previous role", Gary said before pausing.

After a slight sigh, Gary continued "but know that we are past the point when we still make decisions for you, so understand that from now on, it is totally your call, and we will always be a hundred and ten percent behind you. Whatever the decision, I guess us parents will always come to worry and that just comes with territory, so don't mind us and just focus on the things ahead of you. We wouldn't want it any other way".

"Thanks dad. Both your support means the world to me", said Stan with a gentle smile.

After a few more back and forth about the details of the offer, dinner was over. Gary and Martha went on to watch the television, while Monica joined Stan in cleaning up and washing the dishes.

As the two washed plates, Stan noticed how Monica seemed uneasy and quiet. He also recalled how Monica suddenly got quiet, when he told them about the MCG offer. Trying to figure out what was bothering her, Stan asked "is everything okay Monica?"

"Yeah, of course. Just want to quickly get this done so I can still check on some emails. This was a long day and I also need to finish some work before I go to sleep", calmly said Monica.

Confident that something was bothering Monica, but unsure if it was the right time to talk about it, Stan decided to leave it alone for the moment, and just focus on finishing the chore. Shortly thereafter, the two finished washing and went to their opposite rooms, despite the unsettled feelings.

Chapter 18

Fight Between Friends

The following day, Stan woke up earlier than usual, and prepared the breakfast he committed. Just as the table was completely set, Monica entered the dining area for her usual coffee and bread, only to be surprised with the food already prepared. At first, she was surprised that a meal was prepared, but quickly remembered Stan's commitment to prepare it.

"Good morning! Didn't expect you to be up this early", greeted Stan.

"Body clock, I guess", unenthusiastically replied Monica, as she continued towards the direction of the coffeemaker.

Remembering that Monica normally has coffee in the morning, Stan points at the thermos on the table and says "coffee is on the table". Hearing that, Monica stopped walking, quietly took a seat and poured coffee in her mug.

"Everything ok?" cautiously asked Stan. "Yeah, just a bit tired", replied Monica, as she tried to muster a smile.

Certain there was something bothering Monica, but again unsure if it was the time to ask, Stan decided to refrain from asking, and tried to wait for a better time.

"Are you up for a beach day?" asked Stan, while pouring coffee into his mug. Looking silently at Stan for a bit, Monica lifelessly said "sure".

Undeterred, Stan urged on saying "good to know. It's only a few more days before we go back to the city, and I really want to thank you for joining me in this selfish trip of mine. So, I'd like to take you today to the best beachfront around and my personal favorite. It's only an hour from here. So, are you up for a drive?".

Slightly moved by Stan's enthusiasm, Monica forced a smile and said "of course I'm game! Who do you think I am?!"

After laughing at Monica's reply, Stan said back with a smile "never doubted you one bit".

Shortly after the two agreed on their activity for the day, Gary and Martha woke up and joined them for breakfast. The two then prepared for their drive, and before long they were on the road.

As they drove, Stan kept thinking about what was bothering Monica. Wanting to make the drive fun, but trying not to set her off, Stan was the one who initiated most of the conversations. This continued until they arrived at a sandy open space, with just a few cars parked.

The open space was unlike a normal parking lot with lined pavements and guarded gates. It was simply an open lot where cars just parked.

"We're here", joyfully said Stan to a slightly confused Monica. "Are you sure this is the place?" Monica asked. "Couldn't be more certain", said Stan with a big smile.

"Not sure what you were expecting when I said this was my favorite hangout spot, but this is the place. I know it's not a fancy resort, but this is what makes this place special. You'll see", said Stan with a smile as he takes their food and other things from the back of the car.

After looking around, Monica was now a little less confused about the place, as she helped get their things out. After splitting the things they would carry, the two made a short hike from their parking spot, until they reached a clearing that opened to a beautiful beach with pristine green water that extended to the horizon.

"Magnificent", whispered an awestruck Monica. "I have that same reaction every time I come here", said Stan, as he stares at Monica.

"I guess I understand now why you like this place. And I think I now understand why you liked my spot back in the city. They have the same feel, and have a similar beauty", said Monica with a smile.

"Exactly. And just like your spot back in the city, this place is not that developed, and you can just sit under any tree or shade you find", said Stan, as he motions Monica to follow him to a spot he just found.

Although there were a few people in the area at that time, each group was so far away from each other, that one group could not overhear the conversation of the other. The only sound that was evident was the roaring waves as they smashed with the wall of black rocks nearby.

When they got to their spot, they slowly set up their stuff. After the two were done, they looked around the area first, and got their feet wet in the water, before they started to eat. Still enjoying the view and the fresh air, the two settled back to their spot and started sharing their meal.

"You're very fortunate. You know that, right?" rhetorically asked Monica.

Looking at her, Stan replied sincerely "of course. Not a moment in my life, have I ever forgotten how fortunate a life I have. With all the blessings I've been given, it feels like a crime if I don't make the best of it, if only to show gratitude for the things that I've been given".

Despite an intense sincerity in his answer, Monica could not help but feel a sadness in Stan's answer.

"Or maybe all you need to do is just live your life, however you see fit, instead of trying to prove anything to anyone?" she replied.

Struck by Monica's words and unable to come up with a sensible answer, Stan froze as he looked at Monica eye-to-eye.

"Are you okay with me going to MCG?" Stan mustered to ask.

"I don't think you're asking the right question", Monica replied.

"Then what is the right question?!" shouted a frustrated Stan.

"Are you okay going there?!" softly replied Monica.

Before Monica even finished asking the question, Stan already knew the answer. He knew deep down and without question, that the MCG opportunity was not the path he had been wanting. He knew this to be true more than anything, and yet he was convinced that this was the most logical and practical thing for him, lest he risks coming up with nothing, should he choose not to continue. Frozen in a grip of conviction, Stan could not answer.

"I know it's unfair for me to question your decision at this period in your life. Believe me when I tell you that I find no pleasure in having this discussion instead of just giving my congratulations. I know I'm out of line here, but as a friend who has shared both your joy and pain, I hope you chose this opportunity, not because it was convenient or rare, but simply because this was something that you want, above all else", Monica heavy heartedly continued, as Stan froze on.

"Where is this coming from?" Stan asked calmly.

Unsure what her reason was or why she feels so strongly about the matter, Monica was not able to make a quick response. Still searching for answers Monica replied, "I hope I can give you an answer. Really, I do. But I'm also at a loss as to where this is coming from. One thing though that I'm certain, this comes from a place of genuine concern for your wellbeing".

"If this really does come from concern, then why can't you just let me do as I have decided. I think this is the best thing for me right now. It works for everyone, and I'm sure I can be great in this position. That should be more than enough for me. That should be more than enough, for anyone", Stan responded with conviction in his voice, but doubt in his eyes.

"Then what? You stay there for ten good years of your life, earning money and gaining prominence, and then eventually getting consumed with work and life that you quit again. All while wishing each day that you were doing something else, as the years you can't take back, slowly fade away. Or are you just going to wait until you're old and useless, before you get the courage to pursue the life you've always wanted?" said a teary-eyed Monica, as she pauses to get a hold of her emotions.

Still dumbfounded with both the wisdom and emotion in Monica's words, Stan remained quiet as Monica continued.

"I don't think that's fair. Not to you, and not to the people who care for you. Your friends and family will stand by you, whatever path you pursue, and wherever that path may lead you. This is the reason your family chose the life they chose to pursue. To give you the freedom to actually pursue what you want to pursue.

"And I know you understand that more than anyone. Otherwise, what was the purpose of all this resignation and soul searching, if not to rekindle your joy and actually find what you were meant to do? Was all that just for show?" said Monica, as tears ran down her cheeks.

"I'm really thankful for your concern. It means more to me than all the money in the world, and I hope you never forget that. But I've realized in these past few days, that I can't just wait for the world to reveal itself to me, because it really doesn't work that way, nor does the world become easier, if I approached it that way. At some point, I need to grow up and accept the world for both the good and the bad, and do the things I need to do, even if it's not what I wanted", said Stan with conviction, while restraining his tears from falling.

Pausing to compose himself, and to wipe his eyes, he concluded "this is the right thing to do. So, this is what I want to do".

"No, it's not! You are not indestructible, and you shouldn't try to be one. Just because it's a sure-fire thing and a sure win, doesn't mean it's what you need. I know it's hard not knowing how things will work out, and even harder if you run the risk of losing everything you've built your world around all these years. But sometimes, for the right purpose, we deserve to take that risk, lest our hearts cry for the rest of our lives.

"This world is already full of people who've decided to pursue the sure wins, and the sure-fire things. Don't just be another face in yet another generation. Because it probably wasn't life's hardships or struggles that drowns a person in a sea of faces. More than anything, it was probably the sure-fire things and the sure wins that eventually prevented a person from reaching his purest goals and truest purpose.

"If you can find the courage, please choose to pursue what was meant by the heavens to be yours, even if no one wants you to", emotionally said Monica, as her tears keep pouring.

Shaking his head, as tears now poured from his eyes, Stan was deeply saddened. Looking Monica in the eyes with despair and shame, Stan answered "I can't. This is a rare opportunity that will never come again in my lifetime. I owe it to myself and to those who look at my life as a good example, to pursue this course. In this way I can validate the good things that my parents did to raise me. So, this is what I have to do. Besides, my parents chose the sure-fire thing, and they have found contentment and joy, so why can't I?"

"So is teaching. Having the chance to affect not just this generation, but even the new, that's also a rare opportunity. And seeing the passion and joy in your eyes as you gave them that lecture, reminded me of the Stan I once knew. Full of energy, passion and hope, and with utter focus and dedication towards the set goals right before you. But more importantly, in that moment, you were genuinely being you. You were just you. And I think that's worth more than the opportunity that MCG can offer you", said Monica in a sad voice.

"Thank you for your concern. But I don't think I can waste the chance offered to me. As much as I'd like to pursue the teaching job, we both know that it is in the best interest of everyone that I work at MCG", said Stan with a voice that cracked due to sadness.

Looking Stan deeply in the eyes and understanding that there was no longer anything she could say to change his mind, Monica wiped her tears, and began putting their things back in their containers.

"I understand. And I hope that you too will understand why I can no longer support this getaway. I've enjoyed this trip and the good memories will stay with me for as long as I live. But I have already extended my stay, and now I must go back to the life that I had to put on hold", said Monica, as she now stands to go back to the car.

Understanding Monica's emotions, Stan helped pack their things, and without another word, the two went back to the car, and drove back home.

Chapter 19

Early Departure

From a distance, Martha saw a familiar car coming towards the house. As the car got closer, she was surprised to learn that it was Stan's car returning quite early.

"It's just seven past three pm. That was a quicker trip than normal", Martha said to herself, as the car parked and the two got out.

"Is everything ok?" asked Martha, as she noticed some tension between the two.

"Oh, yes. Everything is fine. We just decided to call it a day early because I had an urgent business I have to attend to, so I have to pack and get on the next available plane back to the city", answered Monica, as she noticed Martha's concerned look.

"Oh, okay. That's sad to hear, but I guess, it can't be helped. Gary just went to the farm to check on the crops a bit, but he would probably be back in a few minutes. I'll tell him about your sudden emergency so he can get something for you to take back to the city, to remember us by", said Martha with a smile.

"Thanks Martha! I'd like that", said Monica, with a gentle smile.

"Of course, dear", Martha replied back.

As the two talked, Stan remained quiet, as he sat on the porch, seemingly in deep thought. Shortly after, Monica went to her room to pack her bags, while Martha and Stan remained on the porch.

"Is everything ok, son? What happened? I thought Monica was staying for a couple more days. Is she alright?" curiously asked Martha.

"Nothing happened mom. She just needed to get back to the city all of a sudden, so we went right back home so she could catch the evening flight, unconvincingly replied Stan.

"Doesn't seem like everything is okay, but I do hope you two sort it out somehow", insistently said Martha.

Unsure how, but certain nonetheless that his mom noticed their rift, Stan answered "I hope so too".

After a few minutes passing by, Gary got home, with some delicacies from the market. Asking Stan and Martha about the situation, and getting a vague response, Gary nonetheless accepted the conclusion offered, after figuring some things out from his son's eyes.

Pausing, as he tries to figure out what happened, but at the same time giving Stan some space to figure out his own situation, Gary looked at Stan and said "it'll all work out eventually". Surprised, but appreciative of his father's statement, Stan replied "I hope so too, dad".

When Monica got out of her room with her bags ready, she quickly went to the porch, where Stan, Gary and Martha were waiting.

"Hi Gary, I apologize for the sudden departure and I would really like to thank you for taking such good care of me all this time", apologetically said Monica.

"It was a pleasure having you around. We should be the ones to thank you for going along my son's selfish trip here, and keeping him safe and with great company", said Gary with a sincere smile.

"Don't think too much of it. We were happy to have you here, and you are no longer a stranger, so just feel free to call or visit anytime you want", said Martha.

"Oh, by the way, I bought you these. They are a delicacy of our town, and I heard from Stan that you liked it when you had some at the market", said Gary, before Monica can even answer.

"Thank you, Gary and Martha. It was a delight staying here", said Monica.

"Let me help you with your bags, dear", said Gary, as he reaches for Monica's bags.

"Oh, you don't have to. I can take the bus to the airport, so you don't have to drive me there. I don't want to interrupt your day, just because I had a sudden change of plans", said Monica, as she tries to convince Gary not to take her bags.

"Nonsense. We don't have any plans, and it won't be a bother for us to take you there. Besides, Stan has to stay here to help her mother prepare for dinner, so you don't have to worry about any long goodbyes at the airport", jokingly said Gary.

Checking at how serious Gary was on his offer, and convinced that it was serious enough, Monica conceded, and allowed Gary to help her with her bags. She had no reason to be mad at Gary and Martha, especially with the way they treated her all this time, thought Monica. And the two went to the car and drove off, as Stan stayed silent, as he remained behind.

Still unsettled, but remaining quiet, Stan decided to drive away for a while, as he tried to make sense of how things changed unexpectedly. He decided to just drive towards a random direction, without thought as to where he was going. All he knew at that time was that he wanted to keep driving, until somehow his emotions calmed down.

Playing a calm and composed facade he told his mother that he would not join them for dinner, he tried as much as possible to hide a wave of feelings that kept spiraling and expanding, without any intention of calming down. All he wanted was to make that unexplained feeling stop. And having dealt with this kind of emotion early on in his life, he drove towards a random direction, knowing that after giving himself enough time to think back at what happened and how he acted, his heart and mind might cool off and settle down.

Into familiar horizons he drove, with his mind racing to make sense of what happened, and hopefully rationalize his heart's desires and his mind's designs. Farther and farther he went, until he was passing less familiar paths, but still trying to understand his mind and his heart. Deeper and deeper he went, as night now unfolds, while he passes paths totally unknown.

Unplanned but still grateful, he saw a neon light sign that advertised food on a distant horizon. Feeling the hunger overtaking whatever it was that he was feeling in that moment, he drove towards the neon light, and eventually parked to get something to munch. Checking the place out from the outside, it seemed like a straightforward establishment that was popular for stew.

On the outside he looked calm and collected, and yet despite the hunger, Stan's mind was still unhinged and dazed, as he grappled to find peace. Hoping to at least solve his hunger and hopefully get back to his moping, he got out of the car and robotically had a seat and just ordered the soup that they had. In just a few minutes, his order was already there. Surprised and appreciative, Stan gobbled up the soup as thought it was his last.

Despite the cheap meal, he was surprised at how vigorous he seemingly inhaled it. He was unsure at first if his surprising enjoyment of the meal was due to its flavor, or simply because of how hungry he was at that point in the day.

"Great flavor or just plain hunger, whatever the reason, the enjoyment is real. That counts for something, I guess?" Stan thought, as he finished his meal.

Having satisfied his hunger, he sat back for a moment, and tried to make out where he currently was, and what he should do afterwards. He knew that he was a very long way from home, since he was sure that he had never been to the place he was at. He also understood that if he continued in the same direction, he would eventually have to travel back, because there was nothing for him in the direction he was driving towards. At least that was his conclusion, basing only on his recollection and not on any phone engine search.

For a moment in the uncertainty, Stan was able to get free of the sadness and confusion in his heart. And yet in that moment, the most important thing that stuck out was the thought of how worried his parents would be, if he does not go home that night, regardless of his mood when he comes back.

"They don't deserve to worry about something this petty. I'm a grown man now. I should be able to get past these feelings, and continue as I was. That's what grownups are supposed to do, right? It won't always be peachy or happy, in every moment of my life", he thought, as he stared at the wall.

Calming down as he realized that, he quickly paid for his meal, and drove back the other way. Worrying his parents for his foolishness, would not be how he paid them back, he thought, as he decided to go back.

"If I don't commit to a choice now, I'll be crippled by indecision. Happy or not, I'll make it work. That's what I always do. Happy or not, that's what I'm expected to do. Like the shop I just ate from, I have to understand that I can only go so far, before I have to come back again. Just like the stew they serve, maybe I won't find a memorable meal waiting for me at the end of my journey, and yet even then, I can still find a simple stew that can somehow be enjoyable, and maybe even satisfying. It may not have been what I was looking for, but it gets the job done. And maybe, that's more than enough", he thought as he drove home.

With those thoughts, he convinced himself that what he was doing was right. He continued to rationalize his decision, and reconcile his thoughts with the feelings that he had.

Already past eleven pm, Stan was finally able to arrive home. Despite some light in the living room area, Stan was not sure if his parents waited up, or just kept the light on for when he got back. Regardless of the reason, he was thankful for their concern.

As Stan entered the living room, he immediately noticed Martha and Gary on the sofa, as they woke up to the sound of the door opening. With tired but happy eyes, Stan noticed their relief, as he entered the door.

"How was your drive?" cautiously but playfully asked Gary.

"It was a good one. Took me to a new place, but nothing really beats home", replied Stan, as he tried to give context about his drive, but refrained from giving any detail that might upset his parents.

"Glad to hear. Have you eaten? We saved some curry, if you're hungry", said Martha, as she pointed to some bowls on the table.

"Thanks for saving some curry for me, but I ate on my way back, so maybe tomorrow", replied Stan, as he joins his parents in the living room. "More importantly, it's already late, so you should probably get some rest. I'll put the food in the fridge, so you just go on ahead", continued Stan. And after a brief pause, he added with a smile "and thank you for waiting".

"Of course", said Martha with a smile. "Son, do you want to talk about it?" Gary asked with sincerity.

Surprised at Gary's timing, but also thankful that he asked, Stan struggled to respond, as he was torn between solving things on his own, or seeking his parent's wisdom early on. He could not come to terms in worrying his parents over an issue that he should be mature enough to deal with, but at the same time understood how invaluable his parent's wisdom was, over a matter he was genuinely at a crossroads with.

"I don't know dad", Stan ended up answering.

"Then maybe we should. I also wanted to drink the whiskey that I've been saving, so if not for a good talk, then at least we can make a toast to celebrate this new role that you've been given. What do you say?" said Gary with a smile.

"I'd love that", smiling as Stan replied.

The two then proceeded to the dining area, with Gary taking a bottle of old whiskey and drinking glasses from the cabinet nearby. Martha on the other hand, decided to give the father and son their moment, understanding that it was a rare but precious opportunity for the two to actually share their thoughts and feelings. Besides, she has known both men well enough to understand that leaving the two to discuss what was bothering them, was best in that situation.

"I'll leave the two of you to your whiskey then. Don't drink more than you can handle", Martha said with a smile, as the two just nodded without saying a word.

Gary poured whiskey on both glasses and ceremoniously gave one to Stan, and placed the other in front of him. Raising his glass, and prompting Stan to raise his, they shared a cheer "to the MCG Head of Legal" and "to the souls who may never tire".

"Want to hear a secret?" Gary asked, after taking a sip of whiskey, and after checking that Martha can no longer hear them. "What is it, dad?" curiously asked Stan. "I actually don't like drinking whiskey", said Gary with a blank face, before both of them burst into laughter.

"Then why offer this to me now? And why agonize drinking this?" asked Stan.

"Well, sometimes I just drink it to look tough. But for the most part, I just want to get my money's worth, because this thing costs a lot. When I bought this sucker, I thought it would be proper to have an expensive drink around to celebrate occasions such as this, or if no special occasion comes, then just chug it down like a juice drink, since it should at least taste nice, considering how much money they asked for it. Since I didn't have the taste buds to just chug it, I just tried to take a sip every now and then, hoping that it would eventually run empty. I mean they said on the television that this was for special occasions, right? That this thing was what cultured men drink to celebrate", jokingly said Gary, as Stan laughs.

"Honestly, the tv ads could never have been more wrong. Well, except maybe for now", continued Gary, but now with a more serious expression.

"We never really talk as much as we should. I guess that's just how I thought men should behave. Just take it all in and endure the world's weight, as you carry your family across its rough terrain. Or at least try to. And then make sure that your son does the same thing. And although we make it a point to share meals together, attend the other family gatherings and occasions together, unconsciously, I've made it a point that we both remained walled up, with me always exercising authority, as a father operating in my own elevated tower, and you, always relegated to a lower room, as son", sincerely said Gary, as he tries to find the next words he wanted to say.

"Where are you going with this dad?" asked Stan.

"I'm not quite sure myself, son. We haven't really done this a lot, so I'm still learning as I go", said Gary, before pausing to compose his thoughts, while Stan remained silent, eager to hear what his lifelong idol wanted to share.

"But if you won't mind, I really hope we can talk about it? Whatever it is that's bothering you. I'd really like to know", concluded Gary.

Surprised and at the same time touched, Stan understood where his dad was coming from. In an attempt to start the conversation right, he fiddled with his thoughts somewhat.

"I think you already know what it's about, dad", meekly answered Stan.

"Nonetheless, I'd like to hear it", replied an undeterred Gary.

"Monica and I had an argument about me taking on the new MCG position, and because of our differences, she decided to go back to the city", narrated Stan, as he still tries to temper his revelations.

"Monica seems like a fairly reasonable person, so if she had an issue with the offered position, she may have had her reasons. But why did it escalate?" curiously asked Gary.

"To be honest dad, she was right to have issues with the job. This new position will probably be just as busy, if not busier, than the last post I held, and I guess, she felt that despite the grand opportunity this new role brings, and regardless of the excessive compensation it included, she believed that the teaching job at SC would actually make me happier. And to tell you honestly, she was right", Stan narrated with a heavy heart.

"Then why continue with the MCG role, when you already have one that's better?" asked Gary.

"Because I don't think the world was ever supposed to revolve around me being happy, but more importantly, I have my duties and responsibilities to this family and to your name. And I would be remiss in my obligations to this family, and maybe even to this town, if I let such a great opportunity just pass by me. I'd be a fool, if I let this go. Worse, they'd call you a fool, for raising someone who would just let this go", Stan explained, as his chest now felt lighter with each statement.

"Buy you don't owe the world that. You don't owe anyone that. And you definitely should not owe us for that. We worked hard and sacrificed, precisely to make sure that you won't have to owe anyone, for anything in your life. We worked hard in giving you opportunities, so that you only have to owe yourself for your life. And to come back now and try to pay back what we did, probably goes against our sacrifices, don't you think? Our love was never supposed to be repaid, and having done what we have done, is the end in of itself for us" counters Gary.

"I love you for saying that dad, and with more reason that I should do what I should now do. I know that I may not make sense, and even I don't fully understand myself as well, but despite my uncertainties about this choice, I know that my reasons are right", replied Stan with conviction.

"Son, I can't tell you what you need to do or not, but as a father, understand that I only want what's best for you. I'm not sure what's right or wrong for you, and I guess at this stage, only you can know what's best for you. What I do understand, is that this is the first time in your life that I've seen you this vulnerable. And trust me when I say that it's a good thing. So, if you feel strongly about this decision, then know that we will stay behind you no matter what. We love you, son", said Gary with teary eyes, but still able to hold the tears from falling.

As he felt the love from his father at that moment, he looked him straight in the eyes, and said "thank you dad. I love you".

As the two shared an embrace, their hearts have never been more connected than in that moment. Having expressed their emotions, which they hardly ever do, they found relief and comfort in actually knowing how much their actions have affected the other. And after a few more sips and a few more meaningful conversations, the two returned the ale to the cabinet, and rested their weary eyes.

Waking up the next day, Martha checked the wall clock in their room and saw that it was already past eight in the morning. Understanding that she woke up later than they normally do, but also realizing how late she slept that night, she did not rush to rise up, and waited first for her senses to come back, before she again opened her eyes.

As she lay there in bed, she already noticed Gary slowly waking up, but just like her, was taking his sweet time to rise up. She remembered waking up when Gary joined her in bed last night, and being appraised by him of his conversation with Stan. Despite hearing that his eldest son was deeply troubled by the choices that he was now faced with as an adult, she was nonetheless happy that he and Gary were able to open up with each other, an occurrence, which to her mind had never happened before, between the two walled up and normally composed individuals.

"I'm glad they were able to talk one-on-one last night", she said, as she continued to lay in bed.

As a few minutes had passed by, Martha was now in full control of her senses. Slowly she rose up from bed, with Gary rising up right next to her.

"I'll make some coffee, while you use the bathroom", Martha told Gary, who just nodded back, before standing up to use the bathroom.

As she got out of their room and passed by the dining area, she saw the table already prepared, with fresh hot bread, coffee, sausages, fruits and eggs, already set for eating. She went past the dining area, and continued towards the kitchen, where she found Stan taking out the last pancake out of the pan and into a plate.

"What is all this? What seems to be the occasion?" jokingly asked Martha.

"Good morning mom. Didn't see you there", replied a slightly startled Stan.

"Well, I just wanted to thank both of you for waiting for me last night, and also to say sorry for worrying you", continued Stan, as he and Martha went to the table with the freshly made pancakes in Stan's hands.

"We're just glad you're safe, so you didn't have to do all these. We're your parents so we will always worry, but I guess that's just part of the job. And despite the worrying, your father and I are the most fortunate parents ever, to have you and Gram, as our sons. And we will always be proud of you two, no matter what happens", replied Martha with a smile.

"Thanks mom. I love you both. And I hope you continue to understand why I have to do what I have to do.", replied a teary-eyed Stan.

"After my discussion with dad last night, I've decided to pursue the magnificent job opportunity that has been granted to me and see where it goes, at least for the time being. With this finally decided, I think it is also time for me to start moving, to be able to maximize this blessing that I've been given.

"This being said, I should already start preparing for the new role that I would take on, and I am therefore going back to the city, to be able to settle some matters with my previous firm, and also meet up with my new employers, to discuss the role I am going to handle", continued Stan.

"Of course. So, when do you intend to go back to the city?" asked Martha.

"Today. I've already packed my bags and filled the gas tank of my car, when I went out to get bread earlier", reluctantly said Stan.

"What?" a dumbfounded Martha said.

"I know it's sudden, and that I originally said that I'd stay for another week. But given how big a role and how sudden this offer was given, I'm pressed for time in settling my concerns with my previous employer and studying up for the position that I would be handling.

"As much as I'd like to stay and relax a bit longer, I want to get a head start on this, so I can hopefully be able to manage the role, and if I'm lucky, afford me some breathers in the near future. I know discussing these things may sound like I'm overkilling it, but if my estimations are correct, I'd need every minute of it, just to stay afloat in the months ahead. I guess this is just part of my process in handling new circumstances, as I have been trained in my previous job", Stan stuttered to explain.

"I understand. You don't need to justify what you need to do, so you just do you. I guess I just got caught off guard at how sudden your departure was. But if you think that's best, then just go on ahead", replied Martha, as Gary joined them at the table.

Gary was also surprised at Stan's gesture, but more surprised about his sudden departure. Nonetheless he understood, and gave his full support, and they continued to talk about the departure over breakfast.

"By the way, I think you should also say goodbye to Sheen before you go back to the city. I just don't want you two to drift apart again, after you've just reconnected. Besides, I think you should also talk to him and Julie about you not being able to accept the professor job anymore, considering that you would be staying in the city now, due to your new role", suggested Gary.

"I already did, dad. I feel bad about not being able to teach at SC and having to leave so suddenly, so the least I can do is say goodbye in person, and hope he can understand. I went there this morning when I got the bread, and we were able to talk about this sudden change in plans", explained Stan.

"So, what did he say about it?" curiously asked Gary.

"He was a bit sad that I wouldn't be able to teach at SC and stay a while longer, but he understands how important this move is for me. We then had a couple more discussions about some of the realizations he had about work and about life, but nonetheless kind of allowed me to leave, as long as I return home for our reunions each year", smilingly said Stan, as he pictures his discussion with Sheen.

"I'm glad to hear that, son. Then I guess you're all set", said Gary with some underlying sadness in his voice.

They continued on with their meal, and afterwards, Stan cleaned the table and washed the dishes. As the day continued, Gary and Martha got some delicacies and other items for Stan to bring on his drive back to the city. The two prepared Stan's favorite dish for lunch, and after they ate, Stan said his goodbyes and started on his drive back to the city, that allowed him to live the dream he once had, and unceremoniously, just took it right back.

Chapter 20

Long Drive Back

Now driving in the familiar route that he travelled just a few weeks back, Stan once more saw the landmarks and establishments that they once went past. And although the road and buildings didn't change one bit, as he travelled back, it somehow felt like the feel and view were completely new.

It was not only the outside of his car that seemed different, the inside felt new too. Although the car remained unchanged, Stan understood that the feeling was not the same. And despite everyone saying that new is always better, Stan learned now that it's not always true.

As he travelled and drove, he felt heavy and uptight. He made more pitstops, just to eat more and unwind, as the silence of his car seemed louder now, than it ever had before. And he needed those stops, if only to get some fresh air, and hopefully some new perspective, as he tries to get back to his home.

Despite the silence, he continued on. Driving and resting, but making sure to advance on. He knew he was not fully in tune with his feelings, but nonetheless, he had a deadline, so he had to go on.

Clear all my accountabilities and settle any pending matters in my previous job and study for the new role I'll be having. Those are the tasks at hand that he decided was best to settle, before he begins his new job. This is the most ideal outcome and plan, he already decided. So, it follows that all these preparations should first be done, if he ever wanted to get on top of the operation he was going to run.

There are great benefits to this move, he continued to tell himself, as he lists down in his mind, the different advantages that the role will bring. Such great advantages, he thought, despite not having the one advantage in the world he really wanted.

And he drove some more, and before he knew it, he was once again back inside the familiar parking lot of his house. Already the dead of night, he got out without even taking his things out, went straight to his bed, and just slept till the sun was up.

Waking up the next day, he knew he still did not have the focus to start his tasks. Looking back at the travel he did the day before, he could not believe that despite the same distance and the same travel time, this second trip of his, felt more like a blur. As though he droned off doing something, that his mind just wants to forget.

Unable to shake that feeling, and just barely standing from his bed, he decided to open the television, in hopes that he would find something that could somehow bring him back to life. But as he watched the news, he felt as though he was both focused and distracted. Seeing the images that flashed, but not really caring what they were about, and just wanting for time to pass by. Having felt this way before, although in very short and random times, he understood that it was normal, and was not in any way alarmed. But somehow, he knew, that this was the worst that this feeling has ever been, and that this unfortunate feeling may somehow continue.

Not finding anything satisfying on the television, and remembering how enlightening his eat outs were, he thought that maybe during breakfast his mood can improve, and he can hopefully get some things done. He quickly got a shower, put some clothes on, and was on his way.

Despite already being in his car, he still could not decide where to go. Should he go to his favorite breakfast restaurants near his house and guarantee a satisfying breakfast, or should he go to one of the spots he heard so much about, but accept the risk that it may not give him the satisfaction he was looking for? Although the engine had already started, he remained stuck in the parking lot, still deciding what to do.

Still unsure and confused, he stared through his windshield, as he searched his heart. "Where do you want to go?" he asked himself, as he slowly got frustrated, as time passed by. Eventually he just decided to go to a familiar spot, not wanting another disappointment at that time.

He drove off, parked, went inside the restaurant, ate, left just like that, and was again back at the spot he initially started from. Lying in bed, confused and undecided, without even a sense of how he wanted things to push through.

"At least I'm no longer hungry", he thought to himself with a smile, as he decided to lay in bed and let the night take back the light. With his back laying on the soft bed, he continued in a trance-like state, neither asleep nor fully awake. Just staring into the wall, and just letting his mind imagine how things should unfold.

He tried to resolve his thoughts and his emotions, as he tried to overcome this slump. With things not clearing up, he just decided to talk to himself and believe that what he was doing was ultimately for the best. And yet despite all that, the decision to abandon the MCG post, and just restore everything back before the offer, seemed to keep popping up. "Can I still change my mind at this stage? How should I even tell the executives and even my parents, should I suddenly decide to take my 'yes' back? Is there still a chance that I can teach, should I decide to go back home?" all keep popping up in his head, despite his resolve to continue in the path he was currently on.

And just like that, he was now back.

Chapter 21

The Funeral

Two days went by, and with a few pep-talks to himself, and a few workouts in between, Stan was able to gain a state of mind that can allow him to finally start getting things done. He decided to take a whole day to study the background of MCG and the various laws they constantly had to deal with. He also took the day to familiarize himself with their different operations and checked the backgrounds of the various people in charge.

After a day of reading, he had a light dinner, and decided to grab a beer from his refrigerator. Laying back on his couch as he ate and had a beer or two, he unwillingly remembered his time together with Monica.

"It's been a while since she left, and we really haven't talked again since her trip back. I wonder if she will talk to me if I call her now? Maybe, unless of course if she's busy. But maybe it wouldn't be right to bother her, after all the time I took from her these past few weeks", he thought. "I wonder if she's still mad with me?" he finally ended up asking.

Even after he chugged down a can of beer and finished his dinner, he was still at a standstill, whether it was right to call his friend at that hour. Eventually, he found the courage to try, and started dialing her number.

"She probably wouldn't get any madder than she was before, right? Besides, I owe it to her to check if she got home safely and was not in any sort of trouble at work. After all, I did drag her to join me on my trip home", he thought.

In no minute, Monica's number was ringing, but unfortunately, she was not answering. Every time it rang, Stan's anxiety grew, with one of his fingers always itching to just end the call, just to avoid an embarrassment he was already feeling within him. He was both hoping that she would answer, so that he can check on her, and at the same time hoping that she would not, because he was uncharacteristically nervous, and was not sure if he can actually talk to her, at that time. But alas, the number just rang, with no one answering.

"I don't suppose she's still in a meeting at this time of the day, so it's very likely that she just doesn't want to hear from me", Stan concluded, as he sank his body back to his couch.

"I don't suppose any of the guys have an idea if Monica still hates me?" he thought, as he looked for his friend's numbers on his phone. "Maybe I can invite them for drinks tonight, and hope Monica shows up", he again thought, as his phone now shows Jen's number.

Taking a short pause to finalize his intro and temper his emotions, he then made the call. After a short ring, the call was answered.

"Hi Stan, how are you doing?! How was the vacation?" loudly greeted Jen.

"Hi Jen! It was nice to get away from the city for a while. We should all go to my hometown sometime", replied Stan.

"I'd love that! Let's do that sometime! By the way, word on the street is that you are now the new global head of legal for MCG. Congrats!" Jen cheerfully replied.

"Wow, news really travels fast. I was just about to tell you that. Anyway, considering this big news and since me and Monica are now back, I was hoping we could grab a bite and a few beers later tonight. I'll take care of the beer", said Stan with a chuckle.

"Well, you know how it is with this type of news. But regardless, congrats on the offer! I'm happy and proud of you! But about the dinner tonight, I don't think I can make it. I'd love to, but I have a lot of urgent work I need to get through. Maybe some other time?" replied Jen, with initial excitement at his friend's accomplishment, and eventual sadness, when saying she can't join him to celebrate.

"Yeah, sure. Let's just have it some other time. I don't want to have drinks if one of you can't make it. Well just find another time", reassuringly said Stan.

"By the way, have you heard from Monica since we came back?" Stan quickly shifted.

"Yeah, we had lunch the other day. She gave some souvenirs and had a lot of stories about your trip", narrated Jen.

"What did she say? Is she okay? I mean, why the sudden lunch?" erratically asked Stan.

"Well, we happened to appear before the same judge, so we had lunch afterwards. Of course, we waited first for our clients to leave, before we had lunch, so that they don't get any wrong ideas", jokingly said Jen.

"Anyway, she seems to be doing fine. Very busy thought, with all the work that piled up when she left, so we only had a short lunch. She did however have a lot of great stories that she shared about your trip together, and about the great spots you guys visited. She seemed to have had a blast, during your time there. Kind of makes me a bit jealous of your trip, so you better take us along the next time you go home", emotionally narrated Jen.

"Consider it done. Just let me know when you guys are free, and I'll personally give you a tour of my hometown", reassuringly said Stan.

"By the way, did Monica tell you why she had to go home early? We were actually due to come back to the city next week", said Stan, as he intentionally paused at the end, to wait for Jen to give him any hint if Monica ever mentioned their argument.

"Well, we talked about it a bit when I asked her why she came back to the city early. And I do understand her side on this, but ultimately, she is happy with wherever you decide to go. I mean, she does have a point about going for what actually moves you from the heart, but she's a big girl now, and she does understand where you are coming from. Maybe she just got too invested in seeing you find your happiness, since she did join you on your soul-searching. But she is more than happy to know that a very deserving person, as yourself, will be given this opportunity", emotionally narrated Jen.

"Is she mad at me? I mean, I will understand if she is upset with me. I just wanted to personally talk to her about this, and hopefully clear things out in the best way I could. I tried calling her earlier, but she did not get my call, and I really don't know what to think of this", replied Stan in an uncharacteristically frantic manner.

"She's fine. She's a big girl now. She is genuinely happy for you, regardless of which path you take. She is just more passionate and honest about things than you, so she probably just doesn't want to talk to you, until her feelings have fully settled down, I suppose. Just give it some time. You go way back, so it'll only be a matter of time before you two are back to your normal selves again.

"Besides, she really has a lot of work on her plate right now. It seems like she really put her tasks on hold when you two were on vacation, so that you two will really enjoy yourselves. Not that she was complaining, because she definitely wasn't. But her work just piled up, so now it's time for her to make up with it. So, don't worry. She's not mad at you. She will never be mad at you", replied Jen in a more serious manner.

"Thanks Jen", said Stan, while still trying to understand how to process all that he heard.

"Don't mention it", Jen replied.

"Do the guys know?" curiously asked Stan.

"Of course, they do. They are our friends, so of course they'd want to know about this. We've had a few calls here and there, and we understand where both of you are coming from. But we think this is a matter only the two of you can resolve. My recommendation, just give Monica some time. We're friends, so this will all sort out in the end", Jen reassured.

"I understand. Thanks for your honesty Jen. Let's all meet when all of you are free, and when Monica already forgives me", said Stan with some sadness.

"Sure. See you soon, and congratulations!", said Jen, as she tries once more to sound excited.

Shortly after, the two said their goodbyes and the call was ended. And despite understanding the logic of the situation, Stan could not help but feel disappointed, in himself, and in his situation.

Gaining some insight from Jen, he decided not to call the rest of the gang, as he now understood where they currently stand on the matter. Later on in the night, he did receive messages from them, congratulating him on his new role, and also welcoming him back to the city. Their messages managed to numb the blow of an otherwise sad day.

Finishing the can of beer, and finishing another can for good measure, he continued with his review, until later into the night. No longer able to focus, he eventually went to bed with the game plan to wake up early the next day, to be able to read some more, before going early to collect his last pay from his previous firm.

After a short but continuous sleep, Stan woke up early, got some workouts done, had a light breakfast, studied a bit, and was on his way to his former office. Considering how well known he was to a lot of the people there, and how friendly he was to a lot of the staff and partners, he decided to get his last pay, early in the morning, in the hope that he would only run into a few of his colleagues, as much as possible.

Although the money he would be receiving is actually a return of his capital contribution and some earned profit share, he decided to call them his last pay, since they were the result of his work, and it came in a single check that he would receive for his services and years of loyalty. Besides, it was easier to say, and easier to explain, he thought.

Entering the building that served as his home for a good amount of his life, he could not help but remember the memorable experiences he had along those corridors, elevators and chairs. But more than his memories in the different parts of the building, his fun interactions with the guards and the building staff, seemed more prominent in his mind. Somehow, he realized how their smiles, although immaterial in him drafting pleadings and formulating strategies, always made his day. Smiles and warm greetings, which to most seem inconsequential, and yet to Stan, made all the difference between him being able to carry out the day in high spirit and with more than enough energy to deliver on his tasks, or having a bad enough mood for him to lose focus on his work.

"More than anything, their smiles and greetings will probably be the thing I miss most in this office", thought Stan with a smile.

"Good morning Stan! How have you been?! Saw the game last night?" asked a familiar voice, coming from further inside the building.

"Good morning Mike! Missed the game last night. What happened?" Stan warmly greeted Mike, the lobby security.

"Well, not much of a game, let me tell you that. Our team got clobbered so hard, their screw-up probably counted as two losses", said Mike with an irritated expression.

"We'll get them next time, I'm sure of that", replied Stan with a smile, as he continued on to the elevator.

As he went further inside, he was greeted with warm smiles and heartfelt good mornings. Everyone from the lobby staff, to the elevator attendant, greeted him with warmness. It was like he never left, he thought. And with a smile on his face, he continued towards their firm's floor, went to the reception, got whisked to the waiting area, and without much hitch, was able to get his last pay.

With the check in his hand, and in slight disbelief that he had not yet bumped with any of the partners, he hurriedly went to the elevator to leave. "I already went through some formal gathering of partners and staff for my departure, and it probably would be for the best if he did not have to do that again", he thought.

As he waited for the elevator, he prayed dearly that no partner appears inside the lift, when it opens. Not when he was this close to leaving with his check, without a hitch, he kept on thinking.

"Ding!", sounded the elevator, as the down arrow light kept blinking, and the lift started to open. As the elevator doors ceremoniously opened, Stan's heart raced for a second, as its insides slowly showed. "I'm really not in any mood to have any awkward conversations, so please let me have this", he prayed in his head.

Losing breath for a split-second when he saw the insides of the elevator, he sighed through his nose to release the tension in his chest, before gasping for air as he calmed himself down and regained his composure. "The elevator is empty! Finally, a break!" he excitedly thought.

With that, he quickly went inside, and hurriedly closed the door, so that he could quickly get out of the office, and move on with his plans for the rest of the day. Quickly and with some extra bounce in his step, he went out the elevator, quickly went outside, and in just a few minutes, was already in his car at the parking lot.

"The day is looking pretty bright", he said with a smile, acting as though he was a kid again, who was able to dodge some chores because there was a TV program he liked that was about to start. "Better get going then", he said with a hum in his voice.

As he started the engine, but before his car could move, his phone suddenly rang. "'Granddad' is calling? Does he already know I resigned? Yikes!", he thought when he saw who was calling.

"Hi Granddad! How are you doing?" he blissfully answered, as he tried not to sound suspicious.

"Hi Stan! Doing good as always, although I could use a visit from my grandson every now and then", jokingly replied Lance, Stan's grandfather.

"Good to know you're healthy. I was meaning to visit you. I was actually home a few days back and planned on visiting, but something came up, and I had to come back to the city. But I'll schedule another trip home and visit you and 'grand mom' as soon as I can. Really sorry", sincerely stated Stan.

"That is unfortunate, and we really would have liked to take you around the farm again, but I'm sure it was for something important, so don't mind it. Besides, we can get to see you in the city, and maybe you can show us around", said Lance.

"I don't quite follow 'granddad'?" said a confused Stan.

"We have some sad news for you Stan, and that is the reason we have to go to the city. You still remember my good friend Mr. Paul, right? He passed away two days ago, and in honor of his name, they decided to hold the wake at their office tomorrow afternoon. They wanted all of his friends, partners, and even service providers to all be there for the ceremony to honor his name. He affected all their lives and has treated them all, not just as partners, but also as brothers in craft. So, his family would like to allow all he deemed dear, the chance to celebrate his life one last time, and just have his immediate family present, when they bury him later on. And as a dear friend, I'd like to see him smile one last time", slowly narrated Lance, as the cracks of sadness in his voice were visible through the phone.

Dumbfounded by the news, Stan could not find the words to reply. All he could mutter was "how? How did he die?" despite understanding afterwards, how foolish a question that was.

With a faint chuckle, accompanied by some snorting and wiping of tears that was visible through the line, Lance replied "that stubborn prick went off while doing what he did for most of his life, working late in his office, trying best to manage his company. Janine, his wife, said that he was just reviewing some reports that were up for discussion the next day, but when his eldest came to his office to drive him home, he was sitting in his chair, with his head on top of the desk, and was already lifeless all along.

"She said that James thought that his dad was just taking a nap, given that he had some bliss in his expression, as he laid his head on his table like we normally do when we nap. That stubborn prick, always leaving without saying goodbye".

Despite the physical distance between Lance and Stan, somehow someway, he felt his granddad's sadness through the line.

"Maybe it's for the best. He came out, just as he came into the world, without permission or warning, just the way he wanted. We can just be glad that of all the people the world had to offer, that he chose to hang with us while his time lasted", consoled Stan.

As he said those words, his grandfather listened and the line felt quiet. After a moment of silence, Lance said "maybe you're right Stan. All we can do now is remember the times we shared together, and celebrate the life that this wonderful man lived.

"I understand he was your client, and he was really fond of how you handled their legal needs, and kept talking about how well you were doing. I'm sure he would like you to attend his wake as well, so I hope you can come tomorrow afternoon?"

"Of course. I wouldn't miss it for the world", emphatically replied Stan.

The two went on to talk about the details of their flight, and how Stan would pick them up and have them stay at his place, instead of a hotel. After the details were finalized, they bid farewell and the call was ended.

Still in his car, with the engine on but the car staying put, Stan slouched back to the car seat, as he tried to make sense of the sudden news he just heard. He could not help but recall his interactions with Mr. Paul, and remember how kind and fatherly he was to him.

Despite this, he also could not help but think about the possibility that his old colleagues would be at the wake with him, and how futile his efforts were to avoid them, just to end up in the same room with all of them, on the very next day. And yet he was not sad nor frustrated about that one bit. To him it was worth the trouble, if only he can celebrate the life of a man who lived his life, as free as Mr. Paul did.

The next day, Stan picked up his grandparents from the airport, had them settle down in their rooms in his house, and after changing, they went to the wake of Mr. Paul. His grandparents were both excited to see him and check on him, but they did not seem to know that he had already resigned from his firm. As has been a tradition when his grandparents visit, they still got him his favorite biscuit growing up, and his grand mom, Ann, even gave him some cash for him to spend when he hangs out with friends.

When they arrived at the Roe Family corporate headquarters, his grandparents immediately saw old friends at the entrance, clumped up like a big gang. The group of old men and women were livelier than they normally should, and had a bounce in their step and a glitter in their eyes, as they saw old friends, and discussed the old days. They greeted each other warmly, and seemed well informed about each other's lives, despite not seeing each other for quite some time. They also asked about and shared, about their children and grandchildren's accomplishments, and also the latest news about their businesses. And although they cared deeply about Mr. Paul, and were deeply saddened by his parting, somehow, they no longer show much sadness in their expressions, but more of a calmness in that situation. Like they already went through the same ordeal, and have countlessly went through the wake of one friend to another, saddened by the loss, but understanding that at that point in their lives, they were all going to be crossing that line, and the only question remaining was, who was going to go first, and how. It was a done deal, so why bother the details, and just appreciate the company, while they still had it.

Upon seeing their old friends, his grandparent's eyes lit up, and they somehow gained new energy and speed, and quickly darted towards the pack of old people, just trying to hang on to life, a day at a time. When they joined the group, the group lit up, and there was a frenzy of greetings and pleasantries. As Stan was with his parents, he also got caught up in the barrage of greetings, introductions, and his grandparents parading him through the sea of people, some he knew very well, and others, he only saw on that occasion.

Wanting to appear the perfect grandchild, as he was trained to, and at that point, was already second nature, he smiled, shook hands, and explained his personal and professional details, despite his reluctance, and discomfort. But he loved his grandparents, and he liked the fact that these little things make them happy. "It is still worth it, I guess. Can't put a price on my grandparent's smiles", he thought, as he continued to diplomat through.

After a few minutes, his grandparents and their friends eventually got preoccupied with some other topic. He took the chance and excused himself from the group, telling his grandparents that he also would like to check in on some of his colleagues. And although what he told them was partly true, his main intention for excusing himself was simply to look around the venue, get an idea of how the memorial would be conducted, and find the best seats available for him and his grandparents.

Albeit not his main intention, he did however feel it proper to talk with his former co-partners, as he did in fact wanted to catch up with their lives. And with the wake of Mr. Paul, maybe the discussion would be less about work, he thought. Besides, he was already there, might as well make the most of it, and socialize with his former bosses, so hopefully they would not have to consider him aloof, or trying to avoid them. Two birds with one stone, he again thought.

Shortly after he excused himself, he quickly went inside the conference room of the building, where the wake program would be held. They were supposed to go inside once they got there so that they could quickly find a seat, but his grandparents found their friends first before they could even get close to the venue entrance.

Determined to find a good seat, Stan scanned the conference hall once he got in. It was a big hall, with tables all across it, and a smiling picture of Mr. Paul and several flower arrangements at the farthest end of the room. There were food booths on the side, with a majority of tables in the middle, already filled.

"I better find a seat soon", he thought, as he scanned the area. But no sooner was he inside the venue, a voice called from behind.

"Stan, finally got hold of you. I saw you earlier talking with some big-shot elderly folks, so I wasn't able to approach you. Anyway, didn't expect you to attend, but glad you were able to make it. This was your big client after all", said Shin, who just showed up from nowhere and approached Stan.

"Hey! How are you Shin?! Honestly didn't notice you. I am actually with my grandparents, since they are very close friends with Mr. Paul. They were actually the ones who told me about Mr. Paul's passing, and told me to join them today. Anyway, those are their friends outside, and it seems like Mr. Paul was a well-loved man among his peers. I was just about to get a seat for us, and also try to find out the program for the wake", replied a surprised Stan.

"Don't worry about the seats. I have some free chairs at my table, with a manager from our firm reserving them. It could easily fit the three of you, if you don't mind sitting with us?" said Shin.

"Of course not. Let me check with them first and ask them if they need the seats, or if they would be sitting with their friends. They do seem like they need to catch up a lot, so I'm not sure if they'd stick with me for the duration of the wake", said Stan with a smile, as he called his grandfather.

After just a short call, Stan said "well, just as I suspected. They would be sitting with their friends, so I guess it's just me, if that's okay?" coyly said Stan.

"Of course, it's not a problem. By the way, there would be a program starting in a few minutes, wherein some close friends of Mr. Paul would be giving testimonies and stories about him, while lunch will be served and snacks available on several food booths on the side. And I believe, after the testimonies and some videos and presentations, we all get to go close to Mr. Paul's urn, up front.

"He was cremated shortly after he died, and I think after this wake, his ashes would be carried by his children to the far ocean, and scattered there. Seems like a pretty expensive trip to the ocean just to scatter some ashes, but I guess that's just how they roll", narrated Shin.

"Thanks for the info. That was good to know", replied Stan.

The two proceeded to a table with a familiar manager from their firm was seated, with two chairs on his left side, having notebooks and bags placed over them, to reserve them. When they got near, the manager cleared the chairs, and pleasantly greeted Stan in the most formal way possible. Noticing how uptight the manager was, Stan decided to sit on the chair farthest from him, such that Shin was sitting in between Stan and the manager.

Scouting the table, Stan noticed that all the other chairs were occupied by other guests in the wake, and surprisingly, no one else from their firm.

"Are you the only guys from our firm here? I thought for sure that Mike would make time for an event like this. After all, there are a lot of prominent businessmen attending, and this does pose as a good marketing opportunity for the firm", curiously asked Stan.

Shin looked Stan in a funny way once he asked that, as though Shin was not sure if Stan was just pranking him, or if he was genuinely asking him this concern. Giving Stan the benefit of the doubt, Shin whispered "haven't you heard?"

"Heard what?" replied a confused Stan.

Convinced that Stan really did not know, Shin signaled Stan to follow him to an open area near them, but far away enough from the manager's hearing. Following Shin's lead, and all the more curious about the news that he was just about to share, he eagerly followed him, while trying to figure out what news he could possibly have about Mike.

Unable to figure out what was going on, Stan asked "so, what happened?"

"This was supposed to remain within the knowledge of the partners, but since you're a partner just a few months ago, I guess you still count. But you need to keep this between just the two of us. Got it?" said Shin with a worried expression.

"Of course. You know you can trust me about this, because we were partners just a while back. So, what happened?", reassured Stan.

"The thing is, Mike is no longer with the firm. To put it bluntly, he was forcefully removed from the firm", discussed Shin.

"What?! How come?" a shocked but hushed response from Stan.

"Not everything is as it seems with Mike, apparently. In an audit by our external auditors, they found out that Mike was pumping money out of the firm, and into his personal account. The audit showed that Mike kept signing off on some firm expense, for some technical service offshore, which was layered to be owned by someone else, but was actually fully owned and controlled by him. The firm kept paying exorbitant amounts of expenses to the offshore company, but never actually received any service from them. Mike apparently found a way to always include the expense in our budget, and was able to talk his way to convincing whoever was in charge that the services were actually performed. And the worst part was that the 'services' we received were increased or decreased by Mike, in accordance with the increase or decrease of the firm's earnings for the year. It turns out that the 'shortages' that we needed to fill in our budgets, and that we had to cover for the other partners, were ultimately going into Mike's personal back pocket.

"Not only did we lose significant profits from our profit shares, but a lot of managers and staff, and I guess even you, resigned because of the backbreaking work we had to put through, just to put more money in Mike's already large pocket. It was not like the guy needed more, because his cut in the firm's profit was already pretty big. He also didn't have any vices that we know of. When I asked the truth about it, all he said was that he bought some very expensive houses, cars, watches, etc. and the mortgages were more than what he was making", said Shin with sadness in his eyes.

"That son of a...well, what happened to Mike?" said a visibly angry Stan, while trying to keep his composure.

"The partners confronted him about it, with evidence in hand, but first tried to get some explanation from him. At first, he denied any involvement, but when we showed him the evidence that we had, he quickly turned to tears, and begged the partners for forgiveness, even promising to pay us all back.

"Of course, no one believed his word or promise, not after that discovery, and so we removed him from his position, removed him from the firm, distributed his capital investment among us, and we are now currently seizing all his property, to get back what he took from us. Unfortunately, he really doesn't have much property that is not already seized by a bank or two somewhere. And except for some cash we were able to recover, we really weren't able to get any significant money or property from the man. Which is actually ironic, given how extravagant his lifestyle was.

"As of right now, we already filed several cases in court against him, and will sue him for all that he is worth, and more. But the firm is trying to keep all this under wraps, so that our clients and our staff don't find out about it. I mean, we still are fully operational, and we did not defraud our clients in any way, but still, it doesn't bode well for our reputation if one of our partners actually defrauded the firm, right? Anyway, Mike is currently on bail, but all his assets that we know of, have already been frozen, so he probably is as broke as broke can be, right now, I hope.

"That's also why the firm only sent me and Tim here, as representatives for the firm, so that we can keep a low profile in the meantime. If other executives went here, we thought the Roe family might ask about Mike, and so we thought it best to have a small representation during this wake. Anyway, we can always say that all of the other partners are busy, and make it up by buying the family one of the biggest and most expensive flower arrangements ever created", Shin diligently explained.

"He always presented himself as a mentor to all of us. Even quoting the words of the founders when he discusses with us about our growth with the firm. And all this time he was just making lip service to our faces, while slowly pushing a knife to our hearts. I hope he gets what's due him", Stan rhetorically and sadly stated, as he stared blankly away.

"We'll make sure of that", reassured Shin.

"So, who's running the firm now?" asked Stan.

"Shortly after we figured out what Mike was doing, we immediately elected Peter to take over. But to be honest, I don't envy his position right now. First of all, he needs to run a company without so much as a turnover from Mike, make sure to chase after Mike for everything he has, keep employee morale high, and at the same time keep all these things confidential. All the partners are helping out, and all of us are doing a lot of late nights, just to help out Peter, and keep up with our own engagements, but no burden is heavier than what is on Peter's shoulders. I can barely keep up with current events lately, just to keep up with all the chaos at the firm", replied Shin.

"Peter is less vocal compared to the other senior partners, but he seems like a good man. If my impression is right, then he will be able to handle it. Let's just hope he does live up to his reputation, and not turn out like another two-faced prick like Mike", commented Stan.

"I do hope so. Anyway, let's try not to spoil our night by talking about garbage like Mike. What have you been up to lately?" said Shin, as he got conscious of Stan's souring mood, and tried to lighten it.

"It really sticks a painful pin into my heart knowing how I was played by such a pathetic man such as Mike, and after hearing it now, I can't seem to temper my anger. But what's the point of getting hung up about that loser, right?" said Stan, as he tries to smile awkwardly.

"Anyway, I went back to my hometown weeks ago, to take a breather and have some home cooking, if you will. Oh, and I also got offered the head of legal for MCG", continued Stan, while also trying to change his mood.

"Wow, that's big news! I just heard about their group finding a new head of legal, but I was so busy to find out who that was. You deserve that more than anyone! And the perks and compensation of that position is way better than that of any of our partners", replied a shocked Shin.

"I think so too. I've seen the compensation package, and they really spare no expense on that", said Stan, with a smirk.

"Tell me more!" excitedly said Shin.

But before Stan could continue, the guests were asked to take a seat, as the program was about to start. The two went back to their seats, and Stan just discussed as briefly as possible, how he learned about the MCG offer. And the program continued on, with Stan now focused on the speakers and presentations transitioning from one part to another, while their lunch was served.

On breaks however, whenever a new speaker was taking his sweet time to go to the stage, or when there were video presentations being played, Stan could not help but remember how he was screwed by his former mentor and supposed friend, Mike.

"I can't believe someone like him would cheat us. I don't think I have ever been cheated my whole life. And not one more demoralizing and irritating than the one Mike did to us. We considered him a big brother, a confidant, and a friend. His family is even close to a lot of the other partner's families, and yet he never even hesitated to manipulate and take advantage of that trust. Smiling and weeping with us, all while consciously trying to screw us over, from under our very noses. Who would do something like that?! And for what?! Money?! To what end?!" Stan thought to himself, while trying to remain calm from the outside.

As the program moved on, Stan's thoughts on what Mike continued. Stan was able to distract himself though, each time a new speaker would come up and talk about the life that Mr. Paul once had. With the stark contrast between Mr. Paul's life, and that of Mike's, Stan did find some comfort in the thought that maybe, there are still some people out there who lived life differently than Mike.

Just like that, a couple of hours passed, and after all the guest speakers and friends gave their testimonies and stories about Mr. Paul, finally, his eldest son, James, was on the podium, about to speak up.

"Good afternoon everyone and despite the sudden schedule of our father's wake, we sincerely appreciate your time", said James, before pausing to look around the room, as he readied himself for what he was about to say next.

"As you all know, my father, whom most of you know as Mr. Paul, passed away just a few days ago. He was at the office on his last day, and I was to pick him up from his office so that we can go home together, as we normally do. Sadly, that was the last time I was going to drive my father home from work.

"As sad as it was when I saw my father dead in his office, nonetheless, I find comfort in the fact that he was able to do the thing he was most passionate about his entire life. As you all know, my father is a passionate businessman and one who wanted not only his businesses to prosper, but also wanted every businessman who sought his help to also find success in their endeavors. He was always curious and optimistic of the world that was far beyond our imaginations. Somehow, he always saw some great future which always gave him passion and energy, even at his advanced age, to put forth countless hours planning and executing programs that would lead to the realizations of the things that people only thought were impossible, until he made them come true.

"These past few years, dad was nurturing tech businessmen and emerging social entrepreneurs that focused on sustainable growth, without compromising the welfare of their people. And it gave us great joy seeing how happy he was being part of this new movement of consciousness in the business world. I am truly grateful to be born to such a loving father and a passionate soul.

"Despite his tough demeanor, I would also like to share how funny he can be whenever no one else is around. Beneath the stoic façade, also lies a goofy side to my dad which only those whom he feels truly comfortable with, have had the chance to see.

"He is quick to notice our mood, regardless of how hard we try to hide it, and would joke around or make faces just to make us laugh, whenever no one is around. Despite the global prominence and business influence that my father had, it is the funny side of him that I, and my family, will truly miss. He was more than just a father and mentor to us, he was also our confidant, love coach, cook, and our driver, for most of our growing years.

"He always had a fascination of the high seas, and the vastness of the ocean, and how unexplored it still is. He always thought that there was something rugged and intriguing that lay beyond the deep seas and always wanted to explore it, and using his words, 'stroll around it', when he had the chance.

"To grant his lifelong wish to explore the vast unknown of the ocean, and to concede to his selfish request one last time, we are happy to spread our father's ashes in the deep seas in a few days. We know that he would want that more than anything.

"We thank you for being part of our father's life, and implore your forgiveness if he got tough on you, at times. Trust me, he just gets too passionate at times, and tough on the people he thinks have the most potential to offer. But his intentions are always pure. And we thank you for sticking around and sharing in his amazing life.

"Let us continue to remember the man and also push forward the things he believed in. Have a lovely evening", narrated James.

As Stan's table was situated near the entrance, he was able to catch an acquaintance enter the hall, in the beginning of James' speech. The man seemed frantic and hurriedly went to the front of the hall, near the podium, and stood by the side after signaling a hello to Mr. Paul's family. He seemed to be carrying some cheat pads of sorts, which Stan suspected could be a speech he prepared for the evening. He kept shuffling his cheat cards as he stood, until James went on to the meat of his speech, in which time, he calmed down and returned the cheat pads in his pocket. He seemed moved by the speech, but surprisingly, after James' speech, he motioned to James that he wanted to share his thoughts. After a quick dialogue with James, shortly after he left the podium, he went to the podium, with the announcer asking the guests to welcome some last words from the final speaker.

"Thank you for still giving me this opportunity to talk. Again, I apologize to James and his family for showing up late, and thank you so much for still allowing me to share my thoughts on my mentor, despite my tardiness. And to the guests in attendance, I hope you indulge this fool for a few more minutes of your time", started Marvin, a former and distinct client of Stan, whom he had a very moving conversation, a few months back.

"As some of you may know, Mr. Paul served not only as a mentor and father to his family, but he served as mentor and confidant to a lot of budding businessmen of this generation. He certainly was to me, and I considered his guidance and support, indispensable in my rise in the business community. To say that I owe him my success, whatever that may be worth, would be a complete understatement.

"He had a great passion and curiosity about business, but it was his willingness to teach us new entrepreneurs the ropes that sets him apart from all the rest. He cared about our world, and he cared a lot about the future that we and our children were going to have. And I completely agree with James at how amazingly insightful their father was. Seeing things that we never could have thought was possible.

"But I'd like to disagree with James, just this one time. While it is true that Mr. Paul was deeply passionate about business and his job, especially during the early parts of his life, this I know to be true; that family was his one true passion in life. This became true the moment he met his lovely wife, Val, and the feeling got stronger the moment his children were born", said Marvin, before looking at the table of Mr. Paul's immediate family.

"Although he spent a lot of time with work, he never once missed a recital, or play, or game of any of his children. And although his week was filled to the brim with meetings, believe me when I tell you that his weekdays are that full, so that he would be present for his family during the weekends.

"There are even moments during the lulls in our meetings, when Mr. Paul would ask about the ins-and-outs of dating among young adults, or what was the best shoes out there for basketball. He talks about you, his wife and children all the time, whenever we have consultations. And his eyes light up, every time he talks about his family.

"Although he started off as a young and ambitious entrepreneur, trying to prove his worth to the world with his success, that changed dramatically the moment he had his family. His passion for business changed, and we new entrepreneurs are thankful for it.

"Business was no longer his way of proving his worth. Business was his way of not only providing for his family, but also showing his children how to be great stewards of wealth and power. He wanted to be the best father that he can be, and he wanted to demonstrate that, not only in his household, but also in the way he deals with people.

"Nothing brought more joy to Mr. Paul, than to discuss the potential that his children had within each one of them, and how beautiful a life awaits them beyond the horizon. A world he hoped would have less violence and discrimination, and had a greater appreciation of the limited time that we have, and the beautiful world that we are enjoying.

"His dedication to his craft was not just to carry the torch until his time was up. No. He wanted to contribute to the advancement of an ever-changing world, so that it can turn into the beautiful future that he believed to be possible. And he wanted this future to be his inheritance to his children, more than anything in the world.

"He was passionate about helping the next generation because he knew that even if he were to somehow change the world to the beautiful future he foresaw, it would still be a lonely place, if his children were not able to share its beauty with others.

"From the bottom of my heart I am truly grateful. For all the moments that he shared with me, and all the knowledge he imparted. But most of all, I am thankful for giving me the conscience I needed to be a better person. And for showing me how rewarding it is to have a life well lived. You will never be forgotten", spoke Marvin, as he tried to control his emotions.

Stan could not help but be moved by the sincere speech just delivered by Marvin. And as the crowd stood to applaud him, Stan and Shin joined in. Unexpectedly however, Shin moved close to Stan as they were clapping, and motioned to whisper something.

"Have you heard what happened to their company?" discretely asked Shin.

Turning to look at Shin directly, Stan asked "no. What happened?"

"Wow, you have been out of touch these past few months. Well, to put it bluntly, their IPO did not push through", answered Shin.

"That's hard to believe. I worked with them and saw their financial statements, and they operate in a very specialized and promising industry. Plus, they have a very good support from a lot of industries who also want to push forward what they believe in. And they really wanted to get the funding. So, what happened?" asked a stunned Stan.

Shin signals Stan to move their conversation to a more private area in the hall, and when the coast was clear, they continued their discussion.

"Unfortunately, the public, or rather, investor perception accounted for the decision. When you left the firm, I was assigned to handle their account. We had everything worked out and ready for the IPO, and at the very last week of the IPO, several cases were filed by several prominent pharma, engineering and agricultural multinational companies, contesting the patent claims for several of the intellectual properties of Farmer's Charm. Their most senior researchers and scientists were formerly executives of these big multinationals, and now these multinationals were claiming ownership over the inventions being used by Farmer's Charm. They claim that the designs and ideas for the inventions that Farmer's Charm now use, were developed during the respective executive's tenure with their companies.

"Checking the claims, it was easy to show that all the claims were baseless, but having the news come out just a few days from the IPO, really spooked the prospective investors so bad, that the valuation for the company plummeted during that week. Despite the need for funding so that Farmer's Charm can finally operate on a more global scale, we convinced them to stall their IPO for the moment, until we are able to show that the claims were baseless. The plan now is to wait for the result of these trials, and hope that public perception improves to a point that the stock prices rise enough to sustain their target business model and global scale", explained Shin.

"But what about their current financial needs, how are they going to afford that? And knowing Marvin, I doubt he would want to delay his goals of saving the planet. He doesn't care about money, and of all the businessmen I've worked with, he would be the last one to cheat anyone, just for gain", angrily said Stan.

"It wasn't easy convincing him to back down from the IPO, I'll tell you that. But telling him that he stood to lose all their progress and advancement, not only in their business, but also the impact they had on the environment, should they decide to continue, did seem to make him reconsider his stance on the IPO. Ultimately, he was asked to continue with the IPO, and risk losing all their positive work, or wait a few months, when the estimated stock prices reached a favorable point, and have a better chance at making a bigger impact in the fight for the planet, albeit delayed. And to be honest, I believe he made the right decision to postpone the IPO. At least now we have a better chance of actually making a dent in the greenhouse gas problem we have been dealing with all these years", said Shin, in a surprisingly emotional way.

Seeing conviction in Shin's eyes, and an unusual passion for something other than money, Stan calmed down, and looked Shin straight in the eyes, and said "you did well Shin. You really did!"

"I certainly hope so. Sincerely, I do. But the work is far from done. We have to clear up the cases, as quickly as possible, or at least get to a point in the proceedings wherein we are able to show how baseless they are, and be able to increase the estimated prices of their shares, as soon as possible", said a teary-eyed Shin.

"I have no doubt you will. Of all the lawyers in our firm, you would be the best man to handle this. I do believe in the cause their group is fighting for, and if you need any assistance whatsoever, know that I am always there to help", reassured Stan.

At that moment, the two immediately understood each other's intentions, without any additional words. With convictions in their hearts and purpose welling from within, the two shook hands and separated, with Stan going to his grandparents and Shin going back to his seat. After the ceremony, the guests went to talk to the family of Mr. Paul, and were on their separate ways.

On their way out of the hall, Stan waited outside the entrance, as his grandparents stayed inside to say goodbye to their old friends. As he stood there by the entrance, he was unexpectedly tapped from behind. Composed but curious as to who tapped him, he turned around and saw Marvin behind him.

"Oh, hi Marvin, you startled me for a moment", said Stan.

"My apologies. I didn't mean to surprise you or anything. I saw you on my way in earlier and just wanted to say hello. I know the passing of Mr. Paul was a sudden and sad news for all of us, and I believe his passing was also sad for you, considering how close you too were", said a sympathetic Marvin.

"We do share a deep connection, but I don't think he considered me as that close a friend. I mean he and my grandfather were really close, and was a part of a lot of our social events growing up. But I don't suppose our relationship was as close a bond as the two of you had. Regardless however, I do feel very sad about his sudden departure. He was a good man and a great father. And the world needed a lot more good men like him, that's for sure", stutteringly replied Stan, as he was caught off guard by Marvin's statement, and scrambled dearly to find the right words.

"Not sure about that. Mr. Paul feels deeply about his children and the people he mentors. He is very impressed with your work ethic and talent, and considers you one of the people he is mentoring. He had nothing but praises for you, and he genuinely believed that you have what it takes to change the world for the better. And he was genuinely invested in you, and wants you to grow as a professional, and help improve the way we do things.

"But regardless, it is indeed a sad day for the world, that he is no longer with us. I intend to carry on the work that he started, and would like to help out the others whom he believed in, in any way that I can. So, I just want you to know that I am always here to listen, and to help", said Marvin, with a quiet joy and conviction.

"Thank you, Marvin. That means a lot to me", said Stan with a smile, as he understood how genuine Marvin was with his offer.

Not long after, and after a few more words, the two shook hands and were on their separate ways. Marvin left the venue, while Stan waited on by the door for his grandparents to come out. As he was standing there however, he could not help but be amazed at how calm and happy Marvin looked. He understood the sorrow in his voice, but they probably pertained to the passing of Mr. Paul, more than anything.

What amazed Stan was how Marvin does not seem stressed out, or out of sorts, because of work. Any businessman who had a sudden string of bad things fall on the business they cared deeply about, would be depressed and frantic at that point. Marvin however, had a seemingly unlimited amount of optimism about what the future holds. His smile was still genuine and without a hitch, and that is probably for the best, he thought.

After a few more minutes of waiting, his grandparents joined him, and they were on their way. That night his grandparents treated him for dinner, before they returned home. In all this moment, Stan felt happy knowing that despite all the setbacks that the good guys such as Mr. Paul and Marvin had, they still find happiness and optimism to continue on with their paths. For a world to usher in a bright tomorrow, the world needed more of them to continue to be positive, no matter what surprise the world unfolds, he thought. For us to have a chance, they need to continue to believe in a future that only they can see, no matter how dark the present tends to be.

As he sat alone by his dining table and with a cold beer in his hand, he felt happy that Mr. Paul even considered him a potential leader in the future, he was sure would unfold. And as he finishes the bottle, he thinks back at what Marvin could mean when he said that Mr. Paul thinks that he could change the world for the better. He was just a lawyer, and although he was going to be the global head of legal for one of the biggest companies of the world, taking on that role can hardly be considered world changing. "Only those that take on real risk, and are brave enough to abandon all conventions, can find the strength to truly make a change in this world", he thought.

"I have to take on a lot more risk, if I really want to change the world, even in the slightest. How can I do that if I can't even win my own personal battles? I can't even find comfort in my friends right now, and the one person who joined me in my troubled situation won't even speak to me right now. How did I even lose Monica in all this confusion?" he continued to ponder through the night.

As he sat on the side of his bed, with his elbows placed on top of his legs and his arms supporting his head as he thinks long and hard about the things that transpired, he could not help but feel more confused and uncertain about the things that are happening, and of the things that he must do.

"Eventually I have to move, because the world waits for no one. And as the world goes on, I can't afford to hang on to these thoughts any longer. My emotions have helped push and inspire me to achieve more than I thought I was capable of, and I am thankful I was able to. But maybe this is no longer the time for emotions?" he thought as he paused to internalize his options.

"What I need now is to hang on to life as it goes forward, and be able to take advantage of all the benefits my position now offers. I may not be the happiest I can be, but maybe I can find the rewards of this new life, good enough to carry me by. I only need to temper my emotions and expectations, until I can fully retire.

"This is my new life now, whether I like it or not. All I can do is make the best of it, and find happiness where I can. Even if this life may not be as exciting as I'd like, there is nothing wrong with finding comfort in isolation. Maybe it is easier to live in a familiar space of seclusion, not being too attached, but engaged just enough to affect others in a way that would help my situation. Compared to the chaos that always seemed to follow, whenever I follow my heart, maybe it is best to retain power over myself, and always have control over my thoughts, emotions, and outlook in life. I just need to lock on to a target, and just focus on getting it done, until probably I am old enough for the world to let me retire", he thought to himself, as he slowly raised his head, with full conviction in his decision.

Chapter 22

Long Hard Talk

With a familiar buzzing, Stan opened his eyes to the sound of his alarm clock ringing. It was six am in the morning, and although he had taken a hiatus from his alarm clock in the past few months, waking up to its sound still felt comfortable and familiar. Although it was just the morning after Mr. Paul's wake, having finally settled on a choice, and fully committing to that path, seemed to open up his mind. He seemed to have more energy and focus on the things that he wanted to do, as the goal was no longer the issue, but he was only occupied with how he was going to pursue what he now wanted to pursue. Things are clear, and matters and priorities are in order. And for the first time in a long while, he just knew what he wanted to do.

Taking a moment to collect his thoughts, he quickly got up off his bed and did some push-ups and some planks. After doing a few more reps, he went to the kitchen and had a banana and a coffee. He needed to have energy for the day, because this was the day he was going to sign his contract with MCG. The contract signing was already scheduled a few days in advance, and he was also to have a short meeting with the executives, after his signing.

As he was having breakfast, his phone buzzed to a text that he received. "It's from Sheen. Wonder why he messaged me at this time of the day", a worried Stan, thought to himself as he opened the text. When he opened it, it simply said "hey Champ..if ur free call me". Without losing a minute, Stan quickly called Sheen.

"Hey, good morning! Didn't expect you to call this quickly, but hey, all for the better", answered a cheerful Sheen.

"Yeah, I was already up when I got your message, so I quickly called. So, what's up?", eagerly asked Stan.

"Well, Julie said that SC would be finalizing today, their list of professors for this coming semester, and the dean wanted to know if you still wanted to teach. I understand that you have a position there in the city, but hey, wouldn't hurt to call and make sure, right?" said Sheen.

"No, it's not a problem at all, and thank you for checking with me. But since the position I'll be leading is a full-time job, it's almost impossible for me to travel back and forth from the city to our hometown every weekend to attend class. And as much as I'd love to teach there, I don't think that would be fair for them if I can't do a good job on it. With the responsibilities of my new role, I can't even be a law professor here in the city", replied Stan, with a visible sadness in his voice.

"Well, they won't be finalizing the list of professors until around three pm today, so I'll just tell them that you'd give your answer around one pm", coyly said Sheen.

"I don't think that would be necessary", said Stan in a more adamant tone.

"Well, never hurts to have that option right. Who knows what a few hours might bring? Anyway, just let me know if you change your mind. Take care buddy", dismissively said Sheen.

"Do what you want. It doesn't seem like I can convince you otherwise. Take care!" replied Stan with a laugh before the call was finally ended.

No sooner had the call finished, Stan was greeted by Lance and Ann, who just entered the dining area. "Good morning Stan! Thanks for showing us around the city yesterday and also for driving us to the airport today", said Ann with a smile.

"It's not a big deal. It's the least I can do", replied Stan with a smile.

"You really didn't have to. We can always take the cab, you know. Besides, as you said last night, you have an important contract signing this morning and it wouldn't speak well of you if you suddenly left their building just to drive us to the airport", said Lance with a frown.

"Nonsense. You were a great influence on me growing up, and I won't allow you to take the cab to the airport, as long as I can help it. You don't have to worry about today, because it's only just a contract signing, and although there would be an informal meet and greet with the other VPs, I doubt it would take that long. Those folks are probably too busy to take long talking to me, anyway. I think they'll understand if I told them that I needed to leave early to drive you to the airport. Besides, the museum, the airport, and MCG's office are just a few blocks apart, so I'm sure we won't have any problem with time. I wouldn't have insisted on driving you if I knew I can't deliver on it", insisted Stan.

"What museum?" curiously asked Lance.

"Forgot to tell you, although I was actually just about to wake you up to tell you about that. Well, I knew you two always wanted to visit the biggest museum here in the city, so I planned to drop you two off at the museum, for you two to check it out, while I have my contract signing, and then I pick you up around eleven or eleven thirty, and drive you to the airport. Well, that is if you two can be ready to leave early?" said Stan with a coy smile.

"Wow, I always wanted to visit that place. Sure, that's perfect. But are you sure that won't get you late for your signing?" asked a concerned Lance.

"It won't be a problem. The museum and the MCG office are actually within walking distance from each other, so it really won't be a problem. After you have your breakfast, we can already drive to the museum, and we'll just leave your bags in the car, while you check out the museum and I go to the MCG office. We can even have some lunch near the museum, before I drive you to the airport", replied Stan with a big smile on his face.

"Well, if you say it's fine then okay, I'm fine with that", said Lance.

After Lance and Ann had a light breakfast, they prepared to leave, and the three of them were on their way. They arrived at the museum, shortly after it opened, and after paying the entrance fee, Lance and Ann had their tour of the museum, while Stan was left at the entrance, waving at the two, as they started their tour of the museum.

Checking his designer watch, he saw that his scheduled signing was still an hour away. Since the MCG building was right across the museum, and finding the relaxing feel of the benches just outside the museum, he decided to take a couple of minutes to just sit and feel the morning sunshine beaming through the shade.

There was a park across the museum, with benches on the park that faced the museum's entrance, and a pathway for joggers in front of the benches. Somehow, in the shade of trees with light sunshine beaming through their leaves, as joggers passed by, he suddenly felt at peace and relaxed. It was like he blended in like the trees. And although he did not move a muscle, he was happy to have active people moving about, while he faced a landmark establishment that housed and showed the growth of man, through time.

It was on a long bench at the park, that he encountered this scene just outside the museum, and which he only chanced upon on his way to the MCG building. He initially didn't plan on taking a seat, but as he caught a view of the museum from afar, and felt the cozy ambience of the spot, he just decided to stop walking, and take a seat on the empty spot of the bench wherein he caught a good view of the museum.

"Nice view, right? Always nice to see that there are still people who have an interest in our history", said the only other person on the bench that Stan was sitting on.

Although Stan already saw that the bench had one other occupant, he did not really pay attention to the other person, because he did not want to bother him while he was seated on the far end of the bench, and because he himself did not expect that he would take a seat on that bench at that moment.

Considering however that he was the encroacher of the other person's silence, he thought that it was only proper to be polite by answering "it is indeed a grand view. It feels like it has the same sense of history, as the things inside it".

After Stan's answer, he did not hear back from the man on the other side of the bench, so he continued to enjoy the serenity of the location. He also continued to ponder on the thought brought about by other person on the bench as he enjoyed the cool breeze and warm sun.

"You look like you're doing better than last time. Good for you", said the other person on the bench, after he briefly looked at Stan and returned his gaze at the museum.

Surprised that he was seated with someone who knew him but whom he was unable to recognize, Stan turned his head and gave the other person a good look. At first, he was not able to recognize the man, but as he looked deeper and scanned his memory some more, he realized that he did in fact see the man before, but on only one occasion.

"I'm sorry if I wasn't able to get your name before, but I do remember you. You kind of changed your hair and beard a bit and you do look better dressed today than before, so that's probably why I wasn't able to recognize you. It has been a few months now since we chanced upon each other at the park before and I was almost run over by a lunatic jogger. Thanks for the napkin!" jokingly said Stan, with a wide smile on his face.

"Wow, that's some great memory you have there. I really didn't expect you to recognize someone you casually met on a random spot at the park a few months ago, and I was actually expecting you to just pretend to know me and probably cough up some random stuff, while trying to figure out where we actually met", said the salaryman with a big laugh.

"I'm pretty good with faces I guess, although not with names. Part of my upbringing, I guess. Besides, you are actually harder to forget than you think", jokingly replied Stan.

"Good to know. I think? By the way, just in case you want to know, the name is Vincent", laughingly replied the salaryman.

"My name is Stan. Glad to finally know your name", gleefully said Stan, as they shook hands.

"Glad you also appreciate the beauty of these old structures. I thought only the older generation had some fancy over these types of things", said Vincent, as he turned back to face the museum and returned to a more solemn expression.

"I didn't know that I do. I guess I just felt something wonderful about this spot and just decided to sit back and find out why", replied Stan, as he tries to figure out why he did so.

"Were you able to find your answer?" calmly asked Vincent, while still facing the museum.

"What do you mean?" curiously asked Stan.

"When we first met, I impolitely asked you about what motivates you to work, and although you gave me an answer at that time, I didn't think you were really settled with your answer before. As I too wonder about that thought, I was hoping to know if you were able to find some answer to that question, after all this time", softly said Vincent, who still faced the museum, but has now slumped his head and his eyes looking at the ground.

"To tell you honestly, that question really stuck with me for a long time, and even caused me to think about the foundations of my long-standing beliefs about work, and about life. Despite my youth, I actually thought I had the answers, and had everything figured out. Apparently, that wasn't the case, and I'm thankful it wasn't. How boring it would have been if life were that straightforward, wouldn't it? I guess I needed to feel stupid, to learn a thing or two, every once in a while, right?

"The question wasn't the only reason that I questioned a lot of things in my life, but I guess it probably sparked the flame that grew to be the fire that took down a lot of the things that I believed in. Whether you believe me or not, I actually quit a very lucrative job, to find the answers to some deep questions in my heart and in my mind. And I am happy that I took the leap of discovery when I had the chance.

"But to tell you honestly, I still haven't figured out what motivates me to go to work every day. I decided to quit work to try and find the answer for myself, but despite all this time, I still haven't figured that out.

"What I have come to understand is not everything needs to revolve about me and about these passions of mine. The world continues to move on, and I have to set aside my passion for now and take advantage of the opportunities that arise in life, lest I miss out, and just find happiness where I can. And hopefully, be able to fully satisfy life's requirements, and retire with just enough money and energy to have some alone time in my twilight", narrated Stan, with a sad tone.

Vincent stays silent, as he absorbs all that Stan had discussed, and after a sad sigh, said "that day that we talked was actually a special date for me and my family. And I left work early that day, to have a few minutes in the park to reflect on the things that made that date life changing.

"Three years ago, on the same date that we talked, my son took his own life. It was the third-year anniversary of my son's death, believe it or not".

Stunned by the revelation, Stan tried to grasp his thoughts and try to find a good way to react. Still lost for words, Stan let out what felt the most natural for him in that moment, "how are you holding up", he sincerely asked.

Looking back at Stan, Vincent replied with a bitter smile "frankly, I'm still dealing with grief, and I feel this may never really go away. But I'm dealing with it better these days, thanks for asking. He would have probably learned a thing or two from a smart boy like you, and maybe you would have liked his enthusiasm.

"I really struggled at first to believe what had happened, and to this day I still hope, even at the slightest, that this was just a long nightmare and that I would soon wake up to find my son, alive and healthy, having the time of his life. And I've really tried hard to accept these realities in my life since it happened.

"But I don't think it's fair of me to unload these things on you, so I apologize for that. I just get carried away sometimes".

"Maybe this is the perfect way for you to unburden yourself with this, after all this time. After all the judgmental looks from some of the people around you that you probably had to endure after what happened, maybe it's better for you to express yourself to a stranger, just this time. I promise I won't mind, and I may actually understand you more than you know", seriously said Stan, as he stared at Vincent across the bench.

Looking back and taking a moment to see how serious Stan was with his offer, Vincent looked back at the ground for a moment, before replying.

"You're a really smart guy. You know the right things to say, at the right time", Vincent said with a chuckle.

"I've had my reasons for knowing what to say for different situations, but trust me, this is not one of those situations that I've prepared for. As hard as it may be to believe, you seem to me like a great guy, and after you shared something so intimate, the least I can do is learn from the rest of your experience", half-jokingly replied Stan.

"I've come to understand some things since my son's untimely demise. Over the years I've read books, attended seminars, listened to podcasts and talked to some families who went through the same experience we had, in an attempt to find meaning or reason for his death, and probably find a silver lining in all the things that transpired. Some people keep telling us that we shouldn't blame ourselves for what happened and all that rhetoric. And there are times I believe them, and there are times that I don't.

"But to this date, I still can't understand how a young, positive and talented kid, who has his whole life still ahead of him, can just suddenly consider taking his own life. It still eludes me, or maybe I just don't want to accept the reason why.

"I've talked with his friends, tried learning social media, just to read some of the things that were on my son's head that he was too proud or shy to talk to me about, and try to understand how it came to that. How it came to my son hanging himself inside his room all of a sudden.

"He was a sweet boy, who even from a young age, wanted to be a lawyer, for the simple reason that he wanted to provide his talent and skills to help those that are less fortunate in life. He probably saw a program on TV and was inspired from a young age to become a lawyer. Whatever the reason was, it moved him deeply, and he carried that enthusiasm to school and in all his activities. He was sure that he wanted nothing else than to be a lawyer for the poor. And he was more than on track to reach that dream. He was consistently the top of his class, and put in all the work, for him to be able to attend the best law school in the country. He was determined to be the best lawyer he can be.

"We supported him all the way. Despite our low salaries, we were committed to helping him any way we can. Me and the misses would budget everything we bought, just so we can have some savings from our salaries to support my son's dream. And we were happy to do that. I'd give both my arms and legs, just to send him to school.

"And on the strength of his grades and a scholarship he got, he was able to attend the school he always wanted. It was the top law school in the country, and it was the only school that was acceptable for him. He needed to get the best training, from the best school, if he was going to be the best lawyer that was going to defend the rights of the poor, right?

"Unfortunately, the fairytale ends there. Despite tireless nights of studying, Jason was not able to pass all of his subjects on his first semester in law school. He failed two major classes in law school, and despite his overall average being acceptable, he somehow felt like his life had already ended at that point. He seemed upset at the irreversible failure that would forever stick in his record. In his social media account, he called these grades, 'heartbreaking' and 'unacceptable'. I learned from his classmates that he tried talking with his professor to try and redeem his grade, but he was shot down just the same.

"And maybe those were the last nails in Jason's coffin. Those last moments of rejection and failure probably spiraled things for him. But I still cannot understand how such a stupid and petty thing can push my son to just end his life. With all his life way ahead of him. Why?" said Vincent, as he tries to reach out for answers while sharing his story.

Stan remained silent, listening and intent on helping. Realizing that Stan still wanted to listen on, Vincent continued "I probably don't quite understand failure as much as Jason, and I probably could have listened to him more, instead of just prodding him on to reach for this perfect law school run. I probably am not the best person to share about these high stakes matters with. After all, I'm just a simple employee, happy with my simple job and simple life.

"To some, failure may just result in a nagging feeling of unhappiness. But maybe for others, failure may feel like an inescapable pit with walls quickly closing in, leaving you with only one option to escape its grip, and unfortunately, death was the only option that Jason felt was available. Or maybe Jason was just too caught up with the other things, the inconsequential things, and could not differentiate his true goals from the ones that society piled on to his dreams? Or maybe both?

"He was just a regular sweet kid, who only wanted to be the best lawyer that was capable of serving his client's cases, well beyond their means. And he honestly could have achieved his goals regardless of whichever law school he attended. But somehow society only showed him one way to get to his dreams. That somehow, he needed to complete a checklist of requirements, before he could get to his ultimate goal to serve the underserved. That somehow, he needed a flawless record in law school, be well connected and well networked, and a model citizen, before he could push through with his one simple desire.

"The thing that I regretted about it all, was how I couldn't tell him otherwise. I was useless, because I also believed that there was only one way of reaching the goal that he wanted. After living all these years of my life, I couldn't even see behind the veil of life, and see beyond what society had forced me to see. That there was still some hope out there, and that there was not just one way of getting where we want to be.

"Had I known better, maybe I could have told him that there was always another way of doing things, and success wasn't always reached through a single path. Maybe I could have told him, or showed him how beautiful and abundant life still was, and despite any setbacks, we still had an equal chance to find joy and find life through a different path. That he only really needed to focus on the one thing that set him towards law in the first place; public service. Then maybe, he would still be alive, and living out a life that may not be what the world dictated, but a life that we can all still be proud of", as tears gushed down his cheeks.

Stan shared the sentiment of Vincent, and his chest twitched in pain and fumed with anger at how unnecessary pressure took a toll on another soul that simply wanted to induce change for the better. Deeply saddened, but somehow managing to control his watery eyes from completely succumbing to tears, Stan understood the frustration of another soul, getting lost in the rules of a society that doesn't even know where it really wants to go. And for a few minutes, the two of them embraced their sadness, and quietly mourned over the dead.

After a minute of silence between the two, Stan looked at Vincent and softly said, "I know this won't mean much, but wherever Jason is, I hope he has found his peace. And I also hope you find your peace, really I do. Although this comes from a stranger, but trust me when I tell you that you need not blame yourself for what happened. It may be hard to let go of the memories, both good and bad, that are associated with Jason, but you have to, if you want to continue with the path that is also ahead of you. I'm sure the people close to you would also like you to move forward, and I'm sure Jason would like that too".

With these words, Vincent stopped crying and wiped the tears from his eyes.

"Thank you for listening and thank you for the advice. I guess I already knew that, but I probably needed to hear that from someone else, for it to sink in. I'll try my best, if not for myself, but for Jason's memory, at least", said Vincent, as he tries to smile at Stan.

"Glad I was able to help, and I'm happy that you shared your life with me. I'll cherish Jason's memory and yours. I hope I didn't hold you too long on your way to work", said Stan as he smiles back.

"No need to worry about that, I've been laid off from work, and today is my last day, so I decided to be tardy for once in my life, and enjoy being late, at least this one last time. Anyway, what's the worst that they can do other than deduct a leave of something right? I mean, it's my last day of work anyway, right. Might as well enjoy it a little bit", jokingly said Vincent.

"Oh, don't worry about me, I actually think that being laid off is best for me. I get a severance deal, and me and my wife can now go back to the countryside and live simpler lives. I can also start the small farm I always wanted to have, and the deal they gave is more than enough to fulfill that. There are a lot of things that are unknown, but at least I can actually start living", quickly added Vincent, when he noticed Stan getting worried.

"Well, that's good to know, and I really pray for your success, no matter how you define it. I guess I have to go then. I have a meeting in a few minutes, and I don't want to be late", said Stan, as he readied himself, and already stood up.

"Of course, don't let me delay you", replied Vincent.

Taking a step forward, but remembering something important that he put on hold during their conversation, Stan turned around to face Vincent and innocently asked, "by the way, of all the people you could have asked about their motivation in life, why did you decide to ask me? I'm not angry or anything, and in hindsight, I do believe I became a better person after all that. But despite me not fully grasping my motivations at the time, I did at that time, had a sense of bliss and peace in having the escape of not knowing. So, I do want to know, what prompted you to ask?"

"I actually don't understand myself why I asked such a blunt question like that. And to tell you honestly, you were the only person I ever asked that", answered Vincent, before taking a moment to answer Stan's final concern.

"As I was sitting at the bench at the park at that time, I was reflecting on the life that I have, and how it came about. Looking back at my life, and my son's life, I can't help but question what life is all about. What is it? What is life, but a collection of seconds that we get to perceive and enjoy the world, and the decisions, emotions and thoughts we have in those precious seconds.

"How well then are we spending those seconds? When the time comes that our lives flash before our eyes, will we be happy at the life that flashes before us in our dying moments? What kind of life will we remember, and what memory will we leave behind?

"If this was our only concern, then maybe we would be living differently. Maybe we would only be focused on living a life we can be happy to look back at, in our dying seconds. Better than any social media post or self-promoting video, that would be the only highlight reel that mattered. And maybe, just maybe, we can have one last smile before our time is over", Vincent continued, before pausing as he realized he has gone beyond what was asked.

"I'm sorry if I am rambling again. I have to apologize for disrupting your balance, and I really did not mean to challenge your world views. I guess it just felt right at that moment to ask.

"I've come to believe that there is a penalty when we live a life not our own. And I'm not here to tell anybody how to live their life, but with what little I know, I feel compelled to tell anybody that asks, or is inclined to listen, that there are still other options available. Not just the options we have become accustomed to.

"Of all the people I've met and talked to, you seemed to be the only one who still had the openness to listen to the other options. More importantly, you seem to be the only one brave enough to look past the options that seem apparent, and take a stand for whatever it is you decide on. Some people might call that stupid; I'd like to call that optimistic. And hope makes all the difference", concluded Vincent with a smile.

Stunned and touched at how Vincent sees him, Stan could not understand the sudden change in his feelings. It felt like a gate opened in his chest, and something heavy seemed to have been lifted from within. But despite that, his mind seemed to disagree with what he was feeling. He was sure that he needed to leave, if wanted to get to the signing on time. But somehow, he was already having doubts.

"I'm not sure if your faith in me is warranted. I'm just like any other person. And to be honest, I may even be farther away from the person you may think I am", said Stan, as he tries to hide the lie in his eyes, as he said that.

"You're always that guy, and you will always be that guy. It's who you are, and I'm sure you know that. Regardless of your decisions and actions, you will always be that guy. The only question I guess, is if you are brave enough to be that guy", replied Vincent with a gentle smile.

"A friend told me a few days back, that I've already found my passion and purpose in this world, in teaching. But I've been offered a position that everyone dreams of. Long story short, I'm on my way now to sign the offer of a lifetime, and that's probably the most practical decision I can make at this time. What choice do I have but go for the most practical one?" replied Stan in a defeated manner.

"That choice may be practical, but not necessarily the wise one. And it may be the most sought-after job, but not the one you really dream of. I'm not here to tell you which choice you should make, because those are your dreams and that is your life, and only you can answer that. All I ask is that you actually have a long hard talk with yourself about that, and not just get caught up in the wave of life", answered Vincent.

"That actually poses more questions than answers, don't you think", replied Stan.

"It does, and maybe that's alright", concluded Vincent.

"I have to leave now, so I don't get late. Thank you for your words of wisdom, and I hope you find your joy and peace. Take care", replied Stan, as he turned his back from Vincent.

"Thank you. I will try to find them. And I'm sure you'll find your joy and peace as well. When you do, I hope you can visit me on my farm somehow. I'll be the weirdo who plants tons of chilis, three towns from here", said Vincent, as he waves goodbye and gives a warm smile at Stan.

Stan waves back without turning to look at Vincent, and he continues to walk forward towards his scheduled meeting. As he continued to walk on, beyond the sight of Vincent, his last words sank deeper and deeper within him, and he could not avoid being immersed in them.

As he gets closer and closer to the MCG office, jitters keep growing and growing within him, as he thinks about the type of life he would be living, when he starts working there. "How can I have jitters over a role so coveted and so grand?" he keeps asking himself. "I should be thankful for this chance, and the last thing I should do is waste it chasing some dream that may not even pan out right", he keeps convincing himself.

And yet, despite his mind rationalizing things, his chest pounds harder, and he can't seem to get a grip of the fear and anxiety that has crept out unexpectedly in this signing. His legs seem to buckle under him, and his steps get heavier and heavier, the closer he gets to the MCG building. "If this is the right thing to do, then why does my whole being reject it, despite all of the world's convincing? Will I really find happiness in this path?" he thought, as he was now in front of the MCG tower.

"Is everything okay, Stan?" asked Lance, as he stood beside Stan, who was taking their bags from the back of his car.

"Never better. Why did you ask granddad?" replied Stan with a forced smile, as he tried to reassure Lance that he was doing fine.

"Well, you seem quiet during our lunch, and have not said a word during our drive until we parked here at the airport. I won't say anything to your father, you know that. So, you can always talk to us about it. And although our generations did things differently, you can always talk to us about your problems with the ladies", seriously said Lance.

"We had a different way of handling things back in the day, but maybe we can give some of our insights about dating", Ann chimed in, as Stan just finished taking all their bags.

"No, believe me when I tell you, I'm not feeling sour right now because of a lady. Let's get that straight", quickly replied Stan, with a mild chuckle.

"Then why the bad mood all of a sudden? I mean, it couldn't be about work, because you just signed a very lucrative compensation package just a few minutes ago. I mean, you explained last night how well you're going to get paid, and how favorable this new role is to whatever future endeavor you might fancy later on, so it can't be about that. Which leaves relationship, as the only possible reason for your quietness, right?" a confused Lance explained.

Laughing at Lance's explanation, Stan was somehow able to relieve himself of some of his pent-up emotions, and felt more at ease talking about it. He looked back at his grandparents and smiled.

"Well, there is a close friend in my life who is a woman, and I guess part of the reason I am like this is because of a fight we had a few days back. But to be clear, we are close friends, but are not dating. We did however have a fight because she felt that I may be making a mistake in pursuing this new role at MCG.

"I was invited by SC to be a tenured professor in their new law program, and having seen how much fun I had giving a lecture there, my friend Monica believes that it is best for me to dedicate my talent and time, grooming the new generation of lawyers in our side of the country. And Sheen told me this morning that I still have until one pm today to tell SC if I want to teach there or not", explained Stan.

"Well, that's no longer possible since you already signed with MCG and I doubt your schedule can accommodate teaching in a law school that's so far away, right?", asked Ann.

"It is a waste, but I think the folks in my alma mater can understand why you can't teach there. I mean, you just signed your job contract, and it wouldn't be fair to the people of MCG if you didn't give them your all, after giving you a shot", chimed Lance.

"Well, truth be told, I didn't push through with the contract signing this morning", an ashamed Stan confessed.

"What?!" blurted both Ann and Lance.

"I did not cancel the signing, if that is what you are thinking. But I just couldn't go through with it this morning, and just told them that I wasn't feeling well. I had the signing moved to two days from now", continued Stan.

"But you were already near their office. What did you do then in those hours that you left us?" a worried inquiry from Lance.

"I was actually at the entrance of their building a few minutes before the signing, but I just couldn't go through with it. I probably looked for a sign or a nudge to let me know that this was the right thing to do. I stood at the entrance of the MCG building, hoping that someone I knew would notice me, and maybe that would compel me to push through with the signing, but no one showed and no sign manifested. And a few minutes before my schedule, I just decided to call the HR representative and tell her that I wasn't feeling well, and had it moved to a later date. I then just sat at the park in front of the museum, and tried to think about this next big step in my life", narrated Stan, as he tried to assure his grandparents that he was okay.

Listening to his narration, and their faces finally calming down, as though this situation was something they've already experienced before, his grandparent gave a sigh, and smiled as though everything will be alright. After pausing to analyze what just happened, Lance goes on to ask "is it true? What did your friend Monica believe in, that you enjoyed teaching law? Is it true?"

"It is. I've never felt more alive and with purpose, than when I gave that lecture at SC. And maybe it is the optimist in me, but I would like to see each hopeful graduate at SC's law program become great lawyers in their own rights", declared Stan.

"Then maybe there's no need for you to be confused anymore" replied Lance with a smile, as he looks at Stan with a proudness that Stan has probably only seen once in his life. It was the time he was seven and his father first introduced their whole family to Lance and Ann. And maybe the look that his grandfather gave his dad back then could have a different meaning, but Stan was sure that it was the same look and feel, somehow.

Before he can muster a word, Lance continued "I know a man who once said the same things you're saying now. He was a brave man, who actually pursued his dream over career".

"What happened to him? Was he able to find fulfillment in pursuing his dreams?" curiously asked Stan.

"You tell me. The man I am talking about is none other than your dad. And the dream he pursued were you brothers and your mom", replied Lance with a smile.

Stan was surprised and confused with the revelation. "What is granddad talking about? Dad is a simple man who doesn't seem to be motivated about a lot of things in life. And how can they be the dream?" he thought.

"I don't understand", was all that Stan could muster to say.

"Your father was a talented engineer in the day, and had the chance to be a partner in their firm. However, the only way for him to be a partner at that time, was for him to take on a big project at the furthest end of the country, and manage the construction for a couple of years before he gets his promotion. At that same time, he and Martha were a newlywed couple and you were already a few months inside your mother's womb.

"The senior partner at their firm was a close friend of mine, and he told me that your dad not only refused the offer, but altogether left their firm to look for another job. Naturally, I talked with him and asked him not to let a chance like that get by.

"As a passionate businessman myself, I was so immersed with business and professional growth, that I could not understand why someone as talented as your dad could waste an opportunity, I've had to scrape and bleed for my entire life. I loved my job and really felt strongly about it, so I felt betrayed or let down by Gary, when he decided to just fold and let all his grooming go to waste. It was like he didn't care at all about how I felt about it.

"When I confronted him about his decision, he just told me that his decision was final. When I asked why, he simply told me that it was the only time in his life that he found reason and purpose for living, and would not give that up for anything. He said that 'finally experiencing the joy of being the husband of a loving wife, and having the chance to father another life, I finally found a reason for living, that was truly my own. And I'll be damned if I waste a single moment of it, just to earn a couple bucks. Because as great as my job was, a paycheck was all it ever was. At least to me it was. As nothing is more precious to me than to see my child grow up before my very eyes'.

"As I could not understand his reason at that time, I lashed out and refused to talk to him after that. He lived his life according to how he wanted, and I continued to pursue my passion after that.

"Although his desires differed greatly from the one that I had, in time I've come to understand and respect the desire and decision that he had. It was much later that I came to understand just how admirable his decision was. When you came to our house for the first time in seven years, and seeing just how beautiful and loving our grandchildren grew to be, and how happy your father was at having you, that's when I knew I was wrong to have questioned his path. The path your father took may not have been covered with gold, but what it had in abundance, even the richest of the rich, could only dream to have. And your dad found his reward, in love and life.

"So, believe me when I tell you that the rewards of life may vary, depending on the path you pursue, but the reward never really matters, as long as you're choosing the one you actually want to pursue. My only request is that you always make good with your friends, whichever path you pursue. This one I've come to learn in my years; you have a better chance of getting rich doing something else, than finding happiness without any friends. If you think you already have a path, then just pursue it, easy or not. We will always love you no matter what", Lance narrated, as tears fell from both him and Stan's eyes.

"Understood", said Stan with conviction, as the two embraced and Ann joined in.

After a long embrace, the two wiped their tears and composed themselves. After a few pleasantries, Lance and Ann boarded their plane, and were on their way, leaving Stan who still did not have an answer, but whose fears were no longer there.

Chapter 23

Beyond The Point Of No Return

Two weeks have passed, and in a courtroom, the clerk of court is about to declare the verdict on a criminal case. The courtroom was packed, with tense attendees anxious about what the clerk of court was about to say. As the lady clerk of court raised to read the document containing the verdict, the accused and his family at his back, held hands, as they braced for what was to come.

As the clerk of court started to read the document, the accused and more than half the room tensed up, as though the air was suddenly sucked out of their lungs. Slowly but methodically, the clerk of court continued to read, making sure not to fumble any word, lest he be misunderstood and get on the wrong end of the crowd.

"...find the accused, not guilty", finally declared the clerk of court, as the accused and his family cried in jubilation, as the room was filled with cheers and applause, at the relief and comfort of finding justice to their cause.

Looking to their counsel, the accused can only mouth his thank you, as his voice seemed to abandon him as he sobbed in joy. His family hugged the accused tightly through the bar that separated those who practice law and those who don't, while continuously sobbing as they do.

After a short moment, the judge slightly smashed his gavel on his sound block and cautioned the room to maintain order, to which request, the attendees complied. Yet, despite the caution, their joy remained clear, albeit mummed.

"From the bottom of my heart, I thank you for taking our case. You were the only one to take our case despite our financial situation, and we will forever owe our lives to you", said the accused, as he thanks Monica while still in the embrace of his family.

"I'm sure you'll be able to pay me back. You are a hardworking and law-abiding citizen, and the court has just confirmed that. Besides, I can't allow an innocent man to go to jail just because he doesn't have enough. Justice and the rule of law never discriminated on color or the money one owns, so why should I?", replied Monica with a smile.

Driving out of the court building, Monica could not help but feel happy at the work she just did. Despite the constant heavy workload, and a lot of stressful times, seeing justice served to those who deserved it, makes up for all those hard times, she thought. "This is the reason I took up law", she whispered with a smile, as she drove.

She was on her way back to their office to get some documents she was going to work on over the weekend. She was however caught in the Friday rush hour traffic, so she decided to take a detour instead.

"It's been a while since I last went there, but I guess this is as good a time as any, to relax and sit back. I just wish I had a few cans of beer with me, but I guess I'll just have to settle for the view and the breeze", she thought as she took a right turn.

After parking and walking to the spot on the beach that she normally sits on, she looked towards the horizon and enjoyed the great view, as the sun began to go down, leaving a magnificent hue in the sky. The weather was perfect and the breeze at the right strength. More than a massage or a spa, there was nothing that took away her fatigue, than hanging out in that spot.

"If only the world realized just how cheap pure joy can be", she thought with a sigh. And she continued to stare at the view, waiting for it to peak in its beauty and majesty.

"Still one of the best views around", suddenly said a familiar voice. Too engrossed in the view and her thoughts, Monica was not able to hear the approaching footsteps of the familiar voice's owner. But she was more surprised to figure out who the voice belonged to. Looking back, she saw Stan approaching the spot she was at, and could not believe how that came about. She was not avoiding him, but at the same time, she was still surprised to have chanced upon him at that time.

Unsure how to proceed, thinking that Stan may still be upset with him, Monica made a short but probing reply "it still is".

"Never thought I'd see you here, so if you're still upset with me, I'd understand. I do hope we can be cool again, but if not, then I'll just stay out of your way", humbly replied Stan.

"It's okay, you know. I can't be mad at you for that long, I guess. You have a sweet spot in me, you know that. So, quit being a drama queen already and get your ass over here", jokingly replied Monica, as her previous anger and frustration with Stan seemed to have disappeared now that he was in front of him, giving him an acceptable apology.

"Thanks. To be honest, I did not know you were going to be here, but full disclosure, even if you did not forgive me, I'd probably badger you right now, until we're cool again", said Stan with a coy smile, as he sat very close to Monica.

"I already figured that out already, so to avoid us wasting time, here we are", replied Monica with a laugh.

"Good, because I'd really badger you non-stop, you know that. You're just that important, I hope you understand", sincerely said Stan, as the two friends locked eyes, and understood what they meant to each other.

"So, how's MCG?" asked Monica as Stan stared at him strangely after she asked.

"Haven't you heard?", curiously asked Stan. "Heard what? My hands were tied with a very important case, so I haven't really been in touch with the gang these past few weeks. So, if you were just promoted CEO of MCG, then just spill it out already", pleaded Monica.

Stan locked eyes with her and with a smile replied "I didn't push through with MCG".

"How's that possible? Weren't you decided already?" a stunned Monica replied.

"I was for a moment, but a few feet away from entering the MCG building for my contract signing, I realized that it wasn't really for me. I figured that I was better off foregoing an opportunity I did not want, so someone who can actually enjoy it, can take the job, while I pursue the path, I'd be happy with", confidently said Stan.

"And what path is that?" Monica asked.

"I accepted the teaching job at SC. Class starts in two weeks, and I've been preparing like crazy these past few weeks", smiling as Stan answered.

"That can't be right. If you're teaching there, then what are you still doing here in the city?" asked Monica in disbelief.

"Well, just taking care of the house and other properties I have here, so I can settle them and maybe get enough to buy a decent sized land for my farm back in my hometown. I've decided to work on a farm, on top of my teaching and a small practice back home. I'm also driving my stuff back to my hometown each time we come to the city. Just boring stuff, so let's not get too hung up on that", Stan replied.

"Wow, never thought you'd have it in you, but I'm really happy that you did. Although I won't be as fun without you around. Wish I had some beer to properly send you off somehow", a sad Monica replied.

"Don't worry about the beer. I have that covered. And, here he comes, just in time", said Stan with a smile, as he looks back at an approaching man.

Monica was surprised but happy when he saw who it was. Coming from the parking lot, he saw Sheen walking towards them, with a wide smile as he waved back at them.

"What're you doing here?" an excited Monica asked an approaching Sheen.

"Someone has to be Stan's backup driver as he drives back and forth on those long drives. You know how it is, right", said Sheen as he smiles back at Monica.

"Yeah, I know what you mean. No helping this guy, I guess. But how about the bakeshop? Who's in charge of that?" a snarky Monica replied.

"Haven't Stan told you?" curiously asked Sheen.

"Told me what?" replied Monica, as she gave Stan a mad look.

"Well, Sheen has his own bakeshop. A smaller one, but one wherein he can bake the beloved breads of our hometown, and also some experimental stuff", said Stan, as he and Sheen have a laugh.

"Wow, I'm really happy for you on this new venture", said Monica, as she congratulates Sheen.

"You should also congratulate Stan. After all, we would both be owning that shop as partners", said Sheen with a wide smile.

Monica's eyes grew wide in amazement, as she gave Stan a shove before saying "shut up! Congrats!"

"Thanks! It's not as big a shop as the popular one in my hometown, but it's just enough for the two of us partners to start with. It opens next month, and I hope you can come visit", replied Stan.

"Of course. Just give me a time and a date, and I'll be there. Wow, that is some big news! Sure hope we had that beer, so we can at least have a toast", said Monica.

"Good thing we do", said Sheen, as he raises a pack of mild beers in can.

"Told you I have you covered", said Stan with a wink, when Monica looked at her.

As the sunset peaked in beauty, the three sat down to watch, while they continued to chat. After Sheen passed a can to the two, Monica gave a toast, and again congratulated them.

After a moment of just enjoying the sunset, Monica looks at Stan and says "hey stan, let's have dinner with the gang. I'm sure they'd be just as happy as I am, with these new changes in your smug life".

"Of course. Nothing would make me happier than that", replied Stan with a calm smile.

"How things change so dramatically. We were only here a few months ago, discussing your resignation, and here we are a few months after, discussing how you're taking full control of your destiny. Do you still have any worries that it might not all work out?" sincerely asked Monica.

Facing Monica with calmness and a smile, Stan replied, "when I decided to pursue teaching, I was under no illusion that it would all go according to plan. Maybe it would work out, or maybe it just won't, but either way, I owe it to myself to try.

"Although many consider my path as one leading to a point of no return, I find hope in knowing that the explorers of old were able to find beauty, beyond the so-called 'point of no return'. And this road may have its share of bumps, but never again will I be the person too afraid to go after what I want to be".

-END-

www.ingramcontent.com/pod-product-compliance
Lightning Source LLC
LaVergne TN
LVHW012101160826
845678LV00014B/2898

* 9 7 9 8 3 7 0 2 6 2 3 4 0 *